RARE BIRDS
OF THE WORLD

A Collins/International
Council for Bird Preservation Handbook

This book is based on the ICBP/IUCN Bird Red Data Book compiled by ICBP with the financial assistance of the World Wide Fund for Nature, United Nations Environmental Programme, International Union for Conservation of Nature and Natural Resources, and many other generous donors.

RARE BIRDS
OF THE WORLD

A Collins/ICBP Handbook

Text by Guy Mountfort

Illustrations by Norman Arlott

THE STEPHEN GREENE PRESS

Lexington, Massachusetts

Rare Birds of the World: A Collins/ICBP Handbook

The Stephen Green Press Inc.

Published by the Penguin Group

Viking Penguin Inc., 40 West 23rd Street, New York, New York 100010, USA
Penguin Books Ltd., 27 Wrights Lane, London W8 5TZ, England
Penguin Books Australia Ltd., Ringwood, Victoria, Australia
Penguin Books Canada Ltd., 2801 John Street, Markham, Ontario, Canada L3R 1B4
Penguin Books (NZ) Ltd., 182–190 Waitru Road, Auckland 10, New Zealand

Penguin Books Ltd., Registered Offices: Harmondsworth, Middlesex, England

First published in Great Britain in 1988 by William Collins Sons & Co Ltd.
First published in the United States of America in 1989 by the Stephen Green Press, Inc.
Distributed by Viking Penguin Inc.

CIP Data Available

Colour origination by Bright Arts (Hong Kong) Ltd., Hong Kong
Printed by William Collins & Sons Co Ltd., Glasgow, UK
Set in Garamond

Contents

Foreword

One thousand birds, over 10% of all bird species, are threatened with extinction today. The vast majority of these are found in the tropics, mostly in the forests and islands of developing countries where the destruction of natural resources has too often been perceived as the inevitable price of a better standard of living for growing populations. Loss or degradation of habitat is the single greatest threat to birds and all other forms of wildlife. The loss of the world's plants and animals, its biological diversity, is an international concern that ultimately affects everyone.

To combat this situation, there has arisen an increasingly active conservation movement. The International Council for Bird Preservation (ICBP) has the distinction of being the longest established truly global conservation organisation, having been founded in 1922. For more than 60 years our organisation has played a pioneering role in the promotion of international cooperation in the conservation of wild birds and their habitats. Our original purpose was to protect migratory birds on their flyways and wintering grounds, as well as at home. This was the first clear issue where an international effort was required; it had already been recognised in the Convention on Migratory Birds, signed between the United States and Great Britain (representing Canada) in 1916. The protection of migratory birds throughout their ranges remains an important issue beyond the scope of most national conservation organisations. However, many such groups in countries like Britain, the Netherlands, Germany and Switzerland are active partners with ICBP in raising conservation awareness and assisting with projects in Africa and Mediterranean countries where many northern European breeding birds spend the winter.

Thus birds have played a unique role in the growth of the conservation movement and the quest for a valid environmental ethic. But safeguarding migratory birds for all to enjoy is only a part of ICBP's work. The power of birds to awaken public awareness of broader environmental concerns is one of ICBP's most potent weapons. One of our major objectives is to build and strengthen local bird groups in countries where conservation is virtually unknown. Indeed many of them, like the Malta Ornithological Society to name just one, are now the main voice for environmental concern in their countries.

Since the founding of ICBP, the means and extent of environmental destruction and the speed with which it is being accomplished have grown out of all control. The worst hit countries are those where conservation is least understood. To their governments the preservation of species, and hence of biological diversity, appears a luxury before the overriding need to earn foreign exchange from lumber contracts, cattle raising or cash crops. Yet conservation is far from a luxury, for its central tenets are ecological stability and the sustainability of resource exploitation, and hence real economic balance. For 25 years the provision of conservation know-how and resources for developing countries has been on the agenda of international conservation organisations, and the message is now getting through to the aid agencies: conservation and development must proceed together. The natural riches of a country must be preserved; if they are cherished and wisely used they will be a source of wealth and sustenance for its people forever.

Inevitably there are tough choices to be made. Large populations need land and goods and every effort must be made to enhance their quality of life. Faced with such pressures and with limited funds for conservation, it becomes imperative to identify, as accurately as possible, priority areas where the greatest amount of the world's biological diversity can be saved. It is still true that in general more is known about the world's avifauna and its distributions than about mammals, reptiles, insects or plants. Where high concentrations of bird species occur, it is likely that other forms of flora and fauna will occur in similar abundance and variety. The study of birds can therefore pinpoint areas of exceptional diversity for protection. One of ICBP's crucial tasks is to target these priority areas through the compilation of all that is known about the world's birds that are most at risk. In the majority of cases we can safely assert that sustained conservation initiatives will benefit not just birds, but all the wildlife that exists with the birds and that make each ecosystem a treasure house for the world's genetic diversity. Ultimately, the biggest beneficiary of all will be the human race.

In the last ten years, words like "ecosystem" have entered our everyday language, and concepts such as "genetic diversity" have been broadly received and understood as a good thing. But to me the intrinsic excitement of these concepts is in the beholding of each threatened species, if not in the wild (for few of us are lucky enough to visit their habitats) then at least in our collective thought. Not only are they extremely rare, but many are found only in dense tropical forests or other inaccessible places. It is my hope that this fine book, with its glorious illustrations by Norman Arlott, can in some measure make these beautiful birds come alive and kindle in its readers what Rachel Carson called a "sense of wonder". I am convinced that it is that "sense of wonder" which is the most vital well-spring for successful conservation endeavour.

Much of the information presented here has not previously been available outside the more technical scientific literature. I hope that readers of all ages who take pleasure in the birds around them will find in this account an inspiration for a more international outlook: everything in this world is tied to everything else.

For the 10% of the world's birds that are now under sentence of death, ICBP represents the court of appeal. To present the case for the defence, we could ask for no better advocate than Guy Mountfort, one of the founders of the World Wildlife Fund and a past President of the British Ornithologists' Union. You, the readers of the book, are the jury. In a real way, we all hold the fate of these birds in our hands.

Christoph Imboden
Director, ICBP
Cambridge
December, 1987

For further information on how to join ICBP and help save the world's birds, please write to:

ICBP
"The Mount"
32, Cambridge Road
Girton
Cambridge CB3 0PJ

Introduction

In the course of a long lifetime I have had the good fortune to visit 134 countries; for some years as a soldier, for some as a businessman and finally for the sheer pleasure of exploration, but always at heart as a naturalist. These travels gave me an unusual opportunity to judge for myself the progressive and worldwide deterioration of the natural environment. The destruction of tropical forests alone has reached proportions unimaginable when I was young. Farming was still organic then and chemical pollution an unrecognised menace. Oceanic islands were still for the most part pristine, untouched by the devastation of modern war, mineral mining or the horrors of unlimited touristic development. Many species of birds and other animals, now listed as threatened or which have since become extinct, could still be found in those far-off days. I feel singularly privileged to have seen some of them. My lifetime has, in fact, spanned the period of man's maximum destructive impact on the natural world. Only now is he becoming aware of the consequences and taking steps to ameliorate some of the damage he has caused.

The purpose of this book is two-fold. First, to publicise the comparatively little-known work of the International Council for Bird Preservation (more commonly known by its initials, ICBP). Second, to make available to the general public the accumulating evidence, hitherto circulating only among those concerned with ornithology or conservation, that appalling and increasing losses are occurring among the wild birds of the world, virtually all as a result of human influence. More than a thousand species are now, to a greater or lesser degree, threatened with extinction. The evidence, painstakingly gathered and kept up-to-date by the international network of representatives of ICBP, has until now only been published in its Red Data Books of threatened species. By giving it a much wider circulation in less technical form, it is hoped to generate a greater understanding of the need for improved means of conservation for which ICBP is striving. Although this book may present a gloomy picture, it also shows that techniques to save threatened species have been developed and that, given sufficient resources, ICBP is fully capable of continuing remarkable successes in pulling critically endangered species back from the very brink of extinction. It is not for lack of drive or determination that such successes have been relatively few, but because conservation costs money. Resources are at present so slender that ICBP is constantly having to respond to emergencies, like a fire engine dashing to put out one fire after another, rather than working on measures to avoid more species being added to the threatened list. I therefore hope that this book will create increased support for the vitally important work in which ICBP is engaged. The reader must judge whether this plea is justified. Because of the immense popularity which birds enjoy with the general public, I trust that the book will be regarded not as a tale of woe but as a call for action.

The book is divided into sections. After the introductory chapters the species of threatened birds are treated largely in systematic order by the recognised zoogeographical regions, with their related islands. Species inhabiting the more remote oceanic islands in the Pacific are combined in a separate section. Birds are described zoogeographically because birds within the zoogeographical regions have a common evolutionary history and so exhibit many similar features. Thus the birds of the Palaearctic have evolved independently from those of the Orient. Although these regions are now joined along the Himalayas, and there is considerable migration and range overlap between the two avifaunas, they were once separated by a vast ocean. It therefore makes biological sense to divide up the world's avifauna in this way, although from the practical conservation point of view it will be the artifical political boundaries that will be the important ones.

Each regional account is followed by an appendix of abbreviated entries of additional species which are currently being considered as Candidates for the next editions of the Red Data Book. The classification of the status of species conforms with that in the latest ICBP Red Data Books. They are as follows: Endangered, Vulnerable, Indeterminate, Insufficiently Known, Rare and Of Special Concern. For explanation of these categories see page 211. Obviously, as new information comes in, species may move from one category to another. ICBP uses two further categories: Extinct and Out of Danger. These are self-explanatory and in order to save space I have included species with the former status in an appendix and omitted the latter.

The number of threatened species described for each zoogeographic region varies considerably. There is good reason for this: the differences in total numbers reflects the differences in avifaunal distribution and diversity between the regions, plus the differences of threats to their respective habitats. The differences in the numbers of candidate species (ie. those in the appendices) reflects the current state of Red Data Book research – thus the birds of the Afrotropical region have been recently reviewed and consequently there are few candidate species, whilst those of the Neotropical region are currently under review, hence the great number of candidate species.

Earlier editions of the Red Data Books, published in 1964–71 and 1978–79, were produced at a time when the amount of information available was much less extensive than it has since become. They included both species and subspecies. For the benefit of the reader unfamiliar with the distinction, I should explain that a species is defined as a population of interbreeding individuals which is reproductively isolated from other species. A subspecies (or race) is a geographical variety or subdivision of a species, distinguishable from but capable of interbreeding with other subdivisions; some subspecies differ so little from the original that they are regarded as mere variants, whereas others may differ not only in appearance but in ecology and voice and may be on the way to becoming distinct new species. There is still much scientific argument about the validity of many subspecies.

For the latest edition of the Red Data Books the decision was taken to omit subspecies. It was a hard decision and taken with regret only after long deliberation. The chief consideration was that with the mass of information now coming in, it was obvious that the number of species and subspecies at risk had already more than doubled and that to include subspecies was beyond the available resources of manpower and finance. Moreover, the revised edition was already overdue and the inclusion of many hundreds of new subspecies would cause a further unacceptable delay. A single example will illustrate the problem. Proposals from the region of Papua New Guinea alone called for the inclusion of some 500 new entries, of which 400 referred to subspecies. Although, in conforming with the decision, I have also omitted subspecies from this book, readers can rest assured that they are still regarded as important and deserving of protection by ICBP, if only because of the value of their genetic diversity. The work to save them will, of course, continue.

I acknowledge with gratitude the assistance received from my friends at ICBP, Christoph Imboden, Tom Urquhart, Nigel Collar, Paul Andrew, Tim Dee and Alison Stattersfield, who not only provided the information on which the greater part of the book is based, but freely gave me the benefit of their advice. Tim Dee and Alison Stattersfield were seconded as my research assistants and worked indefatigably to keep me fully informed of the latest information about threatened species, and Alison checked and updated the final drafts with an eagle eye. If, however, from the mass of detail culled from reports from many countries, any error in interpretation has crept in, the responsibility is mine alone. My thanks go too to Jacqui Bellamy, Gina Pfaff and Irene Hughes of ICBP, all patient and tireless typists. Acknowledgements must also be made to the editors of the first and second editions of the Red Data Books, Jack Vincent and Warren King, who pioneered the format and the methods which have since been further developed for the third edition by Nigel Collar and Simon Stuart. I particularly commend Norman Arlott, who had the difficult task of illustrating this book. Many of the species are extremely poorly known and it is a delight to see them in such glorious detail. Finally I thank Crispin Fisher, Director of the Natural History Division of Collins, for his encouragement and for having my untidy manuscript transcribed on his electronic word processor, and Myles Archibald, Natural History Editor of Collins, for his enthusiasm in finalising all the tricky details.

Guy Mountfort. December, 1987

Chapter 1
Birds and Man

BIRDS PAST AND PRESENT

We shall never know how many different species of birds have inhabited our planet, because the majority came and went long before the arrival of *Homo sapiens*. Some authorities have suggested a possible total of one and a half million, but this is little more than guesswork. More recent experts have said half a million occurred during the past 130 million or so years, which seems a more reasonable estimate. It is more interesting to wonder how many species might have existed at any one period, in order to make a comparison with the present. Dr Oliver Austen, in his *Birds of the World*, calculated from a study of fossil records that a peak of 11,500 species was reached during the Pleistocene, about 250,000 years ago. Since then there has been a decline to our currently accepted world total of about 9,000 living species. Many which have not been recorded during the past 50 years are still listed, although now probably extinct. New species are also still being discovered.

The extinction of species is, of course, part of the natural and continuous process of evolution. It is only in comparatively recent times that man has taken a hand in speeding up the process. Unfortunately, he has done so to such an extent that the great majority of recent extinctions are now directly traceable to his influence and activities. The global rate of losses, not only of birds and other animals, but of plants and all forms of wildlife, is steadily accelerating. Some 100 unique species of birds are known to have become extinct during the past 600 years, but today more than 1,000 are considered as nearing extinction. Of these, nearly half have such critically small populations that they seem unlikley to survive for many more years unless vigorous action is taken to save them. The purpose of this book is to draw attention to their plight, to analyse the various threats they face and to describe the results achieved by the efforts of conservationists throughout the world to prevent these devastating losses.

The earliest known feathered creature capable of at least gliding flight was the somewhat reptilian and controversial *Archaeopteryx*, whose complete fossil remains were discovered in 1861 in a German slate quarry and dated back to the Jurassic period of 135 to 150 million years ago. The first true bird, in the sense that its skeleton was entirely comparable to that of a modern bird (for *Archaeopteryx* had almost no breast bone) was a species resembling both a goose and a flamingo. It was discovered in a Lower Cretaceous fossil bed in France, placing it some ten million years later than *Archaeopteryx*, and was

13

named *Gallornis straeleni*. Since then the fossil remains of the ancestors of nearly all today's bird families have been discovered in various parts of the world. None of our present families have appeared in fossil remains earlier than the Paleocene of 60 to 70 million years ago, but about 900 species have been identified in Pliocene deposits of between two and ten million years ago. Some species evidently survived unchanged for many millions of years, while others can be traced as having existed for only 40,000 years, which in terms of the time-scale of the world's evolution is no more than the blink of an eyelid in a man's life-time. James Fisher and Roger Tory Peterson in *The World of Birds* estimated the mean life of a bird species to be as long as two million years, compared with a mean of only 600,000 years for a mammal species. If this is so, it suggests that the greater mobility of birds may have enabled them in the past more readily to survive the drastic climatic and environmental changes which the planet has suffered. Doubtless many species perished during the great fluctuations of the Ice Age in the Pleistocene era, when the ice-cap repeatedly advanced and retreated across the northern hemisphere, reaching as far south as the Thames valley in England and well to the south of the Great Lakes in the United States.

Fossil remains can be somewhat misleading, however, because usually only the bones of birds which died in localities favourable to fossilisation, such as water-laid sediments, have survived. Obviously the remains of the larger species in the Pleistocene beds of the period from 10,000 to two million years ago stand a better chance of discovery than those of smaller or earlier species. We therefore know much more about the prehistoric giant birds such as the colossal American Tetratorn, a bird of prey with a wing-span exceeding five metres, and the giant flightless Moas of New Zealand, which stood nearly four metres high, or the half-tonne Elephant Birds of Madagascar, than about the small birds of the prehistoric forests, whose bones quickly perished. Even today, in the tropical rain-forest the skeletons of dead birds vanish without trace in a few days, because they are destroyed by the hungry multitude of small animals, insects, fungi and micro-organisms. It is again the bones of the larger birds favoured as food by prehistoric man, between 470,000 and 250,000 years ago, which are most likely to be found in his caves or middens of that period.

The extinction of species as a natural process of evolution would have continued even if man had not emerged as the world's most widespread and most successful predator. The ratites, or flightless birds, were particularly vulnerable to him, but those inhabiting islands could also easily be wiped out by tidal waves or volcanic eruptions. Another obvious cause of extinction was over-specialisation, such as gigantism, which led to reduced mobility and therefore to extra vulnerability. The emergence of powerful and invasive competitors for food or nest-sites can also exterminate weaker species, as can be seen today in the success of invasive birds such as the Japanese White-eye

Zosterops japonica, the European Starling *Sturnus vulgaris* or the Indian Mynah *Acridotheres tristis*, which are swamping and supplanting indigenous species on many islands. Over the millennia, the stern rule "adapt or perish" has prevailed. In a changing environment, the ability to fill new ecological niches and to modify feeding and breeding behaviour have been the keys to the survival of species and also to the origins of new species. A classic example is provided by the relatively recent evolution of the 13 species of Darwin's Finches in the Galápagos archipelago, which, from a common ancestor, have developed by adaptive radiation from heavy-billed seed-eaters to fruit-eaters, cactus-feeders, woodpecker-like wood-borers, blood-sippers and fine-billed warbler-like insect-eaters. Even more remarkable is the example of the various Hawaiian honeycreepers, which have evolved from a finch-like original colonist into a multitude of totally dissimilar species, each occupying and morphologically adapted to a different ecological niche.

The association between man and birds has been long and intimate, not merely because birds have provided him with relatively easily accessible sources of food, but because he has always been attracted by their songs, their beautiful plumage and their often confiding behaviour. Their powers of flight have symbolised freedom and their constant activity has been a source of wonder. The tribes of the Americas, Asia, Africa and Australasia still adorn themselves with feather head-dresses. Birds feature prominently in all the early art forms, religions, legends and superstitions. Many species are still locally regarded as sacred, as harbingers of spring or of rain, or as good or bad omens. Prehistoric man may have domesticated gallinaceous birds even before he learned to capture and domesticate wild dogs, pigs and cattle. But until he learned to alter his environment by the use of fire and the axe and to perfect his skill as a cooperative hunter, he made no more than a very local impression on the population of birds or other animals. The influence of modern man and his massive technology, on the other hand, has been progressively more malignant. It is only in recent years that the consequences of his actions as a mass destroyer and exterminator have finally given birth to the now widespread conservation ethic and a sense of moral responsibility for the damage he has caused to the natural environment. He is now beginning to recognise that birds represent important indicators of a healthy environment and that what harms them will also eventually harm the human race.

THREATS TO THE SURVIVAL OF BIRDS

Birds are today suffering at the hands of man in many different ways. He hunts them, traps them, poisons them, takes their eggs and introduces his destructive domestic animals or exotic predators into their habitats. Above all, he alters or destroys their habitats by felling the forests, draining the swamps, polluting and diverting rivers and building dams, highways, airports and cities in what was once unspoilt wilderness. As human numbers and the power of technology expand, so the chances of survival for wildlife diminish. The deliberate persecution of birds pales to near insignificance by comparison with the results of man's present belief in what has been called the unlimited land-development imperative.

The hunting instinct, whether for survival, food or sport, is inherent in man. A tribesman cannot be condemned for killing in order to defend or feed his family, but when twentieth century civilised man kills animals for the fun of it, moral issues are involved and must be faced. Many people today believe no justification can be found for blood sports of any kind. Hunting for sport as practised in some countries of Europe and in North America is now very strictly controlled and limits are placed on the species and numbers of birds or other animals which may be shot. Permitted hunting seasons are also controlled and are often sharply reduced if the populations of game-birds or deer have declined or are threatened by severe weather conditions. Hunters accept these restrictions, by enlightened self-interest, in order to maintain their sport. Game-birds are bred in semi-captivity on a very large scale and none of the species involved is in danger of being exterminated: in fact, the wild populations of several species of game-birds introduced into Europe and North America from Asia are now infinitely larger than in their countries of origin. The same applies to some mammals. The Blackbuck *Antilope cervicapra*, which was almost exterminated in India, is now more numerous in Texas than from whence it was introduced. Sportsmen take conservation seriously and provide large sums of money for the purchase of protected areas where their quarry can breed in safety. In the United States, organisations such as Ducks Unlimited, and fund-raising schemes such as "Duck Stamps" organised by the US Fish and Wildlife Service, raise hundreds of millions of dollars for the creation of protected reserves which, of course, benefit all forms of wildlife. In Great Britain, there is also close and increasing cooperation between conservationists and hunters. Unfortunately, however, the millions of pounds paid for shooting licences in Great Britain are still swallowed up by the national Treasury, instead of being applied to conservation as they should be.

A very different picture of hunting is provided by some other countries, where only a minority respects such protective legislation as exists. The shooting, netting and trapping of wild birds as now practised in Italy, France, Spain and Greece, for example, accounts every year for between one and two hundred million small birds, taken chiefly on migration. A comparable slaughter takes place on Mediterranean islands such as Malta, Cyprus and Crete, where the use of birdlime is also widespread. These forms of mass hunting are completely indiscriminate: birds of prey, storks, herons, owls, orioles, swallows and tiny warblers being taken equally with the so-called "edible" species such as quails, thrushes, buntings and larks. Among them are inevitably many rare species which, in more conservation-minded countries, are very strictly protected.

The killing of birds for financial gain is another problem. It began on a large scale at the turn of the century during the period when it was fashionable for women to wear "aigrette" or "osprey" feathers as head-dresses or in their hats. These extravagant decorations were usually made from the beautiful display plumes which egrets and birds of paradise grow in the breeding season. For this lucrative trade, the plume-hunters raided the breeding colonies of egrets wherever they occurred and very nearly exterminated them, leaving the nestlings to die in their thousands. They also caused severe losses among the birds of paradise in New Guinea. Had it not been for the strenuous efforts of the budding Audubon Society of America, the Little Egret *Egretta garzetta*, or Snowy Egret as it is called in the United States, might have disappeared entirely. Several of the society's wardens were killed by plume-hunters between 1905 and 1908 while defending the breeding colonies. Fortunately, this barbarous trade died out when women's fashions changed. It has recently reappeared in a new guise as tourist trinkets in the form of framed pictures made from the iridescent feathers of Asiatic sunbirds and kingfishers, mist-netted for the thriving workshops of Hong Kong, Singapore and Korea, which are exporting them throughout the world.

The cage-bird trade has become a multi-million dollar source of wealth to the law-breakers and a major threat to the survival of countless species of tropical birds, particularly those of the parrot family, some of which now change hands for thousands of dollars each. In 1983, half a million wild-caught parrots were imported into the United States, Japan and Europe. Twelve species of this family have become extinct in historical times and at least 60 others are now listed as threatened. Though protected by law they are still being smuggled out of South America, the Caribbean and Australia. In spite of occasional heavy fines, it is a highly profitable business. Peru alone exported two million wild-caught birds of various species, including parrots, for a profit of $20 million in 1983. I did not appreciate the sheer volume of this trade, or the degree of mortality involved, until one day in Colombia I saw a consignment of 26,000 small birds from the Amazon forests being loaded into a large freight plane bound for Florida. Hundreds of colourful little corpses already carpeted the floors of the grossly overcrowded cages. The cynical German exporter merely shrugged his shoulders and told me cheerfully that few of the remainder would survive longer than a few months in unskilled hands, but that so long as this valuable source of dollars continued he would be happy to exploit it. All customs officials are now in possession of the lists of birds which, under the Convention on International Trade in Endangered Species (CITES), may not be exported or imported. There is, however, a very real difficulty in teaching busy customs officials how to recognise the prohibited species, which exporters do not hesitate deliberately to misidentify on the export documents. I have included the CITES information in the complete list of threatened species (see Appendix I).

The passion for falconry, as indulged in particularly among the oil-rich sheikhs of the Arabian region, has created another source of wealth for smugglers. Of the various falcons, the Peregrine *Falco peregrinus* is in greatest demand. Some are caught on migration by skilful trappers using tethered doves as decoys in Afghanistan and Pakistan. Others are taken as nestlings in Europe and North America, in spite of heavy fines and the close guarding of occupied eyries. In 1983, American and Canadian guards arrested no fewer than 45 Americans, Canadians and West Germans who were smuggling Peregrines and Gyr Falcons *Falco rusticolus* to the Middle East at prices ranging from $10,000 to $100,000 each. In the same year, several men were heavily fined in Great Britain for taking the eggs or young of Peregrines for sale in Arabia and West Germany. Apart from this trade, Peregrines were almost brought to the verge of extinction in Europe and North America by lethal pesticides. These pesticides are not broken down in digestion and are therefore concentrated in predators that eat contaminated prey. Peregrines, being at the top of the food chain, were thus exposed to very high, lethal concentrations. Fortunately the products concerned were banned by law, and Peregrine populations are now recovering, but they remain threatened by the demand for falconry.

Falconry has been the traditional pastime of the Arab nations since time immemorial and it is not going to be relinquished readily. In Europe and America it is still practised on a very small scale and is so closely regulated that it probably represents no threat to wild falcon populations. Its scale in the Arab countries, however, is a serious threat, not only to the falcons, but to their favourite prey species, the bustards. Having almost exterminated the Houbara Bustard *Chlamydotis undulata* in Arabia, the sheikhs now take their falcons to Pakistan, where the majority of Houbaras that breed in southern Russia spend the winter. The number of Houbaras killed in Pakistan each winter has averaged about 3,000 and Russian scientists have complained of a 75% decline in the breeding population. Pakistan benefits financially from the annual influx of wealthy sheikhs and the Government has not introduced a five-year moratorium on the hunting of bustards, despite recommendations by an international symposium held in Peshawar in 1983. The sheikhs have however agreed to support a captive-breeding project organised by ICBP to restore the population.

Egg-collecting, which was a widespread pastime in Victorian England and elsewhere, is no longer regarded as socially acceptable. Heavy fines are now imposed on anyone taking or possessing the eggs of protected species. Nevertheless, there remains a hard core of unscrupulous private collectors in Great Britain, West Germany and many other countries who are prepared to risk prosecution and who still rob the nests of rare species. Among this international fraternity, clutches of eggs change hands for very large sums of money. Prosecutions are frequent and, at least in Great Britain, magistrates have begun to impose fines matching the black market value of the eggs taken.

The collecting of bird-skins for museums sometimes represents a serious threat to the survival of rare species, but, because the museums concerned are often highly respected institutions, the matter is rarely publicised. It is obviously necessary for scientific purposes that skin specimens should be available for detailed study. Immense and invaluable collections have been assembled during the past 150 years and these are freely accessible to ornithologists. Nearly all of the many great private collections have now found their way to the national musuems. Unfortunately, however, very few countries are yet content with a single national collection and this had led to an undesirable duplication in collecting rarities. In Europe there are still between two and 15 such museums per country, while in the United States there are at least 60. Not all of these are still collecting, but there have been recent instances when collectors from well-endowed museums have bribed officials in Third World countries in order to collect specimens of ultra-rare and officially protected birds. In at least one South American instance, birds have been collected in the full knowledge that they were probably the last survivors of their species. Later in this book instances are quoted where collectors for museums have shot as many as 50 or even 80 specimens of a threatened species known only on one small island. I came across an American collector in the Himalayas who had distributed handbills offering $100 for a fresh specimen of the Western Tragopan *Tragopan melanocephalus*, a pheasant now on the verge of extinction. This sum was more than most hill tribesmen could earn in a year and all pheasants were being shot in the hope of gaining so large a reward. Such behaviour is obviously indefensible.

The best known example of human predation on birds is the extermination of the flightless Dodo *Raphus cucullatus*, the last of which was killed on the island of Mauritius around 1665. These fat and defenceless creatures, which weighed about 20 kg, had no fear of humans and were so easily clubbed to death that the early Dutch mariners called them "Dodaarsen", meaning stupid, hence "Dodo". The Portuguese, who discovered the island in the sixteenth century, introduced rats and pigs, which also fed on the birds and their eggs. Ships' crews of all nations replenished their larders with Dodos until there were none left. Only skeletal remains now survive in museums. The same fate befell the flightless Solitaires, or "White Dodos" *Ornithaptera solitaria* and *Pezophaps solitarius*, on the neighbouring islands of Réunion and Rodrigues, both species being exterminated by 1765. A similar end awaited the Great Auk *Alca impennis*, a flightless, penguin-like seabird of the North Atlantic coastal waters, which were all too easily killed by mariners seeking food or oil from their boiled-down carcasses. The last Great Auk was killed in Iceland in 1844.

Probably neither the Dodo nor the Great Auk had very large populations by the time men started exploiting them. But between 1860 and 1910, the population of the long-tailed Passenger Pigeon *Ectopistes migratorius* of North America, was so enormous that it was numbered in tens of millions. A single flock was reported to have darkened the sky and the weight of roosting flocks to have broken the branches of trees. As the pigeons ravaged grain crops, farmers and professional netters killed them in hundreds of thousands and even dynamited their roosts. Thousands of barrels of pigeons were sold in the New York markets, or the carcasses fed to pigs. The slaughter continued until suddenly the Passenger Pigeon was no more. The last survivor died in the Cincinnati Zoo in 1914. North America's only parrot species, the once abundant and colourful Carolina Parakeet *Conuropsis carolinensis*, which damaged fruit crops, was exterminated in the same year. Nearly all of the many other species which have become extinct in recent times owed their demise directly or indirectly to the influence of man.

Almost 90% of the birds which have become extinct during the past century were island species. Most of these losses were caused by the destruction of or alteration to the native vegetation by agriculture, logging, mining, grazing by introduced livestock, the drainage of wetlands, or the building of towns and harbours. Others were exterminated by the introduction of predatory animals such as mongooses, cats or foxes, or by the rats which had gone ashore from ships and which had multiplied in the absence of their natural predators.

Rats, when they became established on Midway Island during the Second World War, killed all the island's unique rail species within two years. Introduced rabbits on Laysan Island destroyed all the vegetation and thereby exterminated at least three endemic bird species. Huge sums are now being spent on trying to eradicate feral cats, rabbits, goats, pigs, deer and cattle which are causing critical losses to native wildlife and particularly to rare birds on many islands in the Pacific, the Indian Ocean and the Caribbean and Australasian regions.

Two well-documented examples of the vulnerability of island birds to man and his introduced animals can be quoted from New Zealand and Hawaii. It is known from fossil remains that when the early Polynesians discovered New Zealand around 950 AD there were more than 150 species of indigenous birds in the islands, including 20 species of giant flightless Moas. By the time the first Europeans landed with Captain Cook's expedition in the eighteenth century, all but one of the Moas were extinct, this last species being killed off later in that century. One-third of all the other bird species originally seen by the Polynesian settlers were extinct by the beginning of the twentieth century, most of them killed by man, his introduced predators or his destruction of the natural environment by forest clearance and the introduction of sheep, goats and cereal farming. The lonely early settlers also had a passion for introducing the familiar birds of their homelands and 35 such species are now feral in New Zealand, where some have supplanted the declining indigenous species.

The Hawaiian archipelago was probably colonised by the Polynesians around 750 AD, i.e. long before they discovered New Zealand. It is not known whether they exterminated any of the local bird species, whose colourful feathers they used for ceremonial helmets and cloaks. But the Europeans and their descendants who followed Captain Cook's arrival in 1778 exterminated at least 15 species, including eight of the unique honeycreepers. If subspecies are included, the total number of extinctions is at least 50. No other island group in the world is known to have lost a greater number of its endemic birds, nor had more foreign species introduced to compete with them. In spite of the skilled efforts of American conservationists, the islands now have about 30 species and subspecies which are nearing extinction, mainly because of the radical man-made changes to the environment and the ravages of introduced animals such as the Eurasian tree-rat, the mongoose and the feral cat, although continental avian diseases are also believed to have played a major role. The many nectar-eating birds have suffered particularly from introduced invasive plants which are swamping the native vegetation, while huge areas of forest, including the beautiful *Metrosideros* trees whose crowns are smothered in nectar-bearing scarlet blossoms, have been replaced by monocultures of pineapple and sugar cane. Few places now show greater concern for conservation than Hawaii, but the effort has come too late.

Much the same sad history applies to the Mascarene Islands of Mauritius, Rodrigues and Réunion. Having lost at least 17 endemic species, these islands now hold only 16 and of these no fewer than 11 are on the danger list.

Environmental Degradation

None of the previously described threats to the survival of birds is today more serious than man's destruction of their habitats. Birds, like all other animals, are dependent for food and shelter on the kind of environment to which each species is adapted by evolution. Although a few invasive and hardy species such as the European Starling *Sturnus vulgaris*, the House Sparrow *Passer domesticus* and the Cattle Egret *Bubulcus ibis* have achieved almost worldwide distribution, most birds have little tolerance to radical change. A nectar-eating species of the tropical cloud-forest obviously cannot survive in dry savanna, any more than a fish-eating river-bird can survive in a desert. But the wildlife of today is subjected to the sudden and sometimes radical modification or destruction of its habitats on a scale unparalleled in the world's history. The great changes in climate and vegetation which occurred in prehistoric times were usually gradual and most of them measured in millions of years. Wildlife had a chance to adapt to these changes. Today, thanks to the gigantism and power of modern technology, massive changes to environments are being made in less than a decade. Millions of hectares of wetlands are being drained, major rivers are being diverted or dammed and the tropical forests are being felled or burnt at the almost incredible rate of 28 hectares *a minute* worldwide. At the beginning of this century, between the Tropics of Cancer and Capricorn, there was an almost continuous equatorial green belt of tropical rain-forest around the globe, from northern Australia and New Guinea through southern Asia, central Africa and Central and South America. Already this has been reduced to isolated patches and within the next 30 years almost none will remain. The richest and most varied genetic resource on Earth will have been destroyed, and with it countless species of birds, mammals, reptiles and plants, before science has yet studied more than one per cent of them. This is extermination on a grand scale, which will affect at least one quarter of the world's wildlife. It must rank as the greatest ecological tragedy yet caused by man. It may be greater in terms of biological extinction than that which took place 65 million years ago at the end of the Cretaceous period.

The value of the rain-forests has long been recognized. They have provided man with innumerable benefits in the form of foods, spices, gums, fibres, waxes, resins and above all medicinal plants which are the basis of an industry worth $40 billion worldwide. The great rubber industry also came from this source. Recent studies of the uses of tropical plants by primitive forest tribes indicate that a host of invaluable new medicines could be developed commercially. An expedition supported by the World Wide Fund for Nature identified a hundred such plants, all new to the pharmaceutical industry. These included herbal medicines already used, apparently successfully, by the Amazon Indians as treatments for leukemia, heart disease, cancer and also as muscle relaxants and oral contraceptives. Farmers, plant breeders, animal husbandry, the medical profession, many industries and above all biological science will have cause to deplore the destruction of this priceless treasure of source material.

In taking advantage of the soaring prices of hardwood timber and the unprecedented demand for it by the Western nations and Japan, the methods used in clear-felling the rain-forest have been extremely wasteful. Sometimes, only the eight largest trees per hectare are extracted. The remainder are simply knocked down by giant bulldozers with draglines and are left to dry. The following year a match is put to the vast accumulation of dry litter and fires of gigantic proportions then rage for many weeks, consuming everything, including all wildlife. Such conflagrations often get out of hand. Recently in Kalimantan, 35,000 sq km of virgin forest and a national park were consumed before the fire burnt itself out. To get rid of the tree stumps the process is usually repeated in the next dry season. The resultant burnt wilderness is then either taken over by native settlers for growing crops such as bananas, guava, coffee or maize, or is sown with coarse grasses for raising cattle. The soil in tropical forests is both very shallow and lacking in nutrients, most of which are held in the vegetation itself. A temporary enrichment of the top-soil is provided by the ash from the forest fire and this may enable crops to be raised for the first year or two. Thereafter the region becomes a virtual desert, in which only the hardiest weeds and creepers can grow. Any attempt to create grass prairie is likely to fail without a costly input of fertilisers. The wealthy Brazilian and North American beef barons, secure in the knowledge that the American demand for bigger and better beefburgers is insatiable, have bought millions of hectares of the great Mato Grosso rain-forest in Brazil at peppercorn prices and can afford fertilisers in order to sustain the millions of cattle which will replace the forest; but the millions of hungry squatters must move on or starve.

The quite extraordinary variety and richness of tree and plant species in tropical forests, which have been evolving for 65 million years, can never be recreated. Most of South America's 95,000 known species of flowering plants are of tropical forest origin and some tens of thousands of them are now listed as endangered. Some replanting of the destroyed areas is of course being done, but often only with commercially required tree species such as eucalyptus, which are foreign to the original vegetational complex. When I last visited Malaysia I was horrified by the extent to which the magnificent native dipterocarp forests had been replaced by sterile plantations of oil-palm, or alang-alang grass. I was shown regiments of hideously incongruous quick-growing Philippine Pines, which had been imported as most likely to satisfy the Japanese chip-board industry. A quick return in Japanese yen was obviously regarded as more important than the preservation of one of the world's most varied and beautiful forests. Meanwhile, Japan continues to increase its imports of timber from South-East Asia by 20% *per annum*, while leaving its own forests, other than the most biologically important, on Okinawa, intact. Apart from the irreparable losses to wildlife and the inevitable increase in soil erosion, the destruction of the giant forests causes a loss of oxygen and of cloud cover. This in turn permits an increase in the penetration of ultra-violet rays from the sun and will in time undoubtedly affect the local climate. Where African forests have been destroyed, the mean temperature at ground level has risen by as much as 30°C. Scientists are already expressing concern about this in countries which have lost most of their forest cover. India, for example, now has only 14% of its primary forests left, Bangladesh only 9% and Pakistan only 3%. Nepal lost 40% of its superb forests in only ten years and is now suffering from very severe erosion.

Pollution is a topic familiar to us all, though its scale is rarely appreciated. The pollution of land, water and air takes many forms, some all too obvious, some invisible to the naked eye but none the less deadly. Agricultural pesticides and defoliants, oil spills, smog, acid rain, sewage, lethal industrial effluents, such as mercury and lead, and atomic wastes all contribute. Some we are only just beginning to understand. It was not until the publication of Rachel Carson's *Silent Spring* in 1962 that the general public began to realise the extent of the damage done to bird populations by agricultural pesticides. Since then, public opinion has vigorously supported the efforts of conservationists to have the most harmful products banned by law. This has not prevented the manufacturers from doubling their sales in only eight years to a record £13 billion *per annum* by selling these lethal products to Third World countries, which continue to poison their freshwater sources, their people and their wildlife by the run-off from their agricultural land. The extent of this is demonstrated by a recent report that 70% of all the freshwater sources throughout India are now polluted by a combination of pesticides, factory effluents and sewage. Technology continues to develop products which can accelerate man's ability to destroy the natural environment, or alter it to suit his immediate ambitions. Typical of this was the deployment of the infamous "Agent Orange" by the American armed forces during the Vietnam War. Huge areas of verdant forest were sprayed from the air in order to kill all the vegetation in which the enemy found shelter. The result was the creation of a huge, lifeless wilderness of dead trees saturated with arsenical poisons, in which no living thing could survive. The action was justified at the time as a military necessity; but although it may have saved American lives, it had no effect on the outcome of the war.

Oil spills, chemical effluents, untreated sewage and now even atomic wastes are polluting not only many rivers and coastal waters but all the oceans of the world. When Thor Heyerdahl sailed across the South Atlantic he saw oil patches every day of his long voyage. The Mediterranean coastal waters and many of the great lakes and inland seas of the world are seriously polluted and fish stocks have declined steeply. Fish are the mainstay of many human communities and their disappearance because of the combined effects of pollution and persistent over-fishing is becoming an increasing problem. Even the remote polar regions have not escaped. The fall-out from atomic bombs exploded by the super-powers is carried by the circumpolar winds and is now found in the bodies of polar wildlife.

The ingestion of chlorinated hydrocarbons and the even more deadly organophosphates used in agricultural crop-sprays, pesticides and herbicides has taken a heavy toll among insectivorous and seed-eating birds and also among birds of prey and owls which eat poisoned rodents, fish or carrion. The Peregrine Falcon and the Osprey *Pandion haliaetus* in Europe and North America were almost wiped out before products such as DDT and Dieldrin were taken off the market. The much-loved White Stork *Ciconia ciconia* of western Europe is being depleted by eating poisoned locusts while on migration in Africa.

Robert Riseborough recently described pesticides and biochemicals as affecting birds in five ways: they alter or destroy the habitat; alter or destroy the food supply; kill birds outright; damage their reproductive capacity (by causing them to lay infertile or soft-shelled eggs); or kill them over an extended period by the trophic accumulation of poisons in the body tissues. Of these, the most important in the long term is probably the destruction of habitats.

The direct killing of birds with chemicals is sometimes deliberate, although it can almost never succeed in being species-specific. For example, the huge roosts and breeding colonies of the gregarious African Quelea *Quelea quelea*, a small sparrow-like bird which damages crops, are often sprayed from aircraft with lethal Parathion. The colonies are wiped out, but all the other birds in the area are also killed. A recent example resulted in every kingfisher for miles around dying from eating poisoned fish and insects, while hundreds of scavenging birds, mammals and reptiles also died from eating the Quelea corpses.

The extensive use of pesticides to control malaria, or to protect crops such as cotton, which is the mainstay of many Third World countries, is said to be obviously defensible. But the application of more and more of these chemicals, to which insect pests soon develop immunity, cannot be the right answer. According to the Food and Agriculture Organization of the United Nations, the excessive use of pesticides in countries where illiterate farmers cannot read the instructions and take no precautions, is killing at least 5,000 humans a year as well as wildlife. Scientists, farmers and manufacturers must work together to solve this devastating problem.

In Great Britain there are no unchanged native forests left, the landscape having been almost entirely modified by man. This process began during the Iron Age, when the first small clearings were made in the great forests which covered all but the highest hills. Many of the now common trees were introduced after the Roman invasion. Britain now has a smaller percentage of land under forest than almost any nation in Europe, although there are still a few large tracts of ancient and relatively unspoilt deciduous woodland, such as the New Forest, Epping and Savernake. Most of our other forests, particularly in Scotland and many parts of Wales, are now composed of monocultures of quick-growing North American conifers required by industry. Our massive native oaks, from which Britain's navy was once built and which support a greater number of insect and bird species than any other tree, are now regarded as too slow-growing to represent a viable commercial proposition. British hedgerows, which provide a vitally important habitat for many species of birds, are disappearing in order to facilitate mechanised farming and to increase agricultural acreage. No less than 140,000 miles of hedges have gone already, as well as 80% of the chalk downlands and 60% of the heathlands. The beautiful patchwork of small, hedged fields which formed the traditional landscape of England is giving way to huge open fields with wire fences and these, particularly in East Anglia, are beginning to suffer from wind erosion, the fate of the American dustbowl prairies. As well as the insect pests quickly developing immunity to insecticides, the insecticides are also killing the predatory insects which used to keep the pest species in ecological balance.

Our marvellous technology, which makes such a large contribution to environmental degradation, while increasing our yield of crops, thus often backfires. Another form of pollution which affects birds by destroying their habitats is the so-called "acid-rain". This is composed of sulphur and nitrogen oxides from factory and power station chimneys and poisonous fumes from the exhausts of automobiles. These elements are carried by the wind and descend with rain or snow as a deadly combination on far-away regions. Britain is accused of being the primary producer of acid rain in Europe and is rightly blamed for the destruction of forests and the pollution of lakes in Scandinavia; but the problem is by no means confined to one country. The widespread destruction of forests in Germany is undoubtedly caused by the chimneys of the great factory complex of the Ruhr and by the density of automobile traffic on German roads. Factory fumes are also destroying forests in Poland and Czechoslovakia. In Switzerland car exhausts are acknowledged to have caused severe damage to forests. Acid rain in India is attributed to factory chimneys and the widespread burning of wood fuel and dried cow-dung. The truth is that this emotive subject is as yet only imperfectly understood. Meanwhile, forests are undoubtedly dying, lakes and rivers are being poisoned and irreplaceable monuments such as Gothic cathedrals, the Parthenon and the Taj Mahal are being seriously eroded.

Without fresh water it is obvious that all life on earth would disappear. It is astonishing therefore that so low a priority is given to the preservation of the purity of available sources. In many countries, factories are still being built on the banks of rivers and lakes, so that their lethal effluents can be conveniently discharged into the water. In the same spirit, the effluents from holiday camps and hotels are allowed to poison inshore waters by being discharged too close to the shore, as can be seen in Mediterranean and Black Sea resorts and in many "paradise islands" such as the Seychelles. But sewage is only a minor part of the 430 billion tonnes of pollutants which are discharged annually into the Mediterranean. In Britain the once badly polluted and almost lifeless Thames has now been restored to increasing purity, enabling it to be successfully re-stocked with many species of fish, including salmon; but the cost, trivial though it was by comparison with the achievement, has given such work a low priority. Many of the great rivers of Europe, such as the Rhine and the Rhône, remain little more than industrial sewers. Even in the public-hygiene- and conservation-conscious United States, many rivers and some of the Great Lakes remain so seriously polluted that fish have disappeared and bathing is forbidden or restricted.

Heathlands and wetlands of all kinds are the habitats of thousands of species of birds throughout the world. Yet every heath, marsh, water meadow, bog and estuary has a compulsive attraction to the civil engineer and land developer as potential sites for reclamation; more than 50% of them have already been lost in Britain. There are long and costly legal battles to exploit them; their classification by the Nature Conservancy Council as Sites of Special Scientific Interest is again and again over-ruled so that land can be reclaimed for agriculture, or in order to build a factory site, an airfield, a housing estate, or a highway. All the great delta wildlife sanctuaries in Europe are under constant threat of agricultural or industrial development, notably the Camargue reserve on the delta of the Rhône, the Coto Doñana reserve on the delta of the Guadalquivir, and the main breeding grounds of Europe's diminishing population of pelicans on the delta of the Danube. The vitally important wetland reserves of the USSR, Austria, Hungary, Turkey and the Netherlands are similarly threatened. In the Third World, out of 200 major wetland drainage developments funded by the World Bank or USAID, only nine had adequate study made of the ecological consequences, many of which were disastrous.

The conservation of wildlife has to be seen in the context of man's own survival. Where wildlife thrives, it is an indication of a healthy natural environment. Where it declines or has been wiped out, the environment is clearly degraded and man has taken another step towards his own classification as an endangered species. Lest this is thought an exaggeration, consider what is known today about the threats to human survival, apart from the possibility of self-destruction by nuclear holocaust.

First and foremost is the relentlessly increasing pressure of human numbers on the declining natural resources of the world. By 1830 the world's population had reached one billion. Only 145 years later, in 1975, it had risen to four billion. Within the lifetime of today's children it will have doubled again by exponential growth to eight billion. Thanks to medical science, life expectancy continues to lengthen and infant mortality to decline. The gigantic losses caused by two world wars were followed by an immediate boom in births and the millions of lives lost by famines in Asia and Africa caused scarcely a ripple in the soaring graph of the world's population. Although population control is beginning to make progress (in Britain we are nearing zero growth, with births equalling deaths), some African countries are doubling their populations in only 22 years. It is in the impoverished Third World that the tragic consequences of the population explosion are most apparent and already nearly one third of the human race is living at bare subsistence level. In north-east Africa, as I write, millions are actually starving, whereas Western nations are increasingly suffering from diseases attributable to over-eating. Yet some United Nations advisors still encourage some African countries to grow pineapples for the American market instead of food for their own people!

In the rich Western world we are accustomed to read that our farmers are achieving steadily increasing yields and big surpluses from the land they cultivate. But worldwide, the picture is very different. The yield from grasslands, croplands, forests and oceans is declining. Freshwater sources are becoming increasingly scarce, soil erosion is rampant and deserts, which already cover 14% of the world's surface, are advancing. It is clear that unless the wealthy nations of the world devote their technology and wealth to helping the developing nations to overcome the threats to their survival, life in the twenty-first century will be almost unbearable for the poorest countries. Land at present devoted to national parks and wildlife reserves will then inevitably be converted to the production of food. Pessimists are already saying that conservation is fighting a losing battle. Nevertheless, nearly all governments now recognise that the natural resources of the world, if equitably shared and managed on a sustained-yield basis, are sufficient to meet the needs of a world population of double what it is today. What is lacking is agreement that sufficient financial and technological aid will be devoted to the task. It is not yet recognised by the developed nations, which now consume four-fifths of the world's natural resources, that their continuously increasing wealth cannot be sustained without causing catastrophic consequences to the rest of the world. This has been said many times at the United Nations, but has scarcely yet penetrated to the vote-conscious politicians, who by and large suffer from environmental illiteracy and cling to the goal of an ever-rising standard of living for their own nationals. Foreign aid therefore continues to be derisory by comparison with the need and is often far from altruistic. "I'll give you some of my surplus grain providing you buy my tractors with hard currency" is the kind of aid which imposes additional hardship on countries whose exports are banned by the donor nations. On the other hand, many of the poorest nations are far from blameless, preferring to spend vast sums obtained by crippling loans from the West on constructing grandiose state buildings, or on armaments, or on "prestige" developments such as national airlines, instead of on the production of food for their starving people. Getting our priorities right is, in fact, the key to our future in an over-crowded and increasingly hungry world. Public opinion is now well aware of this, even if governments are loath to recognise it. This was amply demonstrated by the immediate and generous response of the general public of many nations who subscribed $1.5 billion to the appeals made by voluntary bodies such as the Red Cross, Oxfam and Live Aid at the time of the Ethiopian and Sudanese famines. The time is coming when politicians will be shamed by the fact that millions died of starvation while they squabbled over the profitable disposal of surplus "food mountains". The quality of life on Earth *can* be maintained and indeed improved if governments get their priorities right and if they combine with religious leaders to control the present suicidal growth of the world's population. The value to man of wildlife and wilderness will then increase rather than diminish as the world becomes more crowded, if for no other reason than that man will need the solace and beauty of nature as a release from the social pressures of what Professor Toynbee called the horrors of the megalopolis existence which he gloomily forecast for the twenty-first century.

THE HISTORY OF BIRD PROTECTION

Conservation is no modern phenomenon. It began with the Moghul Emperor Ashoka, who in 242 BC erected stone pillars on the frontiers of his empire, engraved with the instruction that no wild creature or plant should be destroyed unless required for food. One of these famous Fifth Edict pillars can still be seen in the Gujarat State of India and Ashoka's influence survives in the enlightened attitude of most Indians towards conservation. The idea that areas should be set aside for the protection of birds can be attributed to St. Cuthbert, who in 677 AD created the first sanctuary for seabirds and seals on the Farne Islands, off the Northumbrian coast. At the close of the twelfth century the gentle St. Francis of Assisi preached conservation and focused attention on the beauty of birds as man's confiding companions; it was therefore very appropriate that the 25th anniversary of the founding of the World Wide Fund for Nature was celebrated in 1986 at Assisi.

The first British naturalists to record their observations concerning birds were Martin Martin, who wrote about those he saw in Scotland in 1697, and Mark Catesby, who described the birds of colonial America between 1712 and 1726. The Reverend Gilbert White (1720–1793) devoted his life to the study of living birds. His *Natural History of Selborne* and his posthumously published *Naturalist's Calendar* are models of painstaking observation. They provided the first exceptions to the hitherto prevailing belief that birds could be studied only over the barrel of a shotgun.

By the nineteenth century the number of people interested in birds (though still mainly by shooting them or collecting their eggs) had increased sufficiently for ornithological societies to be formed. The first was in Germany in 1851 closely followed by one in the United Kingdom, where in 1855 the prestigious British Ornithologists' Union was founded by Alfred Newton and others. The oldest society in the United States is the Nuttall Ornithological Club, founded in 1873.

The first credit for organised protection of birds by ornithologists with the support of the general public goes to the Royal Society for the Protection of Birds, founded in 1889, and the Audubon Societies in the United States, the Massachusetts Audubon Society being the first founded in 1896. Others soon followed in different states and the National Audubon Society came into being in 1916. The original conservation organisations are now highly organised and very effective, with membership numbered in hundreds of thousands. They do admirable educational work and have created many hundreds of bird reserves, as well as promoting protective legislation. The first American bird reserve, however, was created in 1870 by private initiative. This was the Merrett Wetlands Reserve in Oakland, California, in an area now almost surrounded by buildings. The United States also created the world's first national park in 1872, the Yellowstone, which, with nearly 2.5 million acres, is still one of the largest and scenically most splendid of any country. The United Kingdom now has 1,600 small but well protected wildlife reserves.

It was not until 1922, however, that the protection of birds on a worldwide scale was made possible by the creation of the International Council for Bird Preservation (ICBP), which today has its headquarters at Cambridge in England. Initially, it had a distinct bias towards Western Europe and North America, from which its founders were enlisted. Its first achievement was the enforcement of the Convention on Migratory Birds by the governments of the United States and Great Britain, a measure aimed chiefly at controlling the over-exploitation of wildfowl. Its activities thereafter rapidly expanded throughout the world. Today ICBP represents a federation of more than 300 member organisations in 100 countries and is recognised as the world authority in its sphere of interests. It collaborates closely with the International Union for Conservation of Nature and Natural Resources (IUCN), the World Wide Fund for Nature (WWF), the International Wildfowl Research Bureau (IWRB) and the various United Nations agencies concerned with conservation, such as UNEP and FAO. From this partnership has emerged a succession of international agreements, treaties and conventions for improving the protection of endangered birds and their habitats in every country. At its periodic international meetings, priorities for action and resolutions for presentation to governments are drafted. The Species Survival Commission of IUCN/WWF made ICBP responsible for the production of the Red Data Book of endangered species of birds, in which all the available information obtained by observers throughout the world is kept constantly up-to-date, so that appropriate action can be taken. Many hundreds of conservation projects have been executed, some involving working in very remote areas or on small oceanic islands. As will be seen in the following pages, some remarkable successes in saving species from almost inevitable extinction have been achieved. Indeed, few organisations have achieved so much with such slender resources, for by comparison with many richer organisations ICBP operates on a very modest budget. Although it now possesses the expertise to save critically endangered birds, many fully documented projects for their salvation are held up by lack of funds. It fully deserves greater support from the public.

Considerable skill in diplomacy is involved in the work of ICBP. Any international conservation project has to deal first with the fundamental imbalance in the distribution of human and financial resources. Strong conservation movements have developed during this century in the affluent industrial countries, for the most part in the northern hemisphere. It is, however, in the developing countries of the Third World, where conservation is rarely practised, that realistic strategies are most desperately needed to fulfil aspirations of long-term economic stability. It is in these largely tropical countries and on their related islands that 75% of the world's threatened species of birds occur.

The world centre for the scientific aspects of conservation of the natural environment and wildlife is the IUCN, which shares the same headquarters with WWF at Gland, Switzerland. After a hesitant start in 1902 it came into being under its present name in 1934. On its various commissions are leading experts drawn from 114 countries, including the USSR, and from Africa, Asia and South America. All national and international societies and United Nations agencies concerned with conservation draw on this source of experience and expertise. Its work is funded in part by WWF, which was created in 1961 as the first international tax-exempt charitable foundation with the objective of raising money on a worldwide basis for conservation. Part of WWF's income is spent on public and governmental education about the need to protect the natural environment and wildlife, part on funding the projects devised by IUCN and ICBP, and part on sustaining the work of the leading national or international organisations involved in similar tasks. Its educational programmes, using mobile cinemas in native villages in Asia, Africa and South America, are of very great value. Thanks to the skill of its founders and trustees, it had raised through its 24 national branches more than $100 million by 1986 and had financed some 6,000 conservation projects in 130 countries. Part of its success is due to its total independence from political or governmental influence as to how or where its money should be spent.

Today conservation is a major topic throughout the world. Although most governments still prefer to give first priority to spending money on armaments or industrial development, the general public in the developed nations is increasingly well informed about the multiple threats to the natural world and is beginning to clamour for action. The "Green" movement has become a political reality in Europe. Nowhere is this awakening more apparent than in Great Britain, where every county now has its Naturalist's Trust, its local branches of WWF and RSPB, and its ornithological society. In addition, there are many specialised national bodies, such as the Wildfowl Trust, the Fauna and Flora Preservation Society, the World Pheasant Association, the Hawk Trust, the Great Bustard Trust and the British Trust for Ornithology, which organises population censuses, ringing and nest-recording. There are similar developments in every continent of the world. As the pressure of public support generated by such societies rises, it is to be hoped that politicians will begin to give the survival of birds and other wildlife the priority it deserves.

Chapter 2
The Palaearctic Region

The Palaearctic Region is bounded in the north, east and west by the Arctic, Pacific and Atlantic Oceans respectively. Iceland is included, but not Greenland, which belongs in the Nearctic, although some of its birds migrate to Europe. All of Europe and Asia north of the Himalayas are included, as is the northern half of China and mainland Japan. The southern boundary extends from Morocco across the northern Sahara, through Arabia and Iran and along the southern boundaries of Tibet and the Gobi. This represents an almost continuous belt of great deserts, which provide a fairly obvious demarcation or boundary to the dispersal of Palaearctic, Afrotropical and Oriental bird species. The northern part of Africa is included because its avifauna, like that in the Sinai region, is composed predominantly of Palaearctic species.

The north-western part of the Palaearctic was greatly affected by the Pleistocene Ice Age and there is still evidence of a north-westerly re-colonising drift of species of plants and birds following the retreat of the last glaciation, although a great area of the region remained ice-free. Today's vegetational zones resulting from the extreme conditions of the Ice Age are clearly apparent. From west to east across Europe and Asia is a northern band of wind-swept and treeless tundra, equivalent to that in Arctic Canada, giving way inland to coniferous boreal forest, which stretches from Scandinavia to Siberia. In Siberia the tundra zone curves southward for a considerable distance. In Europe and western Russia the boreal forest gives way to temperate deciduous forest and in eastern Asia to taiga forest. In Scandinavia the transition from tundra to boreal is still clear-cut, but the landscape and vegetation of most of western and southern Europe is now largely a man-made mixture of coniferous and deciduous woodlands interspersed with agricultural land, canals, dammed rivers and great cities. These varied habitats attract a greater variety of bird species than do the natural forests. In the Mediterranean basin and the Iberian peninsula there are expanses of scrub and maquis, mixed with Mediterranean and introduced tree species. In Central Asia and around the Asian deserts from the Caspian to Inner Mongolia are extensive areas of open grasslands and steppe, parts of which are on clay-pans, sand or stony semi-desert. The high Tibetan Plateau rivals the heights of Arctic Siberia in the harshness of its environment. Throughout much of the Palaearctic there is evidence of a northward drift of deciduous woodlands into the coniferous areas. But nearly all forested areas have been greatly diminished by land-clearance activities in recent times to make way for cereal crops, grazing, or vast monocultures of vegetables or fruit-trees. Great changes have also been brought about by the drainage of swamps and the damming or diversion of major rivers. These have adversely affected many species of aquatic birds. The rocky coasts and offshore islands of northern Europe, where millions of seabirds breed, also suffer from modern man's technology in side-effects such as major oil-spills and the offshore discharge of toxic industrial effluents. Many European and Asian rivers, lakes and inland seas are also seriously polluted and possess greatly diminished fish stocks.

The migration of Palaearctic birds has received intensive study for a longer period than in any other zoogeographical region, although mainly in the European area where bird-ringing originated. Broadly speaking, the majority of western Palaearctic birds which breed in the higher latitudes migrate to the equatorial region of Africa, some wintering on the west coast and others even reaching the Cape. Others fly south-west from the northern regions to winter in the British Isles or the Mediterranean countries. Those breeding in north-eastern Asia, on the other hand, mostly winter in South-East Asia or the Australasian region.

Although the Palaearctic is so large an area, the density of birds and the variety of species within it are relatively low by comparison with the tropical regions. This is largely a reflection of the inhospitable nature of the northern subarctic areas and of the southern deserts. The almost continuous chain of mountains from the Pyrenees eastward through the Alps and Caucasus to the Himalayas has also influenced the dispersal of species. Nevertheless, the Palaearctic has 329 different genera and about 950 species of birds as well as a large number of vagrants from other regions, including a few from the Nearctic which cross the Atlantic with the aid of the prevailing west wind. The enormous region represented by eastern Siberia, Mongolia and China has, as yet, been little studied by ornithologists. However, in the Far East, as in all the Soviet-controlled countries and Western Europe, the study and conservation of birds and the creation of special reserves for them are making encouraging progress.

The **Short-tailed Albatross** *Diomedea albatrus* was prematurely declared to be extinct in 1949. There are now grounds for some optimism in view of a slow, but steady, upward trend in its population since the Second World War. It is known previously to have bred on many islands to the south of Japan, where it was heavily persecuted by feather-hunters. Between 1889 and 1903 many thousands were killed while breeding. Large quantities of bones of the species were found in the middens of coastal North American Indians, which indicates a much wider original distribution. In 1929 1,400 albatrosses were counted on Torishima Island and a decade later only 30–50. In 1945 just a

Chinese Egret

single bird could be found. In 1950 a nest was found and in 1954 six pairs bred, rising to 26 pairs in 1964 and 57 in 1973. The total population is now estimated at about 250 birds and in 1985 51 young were reared, all on Tsubakuro Point on the small volcanic island on Torishima. The island is subject to periodic volcanic eruptions and is uninhabited except by introduced cats and rats, which probably prey on the eggs and young of the albatrosses. A proposal to mine sulphur on the island was refused by the Japanese government in order to save the albatrosses, which have been declared a Special Natural Monument, as had all the island's natural fauna and flora. In 1972 the Short-tailed Albatross was designated a Bird for Special Protection. Current plans include the elimination of the cats and rats and the turfing of the

volcanic slopes to encourage nesting. This is a praiseworthy example of conservation by Japan. The species is listed by ICBP as Endangered.

The **Dalmatian Pelican** *Pelecanus crispus* (Plate II) suffers from human persecution as a fish-eater more than any other of the eight species in its family. Its population has fallen from the millions which reportedly existed at the beginning of this century to only 665–1,000 pairs, about half of which breed in the USSR. In the Romanian Danube delta, which once had an enormous population, there were only about 100 pairs in 1979; in Bulgaria 30–90; in Greece 80–100; in Yugoslavia 55; in Turkey between 90 and 200 and in Iran perhaps 5–10 pairs. In the Volga delta in the USSR the population dropped from 300 pairs in 1949 to 160 in 1974, plus six or seven colonies of about 50 pairs each elsewhere. A few may breed in Sinkiang, China. The Dalmatian Pelican has been eliminated from its former breeding colonies on the Rhine, the Scheldt and the Elbe, from Albania and from seven out of nine of the colonies in Greece. The USSR and Iran have now lost most of their colonies. Persecution by fishermen and the reclamation or pollution of lakes, swamps and other wetlands and the harvesting of reeds have caused these losses. The species is legally and fairly effectively protected in the USSR, Romania, Bulgaria, Yugoslavia, Greece and Turkey, but nesting colonies still suffer from "accidental" fires caused by fishermen. Reserves and national parks protect many colonies and some of these are provided with rafts for nesting. The species is listed by ICBP as Vulnerable.

The **Chinese** or **Swinhoe's Egret** *Egretta eulophotes*, which suffered great losses to the plume-hunters and other forms of human persecution at the end of the last century, now has a very small population. It is listed as Vulnerable. Competition from other egret species may be preventing a complete recovery. It used to be widely distributed, breeding in eastern China and North Korea and as far south as Hong Kong. Today, it is known to breed only on islands on the west coast of North Korea where there are an estimated 250 pairs, and on islands off Shanghai where there is a colony of 20 pairs. A few pairs still nest in Hong Kong in a closely guarded reserve, where they are legally protected. Often confused when in non-breeding plumage with the very similar white morph of the Eastern Reef Heron *Egretta sacra*, the Chinese Egret has a much longer and more luxuriant crest and breast-feathers when breeding. It was these plumes which were its downfall and, unlike the Little Egret *E. garzetta*, which quickly recovered after the massacre by the plume-hunters, this relict species may never recover.

One of the rarest of the world's storks is the little-known **Oriental White Stork** *Ciconia boyciana* (Plate IV) which is given Endangered status by ICBP. Its breeding range in Siberia once extended from Lake Khanka along the Ussuri and Amur rivers to the eastern edge of the Sikhote Alin range and the Krasnoi River in Amurland, in the Soviet Far East and into north-east China, wintering south to Hainan. It has also bred in Japan and Korea. Its numbers in the Amur basin are now very small and because of land drainage it no longer breeds elsewhere in Siberia, nor in Japan or Korea. Hunting and mercury posioning from pesticides wiped it out in Japan and the Korean war probably contributed to its disappearance from that country. The last report from the USSR put the population at 400–500 breeding pairs, but 2,729 birds were recorded on migration in Hopei province, China, in autumn 1986. The

storks are now strictly protected by law in the USSR, South Korea and Japan, where a captive-breeding project has been attempted without success for some years. Special reserves have been created in South Korea and Japan, but all these efforts may have been made too late.

Another stork in trouble is the **White Stork** *Ciconia ciconia*, a species always closely associated with man. Today it is scarce in most of Western Europe, although there remains a good population in Austria and Eastern European countries including the Soviet Union. The most acute problem has been a significant decrease in feeding areas as a result of intensive agriculture. Pesticides, power lines, changes in architecture (favourite nesting sites are on roof-tops and chimneys) and hunting in southern Europe and in the wintering grounds of Africa are all having an effect, whilst in Africa locust control programmes are reducing the White Stork's primary food source. ICBP is very alert to all these compounding problems and their potential impact, and the species, currently a Candidate, may be afforded Of Special Concern status due to the great conservation interest that it generates amongst Europeans.

All the species of the ibis family are threatened by the ambitions of land developers to convert marshes and forests to money-making purposes. One of the two species currently listed as Endangered is the **Northern Bald Ibis** or **Waldrapp** *Geronticus eremita*, which is one of the few birds to have become extinct in Europe in historical times. It now has only two small and widely separated breeding populations, one at Bireček on the upper Euphrates in Turkey, the other in 12 scattered sites in the coastal and Atlas regions of Morocco and one site in Algeria. Until the seventeenth century it bred on the Rhône and the

Danube, in the Italian Alps and in the Swiss Jura. Some survived in Syria until 1930. It may also have bred around the Red Sea and in Iraq. It is legally protected in both Turkey and Morocco, but law enforcement is almost impossible. Nevertheless, strenuous efforts are being made in both countries to save these remarkable birds. At Birečik a joint WWF and Turkish National Parks project provided additional nesting platforms on the cliffs where 85% of the colony nested and, because of the close proximity of houses, protective walls were built to prevent refuse from being thrown on the nests. A traditional festival to celebrate the annual return of the Waldrapps was revived. A captive-breeding attempt has produced many young birds, some of which have joined the now tiny wild colony of five or six pairs. The major cause of decline in Turkey is apparently the massive use of pesticides on the grasslands and marshes where the birds forage for invertebrates. However, climatic and other natural factors may lie behind the long-term population trends, as the species was evidently once abundant in northern Syria, and figures on Egyptian hieroglyphs. The Moroccan population was about 1,000 pairs in 1930, but today is only a few hundred birds at most. Hunting and nest-side disturbance may have been the major factors in the North African decline. The widely scattered nesting sites in the wilds of Morocco make protection particularly difficult, but two of them are guarded and supported by privately sponsored educational campaigns. The related South African species, the Southern Bald Ibis *G. calvus* is also at risk (see page 107).

The second Endangered ibis is the **Crested Ibis** *Nipponia nippon* (Plate IV), one of the world's rarest birds and also perhaps the most beautiful of the ibis family. A century ago it was common in Japan and eastern China, breeding mainly in south-east Siberia and Manchuria southward to Zhejiang and Shanxi Provinces in China and westwards to Xizang (Tibet). It had apparently disappeared from the USSR by 1963, while in Japan the last five wild birds were captured in 1980. In fact, since 1969 there has been a captive-breeding project on the Japanese island of Sado, supported by the WWF. In 1973 there were 14 birds in captivity, but the project gradually failed and only two now survive. In 1981, after a long search by the Chinese Institute of Zoology, a breeding group of seven birds was discovered in the Qinling range of Shanxi Province. It was closely guarded and by 1984 had increased to 17 birds. The Chinese Government has since developed a research, management and captive breeding programme. A breeding facility has been constructed at Beijing Zoo and permission has been granted to take one ibis from the wild each year, in an attempt to preserve the "gene pool" in case some unforeseen disaster wipes out the tiny remaining population.

Many of the species of Palaearctic waterfowl are now giving cause for concern. The population of the **Lesser White-fronted Goose** *Anser erythropus* has declined very sharply since the 1950s and is continuing to do so. It is a Candidate Red Data Book species. Several of its breeding sites in Norway, Sweden, Finland and Arctic Russia have been abandoned and the numbers seen on migration in south-east Europe have declined. Its population size is not known, but is certainly diminishing.

The **Crested Shelduck** *Tadorna cristata* is known only from three specimens but was often featured in early Japanese paintings. Although now usually regarded as extinct, there were sightings in 1964 and 1971 and it may still survive in

36

Scaly-sided Merganser

the remoter Japanese coastal regions or in adjacent Russian waters. Because this species was formerly regarded as extinct it never made it into the Red Data Books but is currently a Candidate Red Data Book species.

Very little is known about the **Scaly-sided Merganser** *Mergus squamatus*, but it is believed to be distributed in small numbers in south-eastern Siberia and north-eastern Manchuria. Like all the sawbills it is rather solitary and may be more numerous than the few reports suggest. It is known to breed in some of the remote mountainous regions of Siberia and Manchuria and to winter in China, Korea, Tibet and Burma, but the majority of its population evidently remains in the main breeding area, on the rivers flowing from the eastern slopes of the Sikhote Alin range in the Soviet Far East. A rough estimate of its population in 1973 was "several hundred pairs". Limited protection is provided for it in the Sikhote Alin Reserve and the Sudzukhe Sanctuary. Its status is given by ICBP as Indeterminate.

The largest of the Palaearctic eagles, the **White-tailed Fish-eagle** *Haliaeetus albicilla* (Plate II), is widely but locally distributed in the northern parts of the region and in Greenland, but is declining in Europe because of human predation, habitat destruction and contamination by the pollution of fish in its feeding areas. Its Asiatic population may be stable but information about it is lacking. It breeds in Greenland, Iceland, Scandinavia and along the northern coast of the USSR to Kamchatka, the Kuriles and Japan. The southern range is in central and north-east Europe and sparsely through the Balkans to Greece, Turkey, Iraq, Iran, the Caspian, Turkestan and eastwards to Mongolia and Manchuria. Immature birds are occasionally reported as far as North Africa, India, Japan and Indonesia. It formerly bred in Austria, Egypt, Israel, the Faroes, Scotland and Ireland. The Greenland population had declined to about 300 adults plus an unknown number of juveniles by 1974, and the total European population to about 500–750 breeding pairs. A decline is reported in the Russian area except around the Caspian Sea, where it is still fairly abundant. It is now rare in Japan and absent from the Yangtze valley in China. The species is notionally protected in almost all countries where it breeds. In Sweden, nest sites are guarded and in Finland pesticide-free food is supplied in winter. An attempt to reintroduce the species into Scotland with young birds taken from Norwegian eyries is now in progress on the island of Rhum and looks promising, two locally-raised pairs having already bred and fledged a total of six chicks over 1985, 1986 and 1987. The species is listed by ICBP as Vulnerable.

Crested Shelduck

The very handsome, white-shouldered **Spanish Imperial Eagle** *Aquila adalberti*, regarded here as a full species, is listed as Endangered and is now restricted to a few areas in Spain and Portugal, where it is subjected to shooting, poisoning, habitat destruction, pesticide poisoning and the danger of striking overhead wires. It formerly occurred throughout the drier regions of the Iberian Peninsula as far north as the Pyrenees and southward to Morocco and the Atlas Range in Algeria. It probably no longer breeds in North Africa, as there appear to be no records for many years. It is now restricted to south, central and west Spain and a few parts of Portugal. Its main stronghold is Cáceres province and Coto Doñana National Park in Andalucía; in the latter about 13 pairs survive under strict protection. Its total population is thought to be about 104 breeding pairs in Spain and only a few pairs in Portugal. Its habit of building its conspicuous nests in solitary trees makes it an easy target for hunters and it has also suffered severely from habitat destruction. It is legally protected throughout Spain, but the traditional Spanish custom of shooting all birds of prey continues in the wilder regions. In 1972 a new management technique was introduced by Spanish conservationists. In nests containing three or four eggs the last two chicks to hatch never survive; they were therefore removed and transferred to nests with only one nestling. Fledgling success was thereby increased by 43%. A new reserve for these eagles in Cáceres province has now been created by the Spanish branch of the WWF.

The **Peregrine Falcon** *Falco peregrinus* is threatened throughout its Palaearctic range by contamination from chlorinated hydrocarbons. Killing and capture for falconry play contributory roles in some regions and loss of habitat is also significant. The species has an almost worldwide distribution except in New Zealand, Antarctica, Central America, northern South America, Micronesia and Polynesia. The status of the Nearctic races is described on page 56. Wherever figures are available they almost all indicate a steady or a steep decline during this century. In some western and northern European countries the populations have fallen by 95% compared with 1940. Of the various subspecies in the Palaearctic Region the European race *F. p. peregrinus* and the Central Asian race *F. p. pelegrinoides* are in particualr demand for falconry, as is *F. p. babylonius* of the Middle East. In Great Britain nest sites are carefully guarded by the RSPB and heavy fines are imposed on those who take eggs or nestlings. However, the very high prices paid by rich Arab falconers continue to encourage this trade in Europe, North America and Asia. The species as a whole is listed by ICBP as Vulnerable although the threat to the different races varies.

Many pheasant species, both in the Palaearctic and the Orient, are at risk. One is the **Chinese Monal** *Lophophorus lhuysii* which, although less brilliantly colourful than its relative the Himalayan Monal *L. impejanus*, is similarly large and short-tailed. It suffers from hunting and is now rare within its restricted range in western China. It is believed still to occur in north-western Siang, western and northern Sichuan, south-west Qinghai and perhaps also in southern Gansu province. In 1877 it was already regarded as rare. In 1910 and again in 1951 it was thought to be near extinction. There has been no reliable information since. It is classified by ICBP as Endangered. The species has rarely been bred in captivity.

Another threatened pheasant is the little-known **Brown Eared Pheasant** *Crossoptilon mantchuricum*. Although no reliable information has been obtained since 1949, it is believed to have become very scarce because of human persecution and deforestation. Originally it occurred in the remote forested mountains of southern Chahar in Inner Mŏngolia and in north-west Hebei and Shanxi provinces of China. Its present range and population size are unknown. In 1862 it was described as rare and by 1931 was extinct in Hebei, but in 1951 was said to be still fairly numerous in the mountains of Shanxi. Wild-caught birds were still being received by the Beijing Zoo up until 1976. There are plenty of Brown Eared Pheasants in private collections in Europe and North America, but all are descended from three originally imported birds, so the gene pool is very restricted. It is classified by ICBP as Endangered.

Several species of cranes in the Palaearctic Region are now seriously threatened. These magnificent birds, which have such delightful courtship dances, are admired wherever they occur. Nevertheless, the worldwide reclamation or pollution of the marshlands they inhabit and the activities of hunters on their migratory routes have brought their populations to dangerously low levels. Some, such as the **Red-crowned Crane** *Grus japonensis*, listed as Vulnerable, have apparently never been very numerous. This species now has two small populations, one breeding in south-east Siberia and Manchuria and migrating to Korea, the other sedentary in Japan, where it is severely threatened by loss of habitat. The mainland Asian population nests around Lake Khanka in Ussuriland, along the tributaries of the Ussuri and Amur rivers and in north and central Chinese Manchuria. The total population in the USSR does not exceed 200–300 birds. Roughly 500 breeding birds have been reported from Manchuria, and a small colony is said to breed in North Korea. In Japan, where before 1890 the species bred on all four of the main islands, a few birds were found breeding on western Hokkaido in 1924 and, as a result of protection, the population has gradually risen from 20 to about 350. The species is fully protected in Japan as a Special Natural Monument. It is also protected by the Japan–USSR Convention on Migratory Birds and by the hunting laws of the USSR and North and South Korea. A Japanese society for the protection of the species promotes supplementary winter feeding by farmers and school-children. In spite of these efforts the habitat of the cranes is threatened by development and they suffer a mortality of 12% per annum from collision with overhead cables. The possibility of burying the cables and enlarging the breeding area is being studied by the Japanese Government.

*Brown Eared Pheasant
and Chinese Monal*

The **Siberian Crane** *Grus leucogeranus* is the largest (standing nearly five-feet tall) and most conspicuous of the cranes with its snow-white plumage and scarlet face. Each breeding pair requires an enormous territory and has a low reproductive capacity. The population is steadily dwindling because of the numbers shot on migration and on the breeding grounds and because herds of domesticated reindeer trample its nests in the tundra. The species breeds in two discrete populations in northern Siberia, one in north-western Yakutia, the other in the lower reaches of the Ob River. The latter population migrates to the Keoladeo Ghana Sanctuary in Rajasthan, India, stopping on the way at the Ab-i-Istada Lake in Afghanistan. The numbers in the population had, by 1985, dwindled to only 37 birds. The Yakutia population has also declined, but in 1985 a flock of over 1,400 was seen wintering in Lake Po-yang in China which may result in a reassessment in its status, currently given as Endangered. Eggs from Siberian birds raised by the International Crane Foundation in the USA have been successfully hatched by Common Cranes *Grus grus* in Siberia and the species is legally protected over most of its range, boding well for the future.

The **Hooded Crane** *Grus monacha* (Plate IV), listed as Vulnerable, is presumed to breed in central Siberia between Tomsk and Lake Baikal, migrating to Japan, Korea and, at least formerly, to the lower Yangtze Valley in China. Its population is still relatively large, but in its Japanese wintering area it has insufficient habitat and has to receive supplementary food. Recently a number have died in Japan from pesticide poisoning. Neither its breeding nor its migration are yet fully known and a nest was not discovered until 1974. There is no recent information from China, but flocks of 50–100 birds were reported in Hebei Province until 1945. In Japan the population fell from 3,435 in 1939 to 250 in 1946; thereafter it rose until 1974 when more than 3,000 were seen. Information from Siberia is lacking but the total population is thought to be about 5,500. In Japan the winter feeding areas have been declared Special Natural Monuments and in South Korea the species was designated a Natural Monument in 1970.

PLATE I Palaearctic Steppe.
1 Sociable Plover (p. 50),
2 Slender-billed Curlew (p. 47),
3 Corncrake (p. 46), 4 Little
Bustard (p. 50), 5 Great Bustard
(p. 46).

PLATE II Western Palaearctic
Wetlands. 1 Marbled Teal
(p. 49), 2 Pygmy Cormorants
(p. 49), 3 White-headed Ducks
(p. 49), 4 Dalmatian Pelicans
(p. 34), 5 White-tailed
Fish-eagle (p. 37).

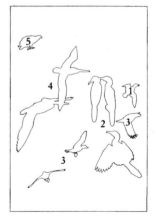

Norman Arlott 87

Norman Arlott 87

Norman Arlott 87

Norman Arlott 87

The **Black-necked Crane** *Grus nigricollis* has been described as the least known of all the cranes, although during the last ten years researchers have shown increasing interest in the species. It is a central Asian species with a breeding range now known to include Ladakh and areas of southern China bordering the Tsangpo River, and in Sichuan and Qinghai Provinces. The main wintering areas are reported to include parts of south-central Xizang (Tibet), southwest Sichuan and Yunnan Provinces in China, northern Vietnam, Bhutan, north-east India and nothern Burma. Recent observations indicate that 500–600 Black-necked Cranes are present in Bhutan in most winters. Wintering areas outside China have suffered markedly over the last 30 years, bombing in Vietnam and shooting in India having all had an effect. In Bhutan the marshland habitat is being improved for agriculture, but the Royal Government of Bhutan is committed to a strong conservation strategy, so perhaps there is a future for this crane. The ICBP has recently changed the Black-necked Crane's status from Indeterminate to Vulnerable.

The **White-naped Crane** *Grus vipio* (Plate IV) is now almost as rare as the Black-necked Crane having been formerly quite abundant. In 1939, 469 were counted wintering in Japan, but in 1955 only 55 were seen there; the number increased steadily to 499 in 1973 and to 732 in 1977. In Korea a flock of 2,300 was recorded in 1961 at the confluence of the Han and Imjin rivers. In this area 1,500 were seen in 1974 and about 2,000 in 1977, nearly half of which later reached Arasaki in Japan. Its main breeding area is believed to be in Mongolia and Manchuria. It is believed still to breed around Lake Khanka and along the Amur and Bureya rivers in the USSR. It formerly wintered throughout Japan but is now apparently restricted to northern Kyushu. A flock of 200 wintered near Lake Po-yang in Jiangxi, China, in 1984. The species may now have a total population of about 2,000. In Japan it was designated a Special Natural Monument in 1952. Its wintering area is a Special Bird Protection Area and the Government subsidises its winter feeding. Similarly, in South Korea it and its staging area on the Han River are protected as Natural Monuments; with winter feeding on an island sanctuary. The

PLATE III Palaearctic Migrants. 1 Black-faced Spoonbill (p. 49), 2 Asian Dowitcher (p. 47), 3 Spoonbill Sandpiper (p. 50), 4 Spotted Greenshank (p. 47), 5 Saunders's Gull (p. 50).

PLATE IV Eastern Palaearctic Wetlands. 1 Crested Ibis (p. 36), 2 Hooded Crane (p. 40), 3 Oriental White Stork (p. 35), 4 White-naped Crane (p. 45), 5 Mandarin Duck (p. 49).

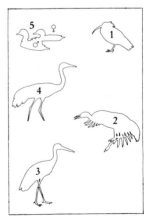

39 km wide Demilitarised Zone provides an excellent additional sanctuary. The species is listed as Vulnerable.

The **Corncrake** *Crex crex* (Plate I) has a widespread range from Europe and Africa to central Asia and used to be fairly common in some countries. Since the introduction of mechanised farming and the reduction of hayfields, combined with the use of crop-sprays, it has declined seriously in its breeding areas (notably in England and Ireland) and has become rare or at least very uncommon throughout the Afrotropical Region. Changes in its African wintering areas are also suspected. It is a Candidate Red Data Book species.

All members of the bustard family have been increasingly threatened by hunting and loss of habitat since the Second World War. One of the most affected has been the **Houbara Bustard** *Chlamydotis undulata*, which is a Candidate Red Data Book species. The nominate race was once numerous in the arid semi-desert regions of North Africa, from Mauritania to Egypt. It is replaced in the Canary Islands by the subspecies *C. u. fuertaventurae* and in the east, from Sinai, Arabia, the north Caspian area eastward to Baluchistan, Afghanistan and Kazakhstan to Mongolia, by *C. u. macqueeni*. The Houbara's present distribution is poorly understood, mainly because of the massive losses which have occurred throughout its range. The Canaries race, confined to the islands of Fuerteventura and Lanzarote, is very scarce but still survives. The nominate race has disappeared from many of its North African strongholds, only Tunisia and Algeria apparently still having a fair number in spite of motorised hunting. In Egypt it is seen only occasionally. In Israel there are about 150 birds. In Jordan it has almost disappeared except in the south around Ma'an but a few breed in the Azraq Reserve. In Iraq, Syria, Oman and the United Arab Emirates only small numbers are now seen. Losses are caused not only by Arab falconers but by locust-control spraying. In Iran numbers have been greatly reduced, though some are still seen in the south; the Iran–Iraq war will undoubtedly cause a further decline. The eastern race is largely resident or nomadic in response to rains in the southern part of its range (including the Middle East), but is migratory in the USSR. The Russian birds winter in Pakistan and the adjacent parts of north-west India, Iran, Iraq and Arabia. However, very few Houbaras now breed in the Arabian region because of the constant and massive hunting. The breeding area in the USSR has contracted greatly and is mainly in the remote semi-desert flats at Kazakhstan, Turkmenistan and Kyzylkum in Uzbekistan, where between 1956 and 1979 the population declined by 75%. Apart from the extensive conversion of virgin steppe to agriculture in the USSR, the main cause of the decline has been excessive hunting in the wintering areas. Arab falconers, having almost exterminated the Houbara in their own countries, have congregated in large numbers every winter in Pakistan (as they do in North Africa) and have killed on average 3,000 of the birds each year.

The **Great Bustard** *Otis tarda* (Plate I), also a Candidate Red Data Book species, occurs in small, fragmented populations in many parts of the Palaearctic Region, from the Iberian Peninsula, Morocco, East Germany and Hungary to Siberia and northern China. Its range increased markedly in central and western Europe in the eighteenth century with the clearance of forested areas, but has declined ever since. Great Bustards became extinct in Britain, France, Denmark and Sweden in the mid-nineteenth century and a little later in what is now West Germany and Greece. The world population is currently estimated at around 20,000 birds. Mechanised farming, the use of pesticides and the great pressure of hunting are all to blame for the decline of the species. In the Russian parts of its range it has suffered particularly severely from the massive conversion of steppe to agriculture.

One of the least known of the world's numerous species of shorebirds is the **Spotted Greenshank** *Tringa guttifer* (Plate III). It is believed to be confined to the coastal mud-flats, swamps and shallow lagoons of North and South Sakhalin Island in the Soviet Far East, but may also breed in Kamchatka, the Bering Islands and on the coast of the Gulf of Okhotsk, wintering in South-East Asia, where it is now rarely reported. Its population size is unknown but the species is evidently rare throughout its range, for which there is no apparent reason, though according to Russian reports, its previous breeding areas have been over-run by human settlements. It is, however, easily confused with related species and may have been overlooked. In Japan, it is a Special Bird for Protection. ICBP give its status as Indeterminate.

The **Slender-billed Curlew** *Numenius tenuirostris* (Plate I), a Candidate spe-

Relict Gull

Audouin's Gull

cies, used to be fairly numerous in its Russian breeding area and also on migration to the Middle East, the Mediterranean islands and North Africa. It is now extemely rare, breeding in unknown but at best very small numbers in the Soviet Union and wintering very locally westward as far as Morocco and Tunisia. A new ICBP project has been launched to find out more about this bird.

Another threatened shorebird is the **Asian Dowitcher** *Limnodromus semipalmatus* (Plate III), listed as Rare by ICBP. It breeds in several small, widely scattered areas across north-central Asia, and migrates to India and South-East Asia. In 1986 4,000 birds were recorded in Sumatra; this must be the species' main wintering location as the 1985 Russian Red Data Book suggests a total population of not more than 5,000–6,000. The habits of this little known species are gradually unfolding as more observations are recorded. One recent discovery was the presence of the Dowitcher at a site in Western Australia, and in spring 1984 approximately 400 were found on passage in Thailand.

Five seabirds are at risk in the Palaearctic (see also p. 50). **Audouin's Gull** *Larus audoinii*, considered Rare, is confined to the islands in the Mediterranean and North African Atlantic coasts. The total population is estimated to be 5,500–6,000 pairs. Its colonies have been subject to harvesting of eggs and young, and disturbance by man.

Four specimens of the almost unknown **Relict Gull** *Larus relictus* were collected in China in the 1930s. A nestling was ringed in 1974 at Lake Alakul, Kazakhstan, and recovered the same year in Vietnam, which suggested that the species may winter in South-East Asia. However, although watched for by Hong Kong naturalists, it was not seen until very recently. The species has now been recorded in China and Vietnam outside the breeding season, and 2,000 pairs are reported from breeding sites in the USSR, although these areas appear to be unstable owing to fluctuating water levels. It is listed as Rare.

The **Chinese Crested Tern** *Sterna bernsteini* has not been recorded since 1937 and may be extinct. It is, however, easily confused with other terns and few ornithologists visit its range. It is believed to breed on islands off the coast of Shantung province, China (where terns are not protected), and to winter in South-East Asia and the Philippines, where there have been a few records, none of them recent. It has always been considered rare, but 21 birds were collected in 1937 on an islet off the coast of Shantung, where it may have been breeding. There is an unconfirmed report of 10–20 in southern Thailand in 1980 and another unconfirmed sighting in Bali in 1986. The species is listed by ICBP as Indeterminate.

In 1960, a new species of nightjar was identified from China, **Vaurie's Nightjar** *Caprimulgus centralasicus*. It is believed to inhabit the sandy foothills of the Kunlun Mountains and the adjoining plains of the Tarim basin in Xinjiang province.

Virtually all we know about the **Eyebrowed Parrotbill** *Paradoxornis heudei*, is from studies dated 1914 and the species is consequently listed as Indeterminate. The species at that time was known to inhabit about 500 sq km of reed-beds along the Chang Jiang between Nanjing and Jingjiang, a distance of 110 km. This is one of the most densely populated parts of the world and the reeds are harvested regularly every year. If the parrotbills have survived, they must be extremely adaptable. In 1914 it was recommended that some of the reed beds should remain uncut, but it is unlikely that any action was taken. In 1972 some parrotbills were collected at Lake Khanka in Ussuriland, USSR and were judged to be conspecific with those collected in 1914 on the Chang Jiang, although given the subspecific name *P. h. polivanovi*. New populations were located in 1983 in Shanghai Province, and in 1987 at Jiangsu and in Mongolia, so it may be that the Eye-browed Parrotbill is not so acutely threatened as once feared.

The **Algerian Nuthatch** *Sitta ledanti* is a recently described bird confined to a single mountain, Mount Babor, in Algeria. In 1982 the population was around 80 pairs. Although Mount Babor has national park status the nuthatch is threatened by loss of habitat through fire, pasturage and wood-cutting. A suggestion to provide bottled gas for local inhabitants to reduce their need for firewood has been taken up and woodcutting is already waning. Mount Babor is a site of outstanding natural value in Algeria, being one of the few localities where the Barbary Macaque thrives and a recently named site for the leopard. It seems that the protection of the park is well in hand, but it remains to be seen whether the Algerian Nuthatch has a long-term future given its tiny population. ICBP list the species as Rare.

ADDITIONAL CANDIDATE BIRDS OF THE PALAEARCTIC REGION

PHALACROCORACIDAE
Cormorants
Pygmy Cormorant *Phalacrocorax pygmeus* (Pl. II) is confined to the Palaearctic, west of the Aral Sea. It is believed to be steadily declining, mainly because of drainage.

ARDEIDAE Herons, bitterns
Japanese Night Heron *Gorsachius goisagi* breeds in low mountain forests on Japan, and winters south to southern China, Taiwan and the Philippines. The preferred habitat of swamps and streams in dense forest is threatened.

THRESKIORNITHIDAE Ibises, spoonbills
Black-faced Spoonbill *Platalea minor* (Pl. III) breeds locally in east China and North Korea, and winters mostly to south and east China. The population has declined greatly in the last few decades.

ANATIDAE Waterfowl
Mandarin Duck *Aix galericulata* (Pl. IV) breeds in the northern provinces of China, the Sakhalin and Kuril islands (USSR), Japan, North and South Korea. It winters south to south-east China and Taiwan. The British feral population represents a significant proportion of the total world population.
Baikal Teal *Anas formosa* breeds in the forest zone of north to north-east Siberia, and migrates to Japan and China. There appears to have been a dramatic decline in recent years.
Marbled Teal *Marmaronetta angustirostris* (Pl. II) is widespread in very small numbers from south Spain to Pakistan but is declining everywhere.
White-headed Duck *Oxyura leucocephala* (Pl. II) has a very fragmented breeding range in Spain, Turkey, Romania, Iran, north Africa and Russia. It has disappeared from many west and south-eastern sites.

ACCIPITRIDAE Hawks, eagles, kites, old world vultures
Red Kite *Milvus milvus* occurs in Europe and some adjacent areas. There has been a marked decrease in its range and numbers in many areas, due to human persecution.
Pallas's Fish Eagle *Haliaeetus leucoryphus* has a range in central and southern Asia. It is declining in the USSR and is thinly distributed in the Indian subcontinent.
Steller's Fish-eagle *Haliaeetus pelagicus* is known from north-east Asia, north China, Japan and Korea. Its numbers are declining.
Black (or Cinerous) Vulture *Aegypius monachus* has a wide though fragmented range in southern Europe and northern Asia, but is nowhere numerous and in many places declining.
Imperial Eagle *Aquila heliaca* occurs very sparsely from south-east Europe to north Pakistan. There has been a marked decline almost throughout its range.

TETRAONIDAE Grouse
Caucasian Black Grouse *Tetrao mlokosiewiczi* is confined to the higher levels of the Black Sea coastal mountains, north-east Turkey and the

alpine zone of the Caucasus and suffers from habitat destruction.

PHASIANIDAE Pheasants, quails, partridges
Altai Snowcock *Tetraogallus altaicus* is confined to Mongolia, a few alpine and subalpine regions in the USSR and is little known.
Sichuan Partridge *Arborophila rufipectus* is known from only two localities in central Sichuan, China.
Blue Eared Pheasant *Crossoptilon auritum* inhabits alpine meadows and forests on the highest slopes in north-central China. Its status is unknown.
Reeves's Pheasant *Syrmaticus reevesi* is recorded in the hills of central and northern China. Its status is unknown.
Lady Amherst's Pheasant *Chrysolophus amherstiae* is resident in north-western China, frequenting wooded mountain slopes and feeding extensively on bamboo.

RALLIDAE Rails
Siberian Crake *Coturnicops exquisita* breeds in the Soviet Far East and winters in China, Korea and Japan. It is very scarce and little-known.

OTIDIDAE Bustards
Little Bustard *Tetrax tetrax* (Pl. I) has a reduced range in Europe, Morocco and the Soviet Union. The main causes are probably habitat changes and hunting pressures.

CHARADRIIDAE Plovers
Sociable Plover *Chettusia gregaria* (Pl. I) occurs from central Asia to north-east Africa, but is declining due to the cultivation of steppe areas.

SCOLOPACIDAE Snipes, woodcocks, sandpipers
Spoon-billed Sandpiper *Eurynorhynchus pygmeus* (Pl. III)

breeds along the north-east coast of the USSR. It winters coastally from south-east India to Singapore and south-east China, but is everywhere rare.

LARIDAE Gulls, terns
White-eyed Gull *Larus leucophthalmus* occurs only in the southern Red Sea and the Somali coast. It is permanently at risk from floating and beached oil.
Saunders's Gull *Larus saundersi* (Pl. III) was first recorded breeding in 1987 in Heilongjiang and coastal Jiangsi, China. It winters along the south and east coasts of China and occasionally in Taiwan, Korea and Japan.

ALCIDAE Auks, murres
Japanese Murrelet *Synthliboramphus wumizusume* breeds on Izu Island and in southern Japan, where its nest sites are threatened by the increase in sport fishing which destroys the habitat and causes disturbance of the birds.

COLUMBIDAE Pigeons, doves
Eastern Stock Dove *Columba eversmanni* breeds in the plains and valleys of central USSR, wintering south to Iran, Afghanistan, Pakistan and north-west India. There are very few recent records from the wintering areas.

STRIGIDAE Owls
Blakiston's Fish-owl *Ketupa blakistoni* is an inhabitant of eastern Siberia, north-eastern China and northern Japan. It is scarce everywhere, perhaps because it is dependent on fast-flowing water which must remain unfrozen in winter.

CAPRIMULGIDAE Nightjars
Red-necked Nightjar *Caprimulgus ruficollis* is restricted as a breeding species to Spain, Portugal, Morocco, Algeria and Tunisia. The populations

throughout North Africa appear to be very sparse.

(MUSCICAPIDAE) TURDINAE
Thrushes

Rufous-headed Robin *Erithacus ruficeps* is known from four specimens, three from north-central China, with a single migrant record in peninsular Malaysia. There are also a few recent records.

Black-throated Robin *Erithacus obscurus* occurs in bamboo thickets in coniferous forests. It has probably been overlooked but is apparently scarce. It is known from very few specimens from central China and in winter from south China, with one migrant record in north-west Thailand.

Hodgson's Bushchat *Saxicola insignis* occurs in the USSR, west China and Tibet, and migrates to northern India. It is considered to be at risk in the USSR.

Amami Thrush *Zoothera amami* is a low density species from Amami, Japan, recently separated from White's Thrush *Z. dauma*.

Yemen Thrush *Turdus menachensis* is restricted to woodlands in North Yemen and south-west Saudi Arabia. The species is strictly montane and threatened by the collection of firewood.

(MUSCICAPIDAE) TIMALIINAE
Babblers

Omei Shan Liocichla *Liocichla omeiensis* is known from central Sichuan in China. Its status is unknown.

(MUSCICAPIDAE) SYLVIINAE Old world warblers

Aquatic Warbler *Acrocephalus paludicola* inhabits fragmented sedge wetlands in eastern Europe. Its winter quarters are unknown but are presumably in tropical West Africa.

Speckled Warbler *Acrocephalus sorghophilus* is confined to north-east China, wintering in south-east China. It has a restricted breeding range and is probably confined to reeds and wetlands.

Socotra Cisticola *Cisticola haesitata* occurs on the island of Socotra, South Yemen, where it is unaccountably rare.

Marshland Warbler *Megalurus pryeri* breeds in north-east China and on Honshu, Japan. It is known from a very few sites on Honshu, and its status in China is unknown.

SITTIDAE Nuthatches

Corsican Nuthatch *Sitta whiteheadi* is endemic to Corsica with a total population of about 2,000 pairs. The species is dependent on old *Pinus* forests which are threatened by the present forest management.

(EMBERIZIDAE) EMBERIZINAE
Buntings

Jankowski's Bunting *Emberiza jankowskii* breeds in north-east China, south coastal Ussuriland, USSR, and north-east Korea. Its status is unknown, but it is listed as threatened in the USSR.

Japanese Yellow Bunting *Emberiza sulphurata* breeds on Honshu, Japan, and winters in east China, occasionally Taiwan, and the north Philippines. It is uncommon.

CORVIDAE Crows

Sichuan Jay *Perisoreus internigrans* is endemic to the spruce and pine forests of the mountains of central China. Deforestation within its range is now a major threat.

Chapter 3
The Nearctic Region

All of Canada, the United States of America, the immense Arctic wastes of Greenland and related islands such as the Aleutians, Newfoundland and Bermuda are included in the Nearctic Region. It is bounded in the north by the Arctic Ocean, in the east by the Atlantic and in the west by the Pacific. Its southern boundary is the northern edge of the tropical forest in Mexico, where it meets the Neotropical Region. Mexico was heavily forested at the time of the Aztecs, but except in the south most of it is now a barren and eroded waste. By contrast with the Palaearctic, the main geographical features of the North American continent run mainly from north to south. From Alaska to Central America is the great Rocky Mountain chain. Down the centre of the continent, from east of the Rockies to the Mississippi valley and from the Canadian Shield southward to Texas, are the vast grasslands known as the prairies. Once the richest grasslands in the world, these are now increasingly eroded and losing their fertility as a result of intensive inorganic farming and over-grazing. Down the eastern coastal regions the Appalachians and other small mountain ranges extend from eastern Canada southward into Georgia. The vegetational zones are well defined in the north but increasingly confusing in the south. North of the Canadian tree-line is a huge belt of cold circumpolar tundra of reindeer moss and dwarf willow, closely resembling its Eurasian equivalent. Next comes the coniferous boreal forest, extending southward along the mountain ranges into the north-western part of the United States. This gives way to the temperate deciduous forests which once covered most of the eastern United States, but which are now much fragmented and survive mainly in the mountains and hilly regions, nearly all the valleys now being cultivated. In coastal California, which has become one of the most densely populated regions, some of the famous Redwood groves have been preserved and it is in the adjacent mountains that the tallest trees in the world are found: the ancient giant Sequoias, some of which weigh 2,000 tonnes. In the semi-tropical climate of Florida and the Gulf Coast are great expanses of lush Bald Cypress and Mangrove swamps, of which the bird-rich Everglades and the bayous of Louisiana are the best known. Thousands of inland freshwater lakes and swamps are located in the Canadian prairies and forests, in addition to the Great Lakes on the Canadian and United States border. There are hot deserts in California, Arizona, Texas and New Mexico and also cold deserts of sage-brush in the south-western United States and western Canada. From

Oregon southward into Baja California is yet another desert-like habitat, the chaparal, which is composed of stunted shrubs and evergreen oaks. Highly mechanised farming and the growth of great cities with tree-lined streets, parks and gardens have transformed a large part of southern Canada and the United States but not always to the detriment of birds, many species quickly taking advantage of the new, relatively safe, habitats provided. Some have even taken to nesting on the roofs and window-ledges of skyscrapers.

The origin of many Nearctic species can be traced to the Tertiary period when the North American continent was isolated. It was connected with Europe by the Greenland land-bridge during the Eocene, which permitted an influx of Palaearctic species. Some Asiatic species also reached the continent during the Eocene by way of the Bering Straits land-bridge, which existed intermittently. From the early Eocene until the late Pliocene the continent was isolated from South America by a broad expanse of sea, but the later Panamanian land-bridge and the many islands of the Caribbean permitted a radiation of some of the early Nearctic species into South America and vice versa. When the southern part of the continent had a warmer climate than it has now, a small tropical North American avifauna was created and by the late Pliocene some of these species had mingled with their Neotropical neighbours. Species from Central and South America are still colonising the southern part of the United States, either by island-hopping across the Caribbean to Florida or by way of Panama to Mexico and California.

The migration of Nearctic birds is being closely studied on an extensive scale, by ringing or "banding" as it is called in North America, and by well organised visual observation which includes the use of sophisticated radar equipment to plot high-altitude nocturnal flight. The majority of the 332 migrant species move south in autumn into the southern part of the United States, or to Central and South America. Some of the Canadian Arctic-breeding waders make very long journeys to winter on Pacific islands even as far as Hawaii, while others reach Argentina and the Antarctic.

Bird research and conservation are highly developed both in Canada and the United States. Perhaps the first practical conservationist in the USA was John Muir, a Scottish immigrant who in 1847 tried to convince the already booming population of California that it was over-exploiting the rich natural bounty of the state. He succeeded not only in putting some of the Redwood and Sequoia forests under legal protection, but went on to create the prestigious Sierra Club, which still plays a major role in the conservation of American wilderness and wildlife. Today there are many hundreds of active local and state societies and foundations in the United States and Canada, all competing for and dispensing research and conservation funds. Both countries have excellent government departments concerned with wildlife and protective legislation. The passing of the US Wilderness Act in 1964, though not entirely successful, was a remarkable national effort to preserve for all time several million acres of unspoilt and undisturbed wilderness. Hunting is strictly controlled, while innumerable wildlife refuges and national parks provide sanctuary.

The Nearctic Region has about 650 species of birds, not counting vagrants from other regions. Its threatened species, by comparison with other regions, are less numerous and on the whole better protected. In view of the wealth of the United States, it is not surprising that millions of dollars have been spent on trying to save the California Condor *Gymnogyps californianus* and on the captive-breeding of threatened species such as the Whooping Crane *Grus americana* and the Peregrine Falcon. In recent years, large sums have also been provided by WWF–US, the Smithsonian Institution and other charitable foundations, as well as by many universities, for the conservation of threatened species in the Caribbean and Central and South America, including the Galápagos Islands, as well as in Asia and Africa.

On the now extensively developed island of Bermuda the early settlers used to rely heavily on a seabird called the **Cahow** *Pterodroma cahow* for food. This little petrel, named after its call, was numbered, at that time, in thousands in its breeding colonies. By 1616 it had been almost exterminated. In 1951 a few were rediscovered breeding on some small islets off Castle Harbour, where, in spite of many difficulties, some have remained ever since. About 18 pairs bred there until 1961 and by 1966 the number had risen to 20 pairs; but only six young were reared because of contamination by the pesticide DDT. In more recent years the population rose to a maximum of 34 pairs in 1984, the number of young fledged varying from 12 to 18 a year. The species is given full protection and classified by the US Government and ICBP as Endangered. Three of the five islets where the Cahows breed are protected sanctuaries, where landing is forbidden and rats are periodically cleared. Artificial nest burrows are provided and fitted with baffles which exclude the aggressive White-tailed Tropicbirds *Phaethon lepturus*. The floodlighting at the nearby US military bases which

Cahow

California Condor

inhibited pair formation has been reduced to an acceptable level. It is hoped
to attract nesting on the adjacent Non-
such Island, where better soil conditions
and the absence of competition might
provide an opportunity for the small
colony to expand. Oil slicks and pollution are, however, problems which per-
sist, being difficult to foresee. Nevertheless, the efforts to save the Cahow could
scarcely be more thorough.

No bird in the world has had more
money or expertise lavished on it than
the **California Condor** *Gymnogyps californianus*. These huge New World vultures have for many years been on the
brink of extinction and the efforts to save
them have been extensive. They once
ranged all along the Pacific coast of
North America, from British Columbia
to Mexico and in prehistoric times as far
east as Florida. By 1800 they were restricted to California, by 1940 the total

population had fallen to about 800, and
by 1971 it was 50. Until recent times the
losses were due to shooting, trapping,
poisoning and egg-collecting. In the last
few years shooting has been the biggest
threat. If the shotgun-pellets do not kill
outright, they cause slow death by lead
poisoning. The last female to die had
eight pellets lodged in her flesh and died
from ingesting a ninth from a carcass,
also a hunter's victim. Museums have no
fewer than 288 skins, half of which were
taken between 1881 and 1910, by which
time the condors were obviously becoming rare. Shortage of rabbits as prey may
also have contributed to the decline.
Eagles and coyotes compete for carrion,
which farmers often poison. The excessive use of pesticides in California probably contributed to reproductive failure,
as has human disturbance near the nest
sites. Condors, although long-lived, do
not breed until at least six years old and

55

then lay only one egg every other year. Between 1967 and 1977 only two nestlings were fledged each year on average and the number of birds seen in sub-adult plumage had declined by 60%. The last surviving wild birds have now all been taken into captivity, bringing the total in captivity to 27, and as a last resort captive breeding is being tried. Twelve condors have already been hatched successfully over the last few years but all from eggs taken from the wild, and it remains to be seen whether the captive Condors can successfully rear young behind bars. The wild population can now be regarded as extinct and their Endangered status is sadly out-of-date.

The **Peregrine Falcon** *Falco peregrinus* (Plate VI) is declining or already rare over large parts of its North American and European range (see page 38) and is now absent from eastern USA and Canada south of the boreal forests. The American race *F. p. anatum* survives in western USA and western Canada, with perhaps 100 pairs in boreal Alaska. There is no estimate for Mexico. About 8–9 pairs survive in California and about 13 pairs in other western states. The contamination of birds and eggs by persistent pesticides and their killing or capture when breeding, on passage, or

Peregrine Falcon

wintering, have caused this decline. This much persecuted bird is fully protected by American, Canadian and Mexican laws. A US Fish and Wildlife Service team and a Canadian team are working on its conservation and captive-breeding projects have successfully released some birds, but these have been of mixed races, no pairs of *F. p. anatum* being available. The status of the tundra race of the Peregrine *F. p. tundrius* is imperfectly known because of the lack of information from Greenland. Its range is from the tundra north of the tree-line from the west coast of Alaska across northern Canada to western Greenland. Intergradation between this race and *F. p. anatum* occurs where the two meet in the

boreal forest zone. The tundra race migrates in winter through the central and eastern states of the USA as far south as Central America, Chile and Argentina. It is mainly on these journeys that it suffers contamination from chlorinated hydrocarbons and other toxic chemicals. In the Canadian tundra the population has fallen from about 2,000 pairs to perhaps 200 and the Alaskan population from 150–200 pairs to only 50–75 pairs. No figures are yet available from Greenland. The race is protected by law in Canada, Greenland and the United States, and some South American countries also give it legal protection. The Peregrine Falcon is listed by ICBP as Vulnerable.

Another North American species on which skill and money have been lavished for many years is the **Whooping Crane** *Grus americana* (Plate VI). For years very close to extinction, it is now beginning to show signs of recovery as a result of an enormous cooperative educational effort to protect it. A separate non-migratory population used to inhabit Louisiana, but was extinct by 1950. A considerable migratory population used to breed from Iowa and southern Illinois northward across southern Manitoba, Saskatchewan and Alberta to southern MacKenzie. These birds wintered along the Gulf coast of Louisiana and Texas and as far south as Central Mexico. Since 1922 breeding of the migratory population has been confined to the Wood Buffalo National Park, northern Alberta and southern MacKenzie, and wintering to the Arkansas National Wildlife Refuge, Texas, and the adjoining coastlands. A second population was created in 1975 by placing eggs under Sandhill Cranes *Grus canadensis* at Grey's Lake National Wildlife Refuge in Idaho; these now winter with their foster parents at Bosque del Apache Wildlife Refuge in New Mexico. The Canadian Wildlife Service is organising a third foster-breeding project. The population of the Whooping Crane was about 1,300 birds in the 1890s. By 1912 there were only 56 in Texas and 32 in Louisiana. By 1918 the Louisiana migratory population was extinct and by 1941 those wintering in Texas had dropped to only 15. This population climbed gradually to 59 by 1971, to 70 in 1977 and by 1987 it was 110. The causes of the high mortality of young prebreeding birds are still not understood. A massive educational campaign organised by the US and Canadian Governments, the National Audubon Society and others has greatly reduced the former heavy mortality caused by hunters during migration. The next priority will be to protect the areas used by the cranes during migration. The species is protected by the US Endangered Species Act of 1973 and the Migratory Birds Treaties between the USA, Mexico and Canada. It is listed by ICBP as Endangered.

The **Eskimo Curlew** *Numenius borealis* (Plate VI) only just escaped the fate of the American Passenger Pigeon and the Carolina Parakeet at the close of the last century when it was shot by the million during migration. It is still extremely rare, with a population which was recently estimated to be possibly only 20 birds, and is listed as Endangered. Its breeding grounds were in the Arctic tundra of the Northwest Territories in Canada and perhaps also in Alaska. The species migrated across southern Labrador, Newfoundland and Nova Scotia, through New England and the Mississippi valley to Brazil, Argentina and occasionally Chile. The return migration was across the Gulf of Mexico and the prairies of central USA to Canada. No breeding or wintering areas are now known, but there are still occasional sightings which give grounds for cautious optimism that it survives. The Eskimo Curlew is protected in Canada and the United States. The species may be conspecific with the Little Curlew *N. minutus* of central Siberia, which winters in South-East Asia and Australia.

At least two of Mexico's parrots are threatened. The **Thick-billed Parrot** *Rhynchopsitta pachyrhyncha* (Plate V) is decreasing rapidly because of logging in its pine-oak forest habitat in the Sierra Madre Occidental and its continuing capture for the pet trade. It is listed by ICBP as Vulnerable. It used to be fairly common from Chihuahua and eastern Sonora southward to Michoacan and during migration as far north as southern Arizona and south-western New Mexico. Its present range is restricted to the mountains of southern Chihuahua, western Durango and eastern Sinaloa. In 1917 as many as 1,500 were seen in a single flock in Arizona, but the largest flock seen anywhere in the last 15 years was only 200 birds. During a four-month survey in 1979, only 55 nests were found. The species is protected by Mexican law but there is little enforcement, and no part of this bird's habitat is protected. As logging increases, the easier access results in more parrots being taken by the pet trade.

Another threatened Mexican parrot is the closely-related **Maroon-fronted Parrot** *R. terrisi*. It occupies a similar pine-oak forest habitat along about 400 km of the Sierra Madre Oriental and southward to the Sierra de Guatemala. It has always been regarded as rare and its total population is believed to be about 2,000 birds. Its forest habitat is being destroyed by fire, logging, grazing and clearing for orchards and crops. It is supposed to be protected by Mexican law but none of its habitat is protected and it is listed by ICBP as Endangered.

The **Imperial Woodpecker** *Campephilus imperialis* (Plate V) of Mexico, largest of all its family, is critically Endangered and there have been no records of it since 1958. Its precarious situation is attributed mainly to shooting and, to a lesser degree, to the felling of the big pines on which it depends. It formerly had a wide range in Mexico, but its present range is unknown apart from a sighting in 1958 on the Sonora–Chihuahua border and unconfirmed reports in 1977 from south-western Chihuahua. An extensive but unsuccessful search was made for it in 1962. Local people say the woodpecker disappeared within a few years when forests were opened up to logging, roads and settlements. It is protected by Mexican law, although this is unenforceable in the remote areas where the species used to occur.

A woodpecker which is probably already extinct in North America is the large (second only to the Imperial) and equally handsome **Ivory-billed Woodpecker** *Campephilus principalis*, listed as Endangered. Only a few unconformed sightings or tape recordings of its characteristic call keep hopes alive that it may still survive. It was always recorded as rare and by 1939 only 24 were known to

Maroon-fronted Parrot

exist in a few remote swamps in Texas, Louisiana, South Carolina and possibly Florida. The last known population (13 birds) disappeared from the Singer Tract in Louisiana following its conversion for the culture of soybeans. Possible confusion with the rather similar and widespread Pileated Woodpecker *Dryocopus pileatus*, combined with the zeal of ornithologists longing to see this fabulous bird, probably accounted for many of the unconfirmed reports of it since then. But it is perhaps still possible that it survives. Today very few mature blocks of swamp forest exist in the southeastern states, but these woodpeckers may be able to adapt to secondary growth. Undoubtedly the loss of its swamp-forest habitat was the main cause of its decline, although commercial collectors wiped out several populations at the beginning of this century. A number of tracts of suitable habitat have been put under protection in Texas and Florida since the disappearance of the species, which is fully protected by Federal and State laws. The species seems likely to survive only in Cuba, where birds of the race *C. p. bairdii* were recently found still to exist in what must be tiny numbers (see p. 86).

Another threatened North American woodpecker is the **Red-cockaded Woodpecker** *Picoides borealis*, listed by ICBP as Vulnerable. In 1985 its population was estimated to be about 3,000. It is found in the coniferous forests of Oklahoma, Kentucky, Virginia and Maryland and southward to Florida and the Gulf coast. It was formerly abundant but is now declining because of the forestry practice of eliminating pines older than 60 years. It normally nests in trees of at least this age. The widespread use of pesticides in plantations to control Fire Ants *Solenopsis saevissima* may be causing reproductive failure or depleting the

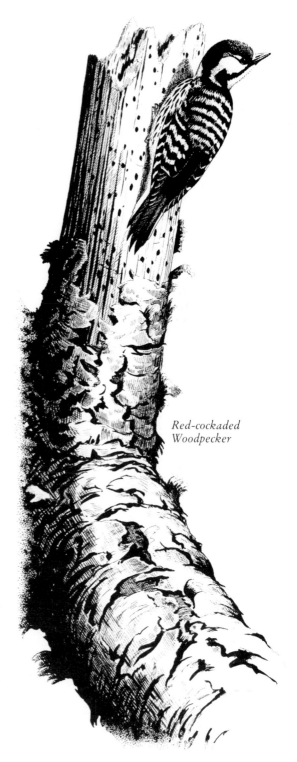

Red-cockaded Woodpecker

59

food supplies of these woodpeckers. A team from the US Fish and Wildlife Service is working on a recovery project, which includes leaving some dead or dying trees and restricting all activity in areas with substantial woodpecker populations. Tax incentives are given to private owners not to harvest mature woodlands and leave corridors between parklands to permit gene-flow between adjacent populations (a good example of imaginative American legislation). The reintroduction of the Red-cockaded Woodpecker into suitable parts of its former range is also being tried. The species is protected by the US Endangered Species Act.

Kirtland's Warbler *Dendroica kirtlandii* is certainly the most thoroughly studied of all warblers in the Nearctic Region and the measures to protect its small and very vulnerable population do great credit to the many organisations involved. These include Federal and State agencies, universities, private companies and several conservation bodies, all cooperating in harmony. As an object lesson to other countries it deserves wider publicity and is worth describing in detail. The breeding distribution of Kirtland's Warbler is severely restricted and only since this cooperative effort was made has a slight recovery been achieved. In historical times the species was known only within an area of 136 by 160 km in northern Michigan. In 1970 this had diminished from 4,860 hectares to about 2,000. The species occurs in burnt-over stands of Jack Pine *Pinus banksiana* between 8 and 22 years old on sandy soil, with low undergrowth and scattered clearings. Its peak population was between 1870 and 1900, when the Jack Pine forests were most subject to fire and lumbering. At that time the great majority of the 71 specimens shot in the Bahamas, where the species winters, were obtained. In 1951 the first accurate census was taken and gave the total population as 500 pairs. In 1961 a similar census showed no change except that the production of young per pair had declined. The 1971 census revealed a sharp decline to 210 pairs, caused by an invasion of the Brown-headed Cowbird *Molothrus ater*, which had parasitised 67% of the Kirtland's Warbler nests. Removal of the Cowbirds began in 1972 and has now reduced the parasitism to below 5%. The productivity of young

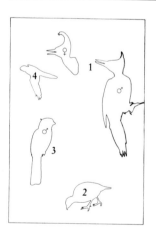

PLATE V Mexican Pine Forest. 1 Imperial Woodpecker (p. 58), 2 Bearded Wood Partridge (p. 66), 3 Eared Trogon (p. 66), 4 Thick-billed Parrot (p. 58).

PLATE VI Nearctic Wetland. 1 Whooping Cranes (p. 57), 2 Eskimo Curlew (p. 57), 3 Piping Plover (p. 66), 4 Peregrine Falcon (pp. 38, 56).

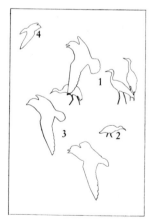

Norman Arlott 87

Norman Arlott 87

Norman Arlott 87

Norman Arlott 87

has increased to more than four per nest, a higher average than is achieved by any other American warbler. Since 1972 the total population has fluctuated between 167 and a maximum of 219 pairs in 1985. About 600 to 800 young are produced each year, thus 1,000 or 1,200 birds should be migrating south each year, but the population has not increased because only about 400 survive to return the following spring. The species is fully protected by law in the USA, Canada and the Bahamas and its recovery is controlled by the US Fish and Wildlife Service. In 1957 the Michigan Department of Natural Resources created three 10 sq km reserves for the warbler and in 1961 the Huron National Forest of 1,620 hectares was designated as a protected Kirtland's Warbler Management Area by the US Forest Service. The forest areas are carefully managed as to felling, planting and fire in order to increase the areas suitable for breeding; and recently the wintering grounds in the Bahamas have been found, giving hope that the reasons for the winter mortality might be discovered. The future of this now famous little warbler looks reasonably bright, but it is still listed as Endangered.

Bachman's Warbler *Vermivora bachmanii*, on the other hand, may now be extinct. It is regarded as North America's rarest song bird and is listed by ICBP as Endangered. Formerly it was locally abundant and bred in Missouri, Arkansas, Kentucky, Alabama and South Carolina, migrating southwards to Cuba, the Isle of Pines and the Bahamas. Its present population size and distribution are unknown, the last nest having been found in Alabama in 1937; the last birds reported up to 1977 were mainly single, in the northern part of the range, without evidence of breeding. Its habitat of bottomland swamp-forest has mostly been destroyed and it is believed that loss of habitat both in the breeding and wintering areas was mainly responsible for the decline of the species. One might assume that excessive collecting also contributed, bearing in mind that at least 192 were shot by American collectors between 1886 and 1892. Bachman's Warbler is protected by Federal and State laws. If the warbler still exists it is most likely to be in the I'On Swamp area in South Carolina. Part of this swamp is now within the protected Francis Marion National Forest.

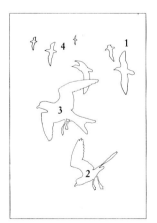

PLATE VII South-west Nearctic Coast. 1 Black-vented Shearwater (p. 66), 2 Least Storm-petrel (p. 66), 3 Black Storm-petrel (p. 66), 4 Townsend's Shearwater (p. 66).

PLATE VIII Localized Nearctic Songbirds. 1 Golden-cheeked Warbler (p. 66), 2 Black-capped Vireo (p. 66).

ADDITIONAL CANDIDATE BIRDS OF THE NEARCTIC REGION

PROCELLARIIDAE Petrels, shearwaters
Black-vented Shearwater *Puffinus opisthomelas* (Pl. VII) is confined as a breeding bird to islands off the west of Mexico and at one large colony it has suffered considerable predation by cats.
Townsend's Shearwater *Puffinus auricularis* (Pl. VII) is in a similar position as the Black-vented Shearwater above.

HYDROBATIDAE Storm-petrels
Least Storm-petrel *Halocyptena microsoma* (Pl. VII) is also confined as a breeding bird to islands off the west coast of Mexico.
Black Storm-petrel *Oceanodroma melania* (Pl. VII) has a breeding colony of 150 birds in California and also breeds off the west coast of Mexico.

PHASIANIDAE Pheasants, quails, partridges
Bearded Wood Partridge *Dendrortyx barbatus* (Pl. V) is a very rare forest species of north-eastern Mexico where deforestation is rampant.

CHARADRIIDAE Plovers
Piping Plover *Charadrius melodus* (Pl. VI) has declined seriously throughout its breeding range in the USA and Canada.

SCOLOPACIDAE Snipes, woodcocks, sandpipers
Bristle-thighed Curlew *Numenius tahitiensis* breeds in a small area in Alaska, and winters in the Pacific.

COLUMBIDAE Pigeons, doves
Socorro Dove *Zenaida graysoni* is now extinct on Socorro Island off the west coast of Mexico, and survives only in captivity.

PSITTACIDAE Lories, parrots, macaws
Red-crowned or **Green-cheeked Amazon** *Amazona viridigenalis* is endemic to a small area of north-east Mexico and has seriously declined, owing to habitat destruction and trapping.

TROGONIDAE Trogons
Eared Trogon *Euptilotis neoxenus* (Pl. V) occurs in the mountains of western Mexico and USA. It is scarce and local.

TROGLODYTYDAE Wrens
Clarion Wren *Troglodytes tanneri* is endemic to Clarion Island off the west coast of Mexico. Recent information suggests this species is threatened.

MIMIDAE Thrashers, mockingbirds
Socorro Mockingbird *Mimodes graysoni* is endemic to the island of Socorro off western Mexico and was thought to be extinct until its rediscovery in 1988.

(EMBERIZIDAE) EMBERIZINAE Buntings
Sierra Madre Sparrow *Ammodramus baileyi* is rare and local in highlands of west-central Mexico.

PARULIDAE Woodwarblers
Golden-cheeked Warbler *Dendroica chrysoparia* (Pl. VIII) is confined to Edward's Plateau in south-central Texas, USA.
Altamira Yellowthroat *Geothlypis flavovelata* has a very restricted range in north-east Mexico.

VIREONIDAE Vireos
Black-capped Vireo *Vireo atricapillus* (Pl. VIII) occurs in Texas northward to Oklahoma, and Mexico. It is becoming very scarce and is suffering badly from Cowbird brood-parasitism.

Chapter 4
The Neotropical Region

The Neotropical Region extends from the tropical rain-forest in Mexico to Cape Horn at the southern tip of South America. The Caribbean islands and offshore archipelagos such as the Galápagos and Falklands are included. The region contains the world's longest mountain range (the Andes), the world's greatest river system, containing two-thirds of the world's river water (the Amazon), and the largest area of tropical forest, amounting to about 400 million square kilometres. It also has the richest avifauna, some 3,000 species, with Colombia boasting the greatest number of any country in the world.

Before the break-up of the super-continent of Gondwanaland, South America was connected with Africa and also with the Australasian landmass. Some evidence for this can be seen in the similarity of the large flightless birds and the parrots of the latter regions. North and South America were isolated from each other by a considerable sea barrier during the Tertiary period, although some birds species were probably interchanged. During the Pliocene the Panamanian land-bridge was formed and this facilitated a larger exchange of species. Like the Afrotropical Region, the Neotropical now has a vast influx of migrant species moving into it in winter. The avifauna of the Caribbean islands is a mixture of species of both North and South American origin, while those of the Galápagos and Falklands are primarily from the adjacent regions of South America, although the latter also has some from Antarctica. Luxurious rain-forest covers most of the northern half of the South American continent. In the southern half are great expanses of open grasslands which, to the south of the Amazon river system, are called the *pampas*. The smaller grasslands in the north are known as the *llanos* and the tropical savannah grasslands of Brazil as *campos*. A narrow band of cold highland steppe lies along the east of the Andes from Colombia and Ecuador southward through Peru and Chile. Between the Pacific shore and the Andes chain is a 2,500 mile coastal strip of virtual desert, the northern part of Chile being perhaps the most sterile desert in the world. The tapering southern extremity of the continent extends into the cold and stormy Antarctic waters and has a mixture of stunted vegetation and open steppe, with glaciers feeding the Beagle Channel in Tierra del Fuego.

The once unbroken forests of Central and South America have already been severely damaged and are being felled at a rate which suggests that within the next few decades very little but secondary growth will survive. Fortunately a few sample areas in each country are now more or less protected as national parks or wildlife reserves, but the losses of genetic resources are already extensive and irreparable. A very large number of species of birds, mammals, reptiles and, above all, plants are at risk of extinction, or already extinct.

The seemingly limitless *pampas* of Argentina, like the *llanos* of Guyana and Venezuela and the grassy *campo* highlands of Brazil, are now mostly devoted to cattle ranching or agriculture. Their avifauna is inevitably declining. Extensive mining activities are destroying many other areas and giving easy access to the hunters who accompany the miners. Although there are relatively few areas of true desert in the Neotropical Region, there are large expanses of high, treeless moors dotted with low shrubs; in this cold and hostile environment a number of unusual birds occur, including several hardy species of hummingbirds. These highlands are called the *páramos* in the north and the *puna* in the south. On Brazil's great tableland is a specialised habitat called the *cerrado*, consisting of low, dense trees and tangled undergrowth. In the Andes there are a number of high-altitude lakes where some of the world's rarest grebes, coots and flamingos live.

Mexico, Central America and the Caribbean islands are also rich in birds, but many of them are gravely threatened by the enormous pressure of logging, agriculture, touristic developments, hunting and the cage-bird trade. The numerous endemic parrots are particularly endangered, in spite of constant efforts by conservationists to save them. The attitudes of governments vary, in some instances being actually obstructive to conservation or paying only lip-service to it. Although most of the countries are parties to CITES, the ignorance or corruption of officials often impede its objectives. Strenuous efforts are being made by IUCN, WWF and ICBP to stress the imperative need to save their threatened natural environments. Some progress has been made, but very many species of birds are nearing extinction. Large parts of South America are still unexplored and much of the information about rare species is still based on very old and out-of-date records.

The **Puna Rhea** *Pterocnemia tarapacensis* was once numerous in the *puna* region of the Andes from southern Peru to Patagonia. It is now believed to exist in small numbers only in three departments of Peru, two in Bolivia and three provinces each in Argentina and Chile and is listed as Endangered, although its taxonomy is in doubt. It is a gregarious, ostrich-like bird which has suffered severe losses from human persecution. In 1977 there were fewer than 100 left in the Tarapaca province of Chile, but on the Peruvian side of the frontier Puna Rheas were said to be still "fairly plentiful". Since that report, however, egg-poaching by the Aymara Indians in the Lauca National Park and hunters around the mining centres have caused further severe losses. Feather dusters made from rhea feathers are still widely sold in Peru and their skins are also burnt in cocoa plantations for supposed beneficial effect. The species is protected by law in Chile, Peru and Bolivia, but with little effect because of the lack of law enforcement.

Tinamous are small to medium-sized, rather solitary relatives of the large, flightless rheas, but have the ability to fly, if rather poorly. They are forest-dwelling and several species are at risk. The **Magdalena Tinamou** *Crypturellus saltuarius* is possibly already extinct, being known only by a single specimen obtained in the Magdalena division of Colombia in 1943. No further trace of this species has been found, and a thorough search of the region is needed to determine whether it still exists. Modern opinion tends to the view that *saltuarius* is a subspecies of the Red-legged Tinamou *C. erythropus*, which is not considered threatened. Meanwhile *saltuarius* is listed as Indeterminate.

Several species of grebe are at dangerously low population levels in South America. The flightless **Junín Grebe** *Podiceps taczanowskii* is confined to Lake Junín at 4,000 metres in Peru. In 1938 it was described as extremely abundant and in 1961 was still common. In 1969, however, the lake was poisoned by the washings from an adjacent copper-mine, which in the course of the year killed one-third of all life in the lake. By 1978 the grebe population had dropped to 300, of which only 100 pairs bred. The Peruvian Government then turned the lake into a National Reserve and, after nationalising the copper-mine, attempted to cleanse the lake. Attempts are now being made to transfer some of the grebes to a nearby unpolluted lake. Meanwhile the species is listed by ICBP as Endangered.

The **Hooded Grebe** *Podiceps gallardoi*, classified as Rare, is endemic to Argentina. This species made headline news when it was first described, as recently as 1974, from one lake in southern Argentina. In 1981 no more than 75 birds could be found but a recent survey has shown the range to be more extensive, with a population nearer 3,000.

Petrels spend most of the year at sea, but when they breed they are very vulnerable to predators as they are colonial and ground nesters. The **Black-capped Petrel** *Pterodroma hasitata* has a greatly reduced range, having once bred on several Caribbean islands. Today it is restricted to certain cliffs of south-east Haiti, and there are also small colonies in the Dominican Republic and on Cuba. Its decline has been attributed to the introduction of the mongoose, but this took place in the 1870s by which time it is known that the population was already in trouble. Capture by man for food and predation by introduced rats were probably the real causes. The breeding habitat in Haiti is confined to areas so steep as to be virtually inaccessible. However, the population pressure is such that Haitian peasants have invaded the pine and cloud-forest above the breeding cliffs, and are even cutting and burning forest on parts of the cliff itself. The Black-capped Petrel is classified by ICBP as Vulnerable.

The Galápagos Islands, 600 miles west of Ecuador, are one of two homes of the **Dark-rumped Petrel** *Pterodroma*

Junín Grebe

phaeopygia. In 1971 there were about 10,000 nest-burrows of this species in the humid highlands of Santa Cruz Island alone and it was also breeding on San Cristóbal, Isabela, San Salvador and probably on Floreana, Fernandina and Pinta. It is now restricted to Santa Cruz, Floreana, Santiago, San Cristóbal and Isabela. The 1971 report stated that only 4,000 nest burrows on Santa Cruz were occupied and only 1,600 contained eggs. From these only 160 nestlings were fledged. It was believed that a similar rate of reproductive failure applied to the other islands. Between 1981 and 1982 there was a decline of 27% on Floreana. The latest information suggests that the total population in the archipelago has declined to as low as about 1,000 pairs. The reasons for this are numerous. Much of the vegetation where the petrels nest has been cleared for agriculture. Introduced predators such as dogs and Black Rats *Rattus rattus* prey on them and their nestlings, and cattle and pigs trample the burrows. Rats are undoubtedly the chief menance, the feral dogs and pigs having now been almost eliminated on Santa Cruz. This island and also San Salvador are within the Galápagos National Park and great efforts are being made to complete the eradication of rats and cattle in order to improve the breeding success of this gravely threatened petrel. The Hawaiian subspecies *P. p. sandwichensis* is also threatened with only about 2,000 birds breeding on the rim of Haleakala Crater, on the island of Maui. Its population was drastically reduced in the 1930s by human interference and introduced mongooses. ICBP lists the Dark-rumped Petrel as Endangered.

Another threatened species on the Galápagos Islands is the **Galápagos Flightless Cormorant** *Nannopterum harrisi*, listed as Rare. It is restricted to only 363 km of coastline on Fernandina

and Isabela islands and has never been seen more than one kilometre outside the breeding range. The present population of about 700–800 pairs shows no signs of changing but such a tiny population, confined to so small an area, is obviously extremely vulnerable. One potential development which is bound to cause fatalities is the change from traditional fishing for crayfish by skindivers to industrial fishing using nets.

Throughout the West Indies bird habitats have been rapidly diminishing under the spread of agriculture, touristic developments and excessive hunting. Many species have disappeared entirely and others are nearing extinction. Potential cage-birds and edible species such as pigeons and ducks are ruthlessly hunted. One such species is the **West Indian Whistling Duck** *Dendrocygna arborea*, listed as Vulnerable. It disappeared from Jamaica in 1960. Cuba and Hispaniola apparently have most of its small surviving population, but hunting is likely to exterminate it in both islands. Hunting is prohibited in Cuba but not enforced and the ducks are not protected in Hispaniola. Barbuda holds a reasonable population and there may still be small numbers in the Bahamas and Cayman Islands. A close season during the breeding period has been proposed in Dominica, where a few may occasionally appear.

The **Brazilian Merganser** *Mergus octosetaceus* is a somewhat mysterious and sedentary species which has probably never been numerous and is now known only in single pairs scattered over a very wide area; consequently it is listed as Indeterminate. During the past few decades it has been reported only rarely in the forested tributaries of the Paraná and Tocantins River in Brazil, the eastern part of Paraguay and the Misiones Province of Argentina. Forest destruction and the present massive damming of

Galápagos Flightless Cormorant and Hawk

the Tocantins River system and other rivers will undoubtedly adversely affect any surviving populations of this little-known fish-eating sawbill.

A number of birds of prey are seriously threatened in the South American and Caribbean region, mainly by loss of habitat and because most hunters of the region cannot resist shooting any birds with hooked bills, despite the laws which are intended to protect them. One such bird is the **Cuban Kite** *Chondrohierax wilsonii*, now confined to eastern Cuba where it is very rare and local. The bird lives in low woodlands and so is vulnerable to habitat loss, and its confiding habits also make it especially easy to hunt. In addition to these threats, the unusual prey species, arboreal snails which are also collected by humans for their beautiful shells, is a limiting factor in this bird's distribution. The Cuban Kite is classified as Rare by ICBP.

A hawk about which very little is known is the **Grey-backed Hawk** *Leucopternis occidentalis* of western Ecuador and adjacent north-western Peru: its status is Indeterminate. It was found in the tropical forests of Ecuador from Pichincha Province southward to the Peruvian border, but its population has declined seriously and it is now seen only in the south of its former range. Agriculture has replaced most of the forests elsewhere. One was seen near the Río Palenque Reserve in 1977 and eight or nine during a four-day search in the Puerto Lopez y Machalilla National park in 1978. These wildlife reserves provide some protection, though only small parts of them offer suitable habitat. No other conservation measures are known.

The closely reated **Mantled Hawk** *Leucopternis polionota*, also Indeterminate, is reported to occur in the Atlantic forest fragments of eastern Brazil, southeast Paraguay and the Misiones areas of Argentina. There is no information on numbers, but these will have declined considerably with the destruction of the species's habitat. Immense areas of its former range have been deforested and are no longer occupied by it. Although conspicuous when soaring, it has not been seen during recent searches in Paraguay. It is legally protected in Brazil and has some protection in the Serra dos Orgãos and Itatiaia National Parks, as it does in the Iguazu National Park in Argentina, where it is apparently still seen fairly regularly.

The **Galápagos Hawk** *Buteo galapagoensis*, listed as Rare, is confined to certain of the islands in the Galápagos archipelago, with a total population of around 130 pairs. Like many Galápagos species it is extremely tame, and this must have contributed to a decrease in its numbers as it was formerly much more abundant. It was an easy target for the early settlers who thought that it preyed on their livestock.

The **Crested Eagle** *Morphnus guianensis* occurs in humid lowland forest from Honduras to Panama, and in South America east of the Andes, south to Paraguay and northern Argentina. In much of its range it is unaccountably rare; because of this, its great size and therefore large territorial needs and its dependence on primary rainforest, it is treated as Rare by ICBP.

The **Harpy Eagle** *Harpia harpyja* (Plate IX), considered to be the world's most powerful eagle, has a similar range to the Crested Eagle with an extension into southern Mexico. It also has similar habitat requirements and so is listed as Rare.

Several species of guans and curassows of South America are now gravely threatened by hunting and loss of habitat. They are all forest birds and represent the South American counterparts of the pheasants in Asia. Their substantial size makes them one of the favourite targets of hunters. One guan which was thought to have been completely exterminated is the **White-winged Guan** *Penelope albipennis*. It was evidently common in Peru in the 1840s, but by the 1870s was rare. Nothing more was heard of it until 1977 when four were seen between the departments of Piura and Lambayeque. Later several groups of 20 were seen. It may still inhabit some of the deep forested valleys on the western slopes of the Peruvian Andes. However, the evergreen forests around the springs which this species particularly favours are rapidly being destroyed by charcoal burning; but part of this habitat is protected by the Cerros de Amotape Reserve in northern Piura. The recent change from military to civil government has left a confusing situation, but a research project is currently examining

Horned Guan

the possibility of saving the species, which is listed as Endangered.

The **Cauca Guan** *Penelope perspicax* (Plate X), also listed as Endangered, is in an even worse position. It used to be found throughout the middle of the forested Cauca River valley in Colombia and on both sides of the Andes in the Cauca and Valle departments. Almost all this forest has disappeared. A few Cauca Guans may survive in the Bosque de Yotoco on the western slope of the Andes and perhaps elsewhere, but even the Yotoco subtropical forest, which a local college has undertaken to manage, has only token protection and is being occupied by squatters. The future looks grim for this species.

The **Black-fronted Piping Guan** *Pipile jacutinga* once ranged throughout south-eastern Brazil to south-eastern Paraguay and parts of Argentina. Hunters have killed very large numbers and deforestation has fragmented its range; it appears to have been migratory, and only a few areas now support viable populations. A few are said to occur in the Iguazu National Park in Argentina. Hunting has been prohibited since 1951, but there is virtually no enforcement and its only effective protection is in the national park. It is listed as Endangered.

The **Horned Guan** *Oreophasis derbianus* of south-eastern Mexico and western Guatemala is another threatened species of this family considered Endangered. It formerly had a fairly extensive range in the cloud-forests of the higher ridges of Oaxaca and the forested slopes of various volcanoes, most of which have since been cleared. In 1965 and 1967 extensive searches discovered none in Mexico and it was seen in only three localities in Guatemala. In 1973 it was rediscovered in Mexico, where it was seen in several localities until 1978; since then no further reports have been received. The species is legally protected in Mexico and Guatemala although hunting still continues everywhere. National Parks and Reserves protect some parts of this guan's habitat, notably the 10,000 hectares maintained at El Triunfo by the Institute of Natural History of Chiapas and a private reserve in the cloud-forest on Volcan Atitlán.

Another member of the Cracidae with Endangered status is the **Alagoas Curassow** *Mitu mitu*, which is separated as a full species from the Razor-billed Curassow *M. tuberosa* and is restricted (if still extant) to one tiny forest in north-east Brazil. It is held in captivity in one collection in Rio de Janeiro.

The **Blue-billed Curassow** *Crax alberti* is steadily declining in northern

Horned Coot

Colombia because of the destruction of the forests and ceaseless hunting pressure. It is mainly restricted to the Santa Marta massif, the Magdalena River valley and the lower Cauca River valley. No steps have been taken to protect it, and no parts of the forests it frequents are protected. It is listed as Vulnerable.

The related **Red-billed Curassow** *Crax blumenbachii* (Plate XI) is listed as Endangered but is very close to extinction. Excessive hunting and the disappearance of its forest habitat are again the contributory causes. Its total population is estimated as numbering a few hundred individuals. It was formerly widespread in south-eastern Brazil, but is now seen only in the forests of Linhares, the Sooretama Reserve and Monte Pascoal National Park. It is legally protected in Brazil, but without enforcement.

About 70 years ago four specimens of a strange little wood-quail were shot in the forest near Bogotá in Colombia. They were named the **Gorgeted Wood-quail** *Odontophorus strophium*. In the 1970s the bird was rediscovered in an oak forest near Virilon. This locality, only 3,000 hectares in extent, is now almost certainly the only one that remains. The species is Endangered.

The **Bogotá Rail** *Rallus semiplumbeus* is another of Colombia's threatened species. It is uncommon to locally fairly common in the marshes around Lake Tota, in the Parque del Florida near Bogotá where it enjoys some measure of protection, and at a few other sites. The decline in its distribution and numbers is attributable to the drainage of wetlands within its range, which is now believed to be restricted to marshes in the savanna at a mean altitude of about 2,600 m in the western Andes of Boyacá and Cundinamarca departments. ICBP lists this species as Vulnerable.

Another threatened rail species is the **Zapata Rail** *Cyanolimnas cerverai* known chiefly from the Zapata swamp in Cuba. Although the swamp has thus far largely escaped drainage attempts, the future of this species is only as secure as the future of the swamp. ICBP lists the Zapata Rail as Rare.

The **Horned Coot** *Fulica cornuta* (see illustration on previous page), also listed as Rare, is found only in a restricted area of high Andean plateau on the borders of northern Chile, western Bolivia and north-western Argentina, and is rarely, if ever, found below 3,000 m. The coot is remarkable not only for its curious appendage or muscular proboscis, which gives it its vernacular name, but also for the original fashion in which it builds its nest. On some lakes a cone-shaped foundation of stones is constructed, up to one metre in height, so that the top comes close to the surface of the water and provides a platform for the nest proper above.

As pigeons and doves are everywhere vulnerable to subsistence hunting, many species throughout the world have become threatened, particularly those which are also sensitive to deforestation. The **Purple-winged Ground-dove** *Claravis godefrida* of south-eastern coastal Brazil is one of the most serious cases and is listed as Vulnerable. It formerly occurred in eastern Paraguay and perhaps also in Argentina, but recent searches have not found it. It is protected by Brazilian law and has some protection in the Serra dos Orgãos National Park, but it appears to have suffered from loss of bamboo thickets and is evidently now extremely scarce.

Records of the **Grenada Dove** *Leptotila wellsi* are scanty and thus its status is given as Indeterminate. Most of the records for this species during the past century have come from the south-western coastal region of Grenada and from Green Island in the north-east. It no longer occurs on Green Island and is very rare in Grenada. The last report was of five birds seen in the scrublands near Grand Anse in 1971, a region now being developed for housing. It has been suggested that competition with other species of doves might have been responsible for the restricted range of the Grenada Dove as several species occupy the same habitat.

The related **Tolima Dove** *Leptotila conoveri* is also a bit of a mystery, and has an Indeterminate status. The size of its population has never been known. It is apparently very locally distributed in Colombia, in an area where deforestation has been very severe. It used to be found on the eastern slopes of the Colombian Andes in the Tolima and Huila divisions, including the headwaters of the Magdalena River, but there has been a great decline in its numbers. It could not be found during a recent thorough search in the upper Magdalena valley. Although none of its forest habitat is protected, there is some hope of its survival because of its known ability to utilise secondary growth.

Almost all the 128 parrot species in South America and the Caribbean region must now be at some risk, either from trappers for the cage-bird trade or from the disappearance of their forest habitats, or in all too many cases from both. So long as bird-fanciers are willing to pay $20,000 for a single specimen such as of the beautiful **Hyacinth Macaw** *Anodorhynchus hyacinthinus* (Plate XII), the largest species of parrot in the world, from Brazil, eastern Bolivia and northeast Paraguay, trapping is likely to continue even if the strictest protective legislation is introduced. Corruption and inefficiency among South American customs officials at present facilitate the

Little Blue Macaw

swamp, is not thought to be much of a problem.

The **Indigo Macaw** *Anodorhynchus leari*, another Endangered macaw, was known only from old museum skins or captives of uncertain origin until 1978, when a small number were discovered by Brazilian ornithologists in the remote ravines of the Rasa da Caterina in Bahía State in north-eastern Brazil. As many as 21 were seen together in a dry river-bed covered with low, thorny vegetation. Fortunately the region is within an existing ecological reserve which may provide some protection from collectors, but the total population is believed to be only around 60 individuals.

Although there are several examples of the attractive **Spix's** or **Little Blue Macaw** *Cyanopsitta spixii* in captivity, virtually nothing is known about its behaviour in the wild. In contrast to the great majority of the parrots and macaws of South America, which are threatened by a combination of loss of habitat and the cage-bird trade, this naturally rare species appears to have been exterminated entirely by the activities of the bird-traders. The macaw's preferred habitat, *Buriti* palm swamps, is usually left undisturbed, being of little use for agriculture. It used to be reported from several parts of central Brazil, and wild-caught birds were still being illegally offered for sale as recently as 1986. The only recent record from the wild is of three birds. Clearly ICBP will be classifying it as Endangered in the next Red Data Book.

The **Blue-throated Macaw** *Ara glaucogularis* (formerly called Wagler's Macaw *A. caninde*) is presumed still to exist, but there are no recent records from the wild and the origins of those in captivity are in doubt. It is a Candidate Red Data Book species. If it still survives, it is likely to be in south-eastern

work of smugglers, and threatened species are still being exported by the hundred. Thanks to CITES this trade has become more difficult, but it is still thriving. It is said that in 1982, 1,000 Hyacinth Macaws were smuggled out of Brazil. The drastic decline in the population of this species must be largely attributed to trade as destruction of its favoured habitat, gallery forest and

Bolivia, where confusion with the closely related Blue-and-Yellow Macaw *A. ararauna* is likely, and perhaps in north-western Argentina. The last report of the Blue-throated was in the late 1940s, from Salta province in Argentina, but this may have been a Blue-and-Yellow Macaw. There are still some substantial tracts of the dry deciduous forest, which is believed to be the habitat of this species, in north-western Argentina and south-eastern Bolivia, where it may perhaps survive. Only five specimens are known in museums.

Another species in great demand by the cage-bird trade is the **Golden Conure** *Aratinga guarouba*. It lives only in a very restricted area of north-eastern Brazil, primarily in eastern Partá, but also in adjacent western and northern Maranhão. Because of the high prices paid for this spectacular yellow and green bird it had become rare by 1946 and is today further threatened by the destruction of Brazil's forests. Its distribution has become fragmented as a result of widespread forest destruction. It is legally protected in Brazil, but still obtainable at a high price, being one of the most desirable birds an aviculturalist could possess, from the illegal traders. It is listed by ICBP as Vulnerable.

The **Golden-plumed Conure** *Leptosittaca branickii*, a Candidate Red Data Book species, and **Yellow-eared Conure** *Ognorhynchus icterotis*, listed as Vulnerable, are parrots which are sparsely distributed in the Andes of south-west Colombia and adjacent northern Ecuador in upper subtropical and lower temperate zone forests. The Golden-plumed Conure also ranges into Peru. Both are equally at risk and neither has any legal protection. The Yellow-eared Conure was once very numerous but has suffered a substantial decline owing to the deforestation of the mountain slopes

it occupied. By 1956 it had become scarce and the alarm was sounded for the species. A few were seen during 1975 in the Purace and Guacharos National Parks in Colombia, where they have some measure of protection, but the population is now very local and must be very small. A new national park has been proposed in the Nevada del Huila area, in which this species might be expected to occur.

The **Rufous-fronted Parakeet** *Bolborhynchus ferrugineifrons* is one of the least known Neotropical parrots. It used to be recorded in Colombia from the Tolima and Cauca divisions to the high slopes of the central Andes. There have been a few recent reports in the high-altitude scrublands on the Tolima–Caldas boundary, which might have involved this species. The temperate *páramo* scrub-forest on the Andes slopes which it used to favour has now been reduced to small isolated patches which provide very limited habitats. Nevertheless there is still some hope that the species may not have disappeared since it has been suggested that its preferred habitat might in fact be scrubby mountain slopes, of which plenty survive. It therefore has Indeterminate status.

The **Blue-chested Parakeet** *Pyrrhura cruentata* (Plate XI), listed as Rare, occurs in a circumscribed area in south-eastern Brazil. The primary forest in this region has mostly been cleared, only relict patches remaining. However, it appears to be not uncommon in one or two reserves.

The **Brown-backed Parrotlet** *Touit melanonota* is also restricted to south-eastern Brazil. It too occurs in reserves and the habit of birds in this genus of remaining inconspicuous, high in the forest canopy, may partly account for the presumption of Rare status.

Another little-known parrotlet which

*Red-spectacled
Amazon*

is endemic to the lowland forests of coastal eastern Brazil is the **Golden-tailed Parrotlet** *Touit surda*. Its population has inevitably declined in pace with the destruction of forests within its range. Only a few small areas of suitable habitat now remain and this delightful little bird is, in consequence, greatly at risk. There have been no recent reports about its status. It is protected by Brazilian law and may be afforded some additional protection in the Monte Pascoal National Park in Bahía State, which has some suitable habitat but it is not known whether any still surive there. The species is listed as Indeterminate.

Almost as little is known of the **Rusty-faced Parrot** *Hapalopsittaca amazonina*, a Candidate Red Data Book species. It has a discontinuous range in the northern Andes and is currently considered to consist of four subspecies. Found primarily in temperate zone forest, from 2,300 to 3,500 m, it is scarce throughout its range. The rarest subspecies *H. a. fuertisi* is known only from a very limited area in Colombia's northern central Andes. It was rediscovered there in 1980, having not been seen for 70 years.

Everything possible is being done to save the gravely threatened **Puerto Rican Amazon** *Amazona vittata*, which used to inhabit all the forested parts of Puerto Rico. Its total population declined as soon as the lowland forests began to be felled. By 1969 only 20

remained and by 1976 only 13. In 1977 only three pairs bred, but in 1982 the species recovered to 29 birds. It is now fully protected by Puerto Rican and US Federal Laws. Its survivors are within the boundaries of a US National Forest and are being closely studied by experts from the US Fish and Wildlife Service. A captive-breeding project has been started in the Luquillo Forest and in 1985 12 young were successfully fledged, five of which were from captive-bred parents. It is known that the factors influencing the survival of this parrot are the lack of suitable nest-holes, the flooding of holes by heavy rain, competition for nest-holes from Pearly-eyed Thrashers *Margarops fuscatus* (which also prey on eggs and young), predation by rats and hawks, and the infestation of nestlings by bot-fly warbles. Efforts are being made to reduce all these factors. The possible threat of hybridization with the recently established Hispaniolan Amazon *A. ventralis* is also being studied. This detailed research is a good example of what is involved in making a last-minute effort to save a species of bird near the brink of extinction. Had it been undertaken 30 or 40 years ago, this parrot might not now be classified as Endangered.

The now rare **Red-spectacled Amazon** *Amazona pretrei* is threatened by the destruction of its forest habitat and formerly by hunting which reduced its original small population. It is especially vulnerable because what appears to be its entire population congregates in a single patch of forest in winter. It was formerly common in south-eastern Brazil, the adjacent Misiones Province in Argentina and possibly also in northern Uruguay. Its range in Brazil is now greatly reduced and its status in Argentina and Uruguay unknown. Hundreds used to be shot in the hope that a few winged birds might be sold to the pet trade. In 1971 numbers at its winter roost in Rio Grande do Sul were estimated at between 10,000 and 20,000, but by 1976 only 2,000 could be found roosting a few kilometres from the original site. The Rio Grande do Sul State Government has proposed a research and conservation project and has turned the *Araucaria* grove used for roosting into a protected reserve. ICBP lists the species as Vulnerable.

The **Red-tailed Amazon** *Amazona brasiliensis* is another gravely threatened mainland Neotropical parrot and is listed as Endangered. It is endemic to south-eastern Brazil, where forest destruction has been extensive. The only recent reports are from São Paulo. The size of its population is probably no more than 4,000 individuals. Its habitat is believed to be coastal lowland forest and stands of *Araucaria* pine, which it shares with the related and now vulnerable Red-spectacled Amazon *A. pretrei* (see above). It is protected by Brazilian law, but like other parrots is still freely offered for sale.

Its close relative, the **Red-browed Amazon** *Amazona rhodocorytha*, which replaces it in the coastal region of Brazil from Alagoas to Rio de Janeiro, is probably equally at risk as it is much traded and its forest habitat is fast disappearing. It is a Candidate Red Data Book species.

On the small island of St. Lucia in the Caribbean a promising effort is being made by the WWF (US) and by the local government to save the Endangered **St. Lucia Amazon** *Amazona versicolor*. Like most of the parrots of this region it has nearly been wiped out by illegal hunting and diminution of habitat by logging and agriculture. It used to occupy all the forested slopes of the island, but is now restricted to between 50 and 65 sq km of forest to the east of Morne Gimie, where about 100 birds survived in 1977. The population has declined, mainly because of shooting and capture for the pet trade but also as a result of the destruction of its forest habitat. The recent creation of a strictly controlled nature reserve at Morne Gimie is, however, proving a great success (250 birds in 1986) and is well supported by tourists. A study of the breeding biology of this and other endangered species and a captive-breeding project supported by WWF and Jersey Wildlife Preservation Trust are giving encouraging results.

The **Red-necked Amazon** *Amazona arausiaca* and the **Imperial Amazon** *A. imperialis* (Plate XII) are known only from Dominica in the Lesser Antilles and both are considered Endangered. The former was once abundant throughout the island but is now seen only in the regions of Morne Diablotin and the Picard River, usually in lowland forest or mangroves. In 1978 its population was estimated at 300 birds. Both species are threatened by a number of pressures, notably forest modification by humans compounded by hurricanes. Hunting and trapping for trade have been excessive, but Red-necked Amazons also suffer from competition for nest-sites and predation of their eggs and nestlings by Pearly-eyed Thrashers *Margarops fuscatus*. In the lowland forests the Red-necked may be restricting the Imperial to the dwarf rain-forest in the mountain tops by competition for nest-sites. The Imperial, which numbered only 60 birds in 1987, is in the greater danger. A national park has been established at Morne Anglais to the south of the island, but probably neither species is within its boundaries. The Canadian Nature Federation is working with the Dominican Government on the legislative groundwork for a parks system and on a study of the endangered parrots of the Antilles. During 1987 money for conservation studies was raised by a "Parrots in Peril" appeal sponsored by the National Federation of Zoos on behalf of ICBP.

The **St. Vincent Amazon** *Amazona guildingii* is found only on St. Vincent island in the Lesser Antilles and is yet another Endangered Caribbean parrot. It has a small and declining population which is illegally hunted and its young are taken every year by the pet traders. Its potential breeding area has been reduced to only 30 sq km in the centre of the island, parts of which have already had the large trees extracted, thus depriving it of nest-holes. Its population had fallen steeply to around only 420 birds by 1982 and on average 30–40 young are still taken by the pet trade each year. Although protected by law, hunting and nest-robbing continue unchecked (I saw one being bought by an American tourist in Panama). The establishment of a protected forest reserve is being considered.

The **Puerto Rican Nightjar** *Caprimulgus noctitherus*, is found only on the island of Puerto Rico and was thought to be extinct from about 1911 until 1961, when it was rediscovered. The former distribution is known to have included the moist limestone forest of the northwest coast, while the most recent records are all from the dry limestone forest of the south-western coast. The mongoose, introduced in 1877, is presumed to have extirpated the bird from those areas of its

Hook-billed Hermit

former range having sufficient rainfall and standing water to support mongooses. The remaining habitat of lowland scrubby semi-arid forest is threatened by an expanding human population and rapidly developing industry. The survival of the Puerto Rican Nightjar population, numbered at 450 to 500 pairs, will depend on the preservation of this habitat. ICBP lists the Puerto Rican Nightjar as Rare.

The hummingbirds are confined to the Nearctic and Neotropical Regions and many of the 315 species are highly specialised, or have very restricted distributions. They are particularly vulnerable to the destruction of the nectar-bearing forest plants on which they depend for food. The **Hook-billed Hermit** *Glaucis dohrnii* is known from only two areas of primary forest in eastern Brazil and is consequently listed as Endangered. It used to be found throughout the region from southern Bahía to

Rio de Janeiro. In 1938 its range was 35,000 sq km, but by 1967 it was thought to have been reduced to only 100 sq km, most of its forest habitat having been converted to cattle pasture. By 1976 it was known only from a forest tract, now unsuitable for the species, on the Klabin (now São Joaquim) Farm estate, on the border between Espírito Santo and Bahía States, and from the Monte Pascoal National Park in south-east Bahía. But in 1986 it was also found in a previously unknown patch of privately owned forest near Porto Seguro, also in Bahía.

Yet another hummingbird with a very restricted distribution is the **Black-billed Hermit** *Phaethornis nigrirostris* from the Nova Lombardia Reserve in Espírito Santo, Brazil. It too is dependent on primary forest and is outnumbered in its range by another hermit *P. eurynome*, so increasing the pressure on the available resources. It is listed as Rare but its taxonomy is in doubt.

The **Black Inca** *Coeligena prunellei* is a typical example of a threatened hummingbird. Most of the existing museum specimens were collected in the nineteenth century and are presumed to have been taken on the slopes of the Andes in central Colombia, where the subtropical forests have now been almost destroyed. It was seen in 1974 near Facatavá and again in 1978 in Boyacá at an altitude of 2,300 m on the slopes of Cerro Carare, where there were thought to be several hundred. Recent work suggests that it is a good deal more widespread in relict forest patches than had been thought. However a serious decline from the substantial nineteenth century population has taken place and the species is listed as Indeterminate.

The **Juan Fernandez Firecrown** *Sephanoides fernandensis* is a hummingbird that is now confined to a single island. There were thousands of these delightful birds on the Juan Fernandez Islands of Chile 15–20 years ago. Today the numbers have been reduced to a mere 250 on Isla Robinson Crusoe. In this case it is not vegetation destruction which has caused the decline (introduced plants are a good food source), but nest predation by Black Rats *Rattus rattus* and Coatimundis *Nasua narica*. It is a Candidate Red Data Book species.

The **Chilean Woodstar** *Eulidia yarrellii*, has an extremely restricted distribution in Tarapacá, the northernmost

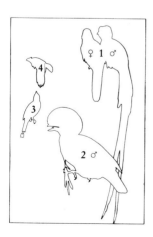

PLATE IX   Central American Forest. 1 Resplendent Quetzal (p. 85), 2 Bare-necked Umbrellabird (p. 88), 3 Keel-billed Motmot (p. 97), 4 Harpy Eagle (p. 72).

PLATE X   Northern South American Forest. 1 Cauca Guan (p. 72), 2 Recurve-billed Bushbird (p. 98), 3 White-mantled Barbet (p. 97), 4 White-chested Swift (p. 95).

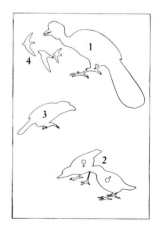

Norman Arlott 87

Norman Arlott 87

Norman Arlott 87

Norman Arlott 87

province of Chile, where it is most often seen in the suburban gardens of the city of Arica and in the agricultural areas of the Azapa and Lluta valleys. Vagrants have occurred up to 130 km away. Until 1948 it was regarded as common, but by 1971 had become scarce. Between 1972 and 1973 it was seen only three times, in the Azapa valley; more recently, it has again been found to be common. The region is surrounded by inhospitable desert, offering no habitat to the species. Meanwhile it is still on the Endangered list.

The beautiful and unique emerald-green **Resplendent Quetzal** *Pharomachrus mocinno* (Plate IX) is one of the most famous of South America's many unusual birds and has a range extending from southern Mexico to Panama. It is threatened by the destruction of tropical cloud-forests, and the persistent activities of the cage-bird traders, and is currently listed as Vulnerable. Its decline is most marked in the mountains of Costa Rica and Panama. Although legally protected in Mexico, Costa Rica and Panama, enforcement is almost impossible in the high and remote regions where these birds occur. The designation of the

Quetzal as the "National Bird" of Guatemala was intended to gain public support for its protection, but only tended to encourage its capture for trade. In Costa Rica alone one dealer exported 100 Quetzals in 1973 and there is a ready market for such illegal trade. Quetzals benefit from a number of reserves and national parks and a few patches of cloud-forest are also under protection; but huge areas have been destroyed to make way for shifting subsistence agriculture, coffee plantations, or cattle ranching.

Another species severely threatened by the cage-bird trade is the attractively coloured **Toucan Barbet** *Semnornis ramphastinus* (Plate XII) of north-western South America. It is found chiefly in the foothills of the western Andes in Colombia and north-western Ecuador and is declining in all the accessible parts of its range because of the demand for it as a cage-bird. Little of the forest of the upper tropical and subtropical zones is protected and this barbet is very easily trapped. A few parts of its habitat are protected by the Los Farallones National Park and along the Rio Anchicaya valley in Colombia. The

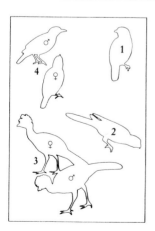

PLATE XI Neotropic Atlantic Forest. 1 Banded Cotinga (p. 88), 2 Blue-chested Parakeet (p. 76), 3 Red-billed Currasow (p. 73), 4 White-winged Coptinga (p. 88).

PLATE XII Neotropic Bird Market. 1 Hyacinth Macaw (p. 74), 2 Red Siskin (p. 91), 3 Toucan Barbet (p. 85), 4 Yellow Cardinal (p. 102), 5 Imperial Amazon (p. 78).

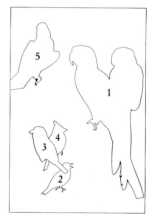

proposed Cotacachi–Cayapas ecological reserve in north-west Ecuador will also give some protection. But this species, like the Long-wattled Umbrellabird *Cephalopterus penduliger* and the Red Siskin *Carduelis cucullatus* (see pages 88 & 91), is more seriously threatened by human persecution than by loss of habitat. It is listed by ICBP as Vulnerable.

A number of woodpecker species are threatened by a combination of hunting and loss of habitat, and especially by the felling of the mature trees in which their nest-holes are made. For the last 20 years there have been very few records of the **Helmeted Woodpecker** *Dryocopus galeatus* and it may well be in danger of extinction. Until the 1950s it was recorded in the lowland forests of Brazil, Paraguay and the Misiones Province of Argentina. Despite several searches, its present distribution and status are unclear. Much of the lowland forest in all three countries has been seriously depleted, but there are still some substantial forested areas within this woodpecker's former range where it may survive. It has been described as the world's least-known woodpecker and is appropriately listed as Endangered.

The **Ivory-billed Woodpecker** *Campephilus principalis*, probably extinct in North America (see page 58), still exists in Cuba; but a population of probably fewer than six pairs is all that remains of a species believed to have been formerly common in suitable lowland and montane habitat throughout most of the island. It is confined to the region of the Cupeyal Reserve in the Oriente Province. Forest reservations were established by the Cuban Academy of Sciences in 1963 and no further felling is permitted, but most of the mature timber had already been extracted. An expedition in the spring of 1986 sighted two and very likely three birds in very disturbed

Ivory-billed Woodpecker

forest, giving some hope. It is listed as Endangered.

The antbirds, confined to Central and South America, are small and sometimes rather drab little birds which live in the dense undergrowth and thickets of forested regions. Because of their skulking behaviour they have often been overlooked and are very imperfectly known. Nevertheless, there are no fewer than 223 different species, some of which are certainly now very rare because of the widespread destruction of their habitats.

The **Black-hooded Antwren** *Myrmotherula erythronotos* was known with certainty only from museum material collected near Nova Friburgo, between Rio de Janeiro and Campos, where almost all the tropical forest has since disappeared. It was searched for by the British Ornithologists' Union (BOU)-WWF expeditions of 1980–1982 without success but was rediscovered in a new, secret locality in September 1986 by members of the Rio de Janeiro Birdwatchers Club. It is listed by ICBP as Endangered.

The **Narrow-billed Antwren** *Formicivora iheringi*, listed as Vulnerable, is known only from the interior of southeastern Bahía in Brazil, where its habitat of dry ridge woodlands with terrestrial bromeliads is being progressively cleared. Its habitat is shared by the equally scarce Slender Antbird *Rhopor-*

nis ardesiaca (see below). They are protected by Brazilian law, but no part of their habitat is protected.

Another antbird which is only just managing to survive the massive destruction of Brazil's forests is the **Fringe-backed Fire-eye** *Pyriglena atra*. It has been recorded near Salvador in southern Bahía State and is now known only from two small populations on either side of a road near Santa Aman to the north of Salvador on the Atlantic coast. It is protected by Brazilian law and a reserve to protect this species and others has been proposed, but no action has yet been taken. It is listed as Endangered.

The **Slender Antbird** *Rhopornis ardesiaca*, considered Vulnerable, has been recorded from four localities in eastern Brazil but might be found in others. Only four specimens have been collected, but it was found again in 1974 and 1977 in the same habitat of dry forest with terrestrial bromeliads. Little of this habitat has escaped clearance for cattle pasture however. The species is protected by law in Brazil, but enforcement does not exist in remote areas where it might survive.

The **Moustached Antpitta** *Grallaria alleni* is known from a single specimen collected in 1911 at an altitude of 2,100 m in the Caldas division of Colombia, on the western slope of the central Andes. The forest in this region has been seriously reduced and it has been recorded at only two localities. Its status is given as Indeterminate.

Two related antpittas are known from the same general region, the **Bicoloured Antpitta** *G. rufocinerea* and the **Brown-banded Antpitta** *G. milleri*. Both are now threatened by forest destruction. The former is a Candidate Red Data Book species and the latter is considered Indeterminate. The Brown-banded Antpitta is known only from seven specimens collected in 1911, which suggests that at that time it was not uncommon. There have been no other records since.

The tapaculos belong to a family that is related to the antbirds and are characterised by their long legs, short, rounded wings and cocked tails; some also have movable flaps covering their nostrils. **Stresemann's Bristlefront** *Merulaxis stresemanni* is, or perhaps was, one of these, for it may now be extinct, although its status is still given as Indeterminate. It is known only from two Brazilian specimens, one collected in 1831 near Salvador in Bahía State, the other in 1938 some 250 km south of Salvador. Most of the forests of the eastern coastal region of Brazil have since been cleared and there have been no further reports of this species, although a search for it was made in 1977. It is protected by Brazilian law but none of its potential forest habitat is protected.

Its relative the **Brasília Tapaculo** *Scytalopus novacapitalis*, also listed as Indeterminate, was known from three specimens collected in 1957 in dense, flooded thickets surmounted by gallery-forest of palms. This area is now occupied by the capital city of Brasília. No further trace of the species was found until recently when it was rediscovered near the city. There are still some similar areas within the millions of square kilometres of the Brazilian plateau where it might occur.

Moustached Antpitta

The cotingas are confined to the tropical forests of Central and South America. Many of the males have bizarre head-ornaments or are brilliantly coloured. A species currently listed as Indeterminate but which is almost certainly extinct is the **Kinglet Cotinga** *Calyptura cristata*. It was known in the last century only in the Nova Friburgo and Rio de Janeiro areas, where deforestation is now almost complete; there have been no reports of it during this century. It is legally protected in Brazil and some 5,000 hectares of suitable habitat exist in the Serra dos Orgãos National Park, although it has never been recorded there, and there now seems little likelihood that the species still exists.

The **Banded Cotinga** *Cotinga maculata* (Plate XI) has been greatly reduced in numbers and distribution as a result of forest destruction. It is absent from

Long-wattled Umbrellabird

much of its former range, but still exists in the Linhares and Sooretama reserves (Espírito Santo) and near Porto Seguro (Bahía) in south-eastern Brazil. It is protected by Brazilian law and listed by ICBP as Vulnerable.

The **White-winged Cotinga** *Xipholena atropurpurea* (Plate XI) is in a very similar situation, being now confined to Linhares and Sooretama (Espírito Santo), the Monte Pascoal National Park, the Porto Seguro area and Una Biological Reserve (southern Bahía) and one forest in Alagoas. It is also listed as Vulnerable.

The **Long-wattled Umbrellabird** *Cephalopterus penduliger* is avidly hunted for the cage-bird trade and is also large enough to be shot for food. It has a limited distribution in western Colombia on the slopes of the Andes and southwards into western Ecuador. It is quickly exterminated around all human settlements. There is, however, still a considerable amount of undisturbed forest within its range where it may maintain a reasonably large population. However, nothing is being done to protect it and it is considered Vulnerable. The **Bare-necked Umbrellabird** *C. glabricollis* (Plate IX) of Costa Rica and western Panama is also at risk, and is a Candidate Red Data Book species.

It is something of a relief to turn to the swallow family and to realise that out of the world's 78 different species only five are considered threatened. That swallows and martins feed on flying insects, and are therefore less vulnerable to the worldwide destruction of forests and other wild vegetation, is a significant factor in the survival of their many species. They are, however, vulnerable if deprived of nest-sites, as is evidently happening to the beautiful **Golden Swallow** *Kalochelidon euchrysea*, whose blue-green upper parts are strongly glossed with gold. The Jamaican subspecies *euchrysea* was formerly common in the mountainous interior of the island, but by 1916 it was restricted to Cockpit County in the west. In recent years its population has fallen even further and it is now seen only in the Ram Goat Cave region in that county. Since 1961 it has been recorded only six times and may be heading for extinction. The reasons for its decline are not clear, but competition for nest-sites by the introduced European Starling have probably contributed. Its other population *sclateri* may also be threatened in Haiti and in the Dominican Republic where it is local and found chiefly at higher elevations. The species is a Candidate Red Data Book species.

The **Rufous-throated Dipper** *Cinclus schulzi* is a declining species with an Indeterminate status. Although there is an abundance of suitable water-courses in Argentina, its major habitat, it is restricted to the north-western provinces of Jujuy, Tucumán, Salta and Catamarca. In 1983 it was discovered that the species's plight was not as grave as had been thought, and it has been predicted that it should be found in the valleys of the Aconquija system. All the regions where it occurred in the past are in relatively dry parts of Argentina, where there are few fast-flowing streams. Some of these have been tapped or diverted, while others are now polluted, which may explain the gradual disappearance of this dipper.

Another rather puzzling bird is the little **Apolinar's Wren** *Cistothorus apolinari*. It is restricted to the north portion of the Eastern Andes in Colombia. Most of the recent records come from the Parque del Florida and the shores of Lake Tota in this region. The species is fairly common but very local in tall cattails bordering waterbodies. Its status is given as Vulnerable.

The **Zapata Wren** *Ferminia cerverai* is restricted to one area of swampland, the Zapata Swamp, in Cuba. It is thought to be at risk because of the ease with which its habitat could be destroyed by large-scale drainage and it is listed as Rare. Although no drainage scheme has taken place, the species declined to near extinction in the 1960s and 1970s owing possibly to burning of the habitat by local people, but some records in the 1980s offer some hope that it may be recovering.

The **White-breasted Thrasher** *Ramphocinclus brachyurus* has suffered severely on Martinique from the popular local passion for hunting small birds. Neither the bird nor its habitat is protected and it is now rare and restricted to a single peninsula on the north-east coast of the island, where mongooses, rats and hunters still prey on it. A second population, distinguished as the subspecies *R. b. sanctaeluciae*, occurs on St. Lucia. They are the only representatives of this unique West Indian genus. The St. Lucia White-breasted Thrasher apparently suffers less from human persecution, but in 1971 a survey showed that only about 75 pairs remained and that these were restricted to five small ravines spanning 8 km and ranging inland for only 1.5 km from the north-east coast. The future of this population depends on the preservation of the scrub-forest in these valleys. They are at present part of a forest reserve, which provides a little protection. Mongooses occur in the forest and the Fer-de-Lance snake *Bothrops caribbaeus* is abundant and undoubtedly preys on the largely terrestrial thrashers. The species is listed as Endangered.

The **Zapata Sparrow** *Torreornis inexpectata* occurs in three races in three widely scattered but restricted areas of Cuba; nominate *inexpectata* in the Zapata Swamp, *sigmani* along the arid south-easternmost coast where it is greatly at

Mangrove Finch

risk from fire, and *varonai* on Cayo Coco, an island off the central-northern coast. Disturbance of the habitat within any of these circumscribed ranges might quickly result in extinction. The species is classified as Rare.

The **Tumaco Seedeater** *Sporophila insulata* is almost certainly extinct, although currently listed as Indeterminate. It is known only from the small island of Tumaco, off the south-eastern coast of Nariño, Colombia, where four specimens were collected in 1912. The island at that time was covered with mangroves and stunted vegetation. It is now covered by the city of Tumaco.

In 1911 two specimens of a very distinctive small finch were collected in a forest at an altitude of 2,175 m in the Rio Toche, in Colombia. They were given the name **Olive-headed Brush Finch** *Atlapetes flaviceps*. Most of the forest where the specimens were collected has disappeared and it is probable that the widespread destruction of the tropical forests elsewhere in Colombia has exterminated the species. However in 1967 three birds were netted and photographed and so it might perhaps still survive in the remaining forests. The species has an Indeterminate status.

Another vulnerable finch is the **Mangrove Finch** *Camarhynchus heliobates*. It is restricted to mangroves on the

islands of Isabela and Fernandina in the Galápagos Islands where its population is very small and restricted. It is classified as Rare.

At least three of South America's colourful tanagers are at risk, one of which, the **Cherry-throated Tanager** *Nemosia rourei*, may indeed be extinct, although currently listed as Endangered. It is known only from a single specimen collected in 1870 on the north bank of the Rio Paraíba in Rio de Janeiro state, Brazil, and a flock seen in Espírito Santo State around 1940. Both these areas are now reportedly cleared of forest.

The **Azure-rumped Tanager** *Tangara cabanisi* has a very restricted range from the cloud-forest of southern Chiapas in Mexico to part of the highlands of western Guatemala. Until recently it was known only from three skins, one of which was taken in Guatemala; but between 1972 and 1977 there were several sightings in the Chiapas region of Mexico, one of which was of a flock of 16 birds. A reserve of 10,000 hectares at El Triumfo, owned by the Institute of Natural History of Chiapas, protects some of the cloud-forest habitat of this species. Its range has not yet been thoroughly searched and its population may be larger than thought. It is listed as Indeterminate.

The even more striking **Seven-coloured Tanager** *T. fastuosa* is listed as Vulnerable. It is restricted to part of the north-eastern Brazilian coast in Pernambuco and Alagoas States. Thirty years ago it was common, but constant collecting for the cage-bird trade and the reduction of forests have greatly reduced its numbers, although it has been observed in forest fragments and in degraded forest. There are a few protected forests within the tanager's range but it is protected by Brazilian law, though this has little effect on the illegal bird traders, from whom nearly all the tanager species suffer.

Semper's Warbler *Leucopeza semperi* is endemic to the island of St. Lucia, in the Lesser Antilles, where it used to occur in all the montane forests.. Its numbers declined until it became scarce and it was seen only occasionally up until 1972. There have been no subsequent reports, despite a search as recently as 1987, suggesting that it is now gravely threatened and consequently it has Endangered status. As this species nests on or near the ground and frequents the forest understorey, it may have fallen victim to the introduced mongoose.

Both races of the **Yellow-shouldered Blackbird** *Agelaius xanthomus* are struggling for survival on the West Indian islands of Puerto Rico and Mona, the latter lying between Puerto Rico and Hispaniola. Their combined population does not exceed 1,500 and they are listed as Vulnerable. The Puerto Rico race *A. x. xanthomus* was common in the coastal lowlands until 1940 but is now confined to small areas on the south-west and east coasts, where its population is declining at a rate of 20% per annum. Nesting on the mainland is rare, most of the birds breeding in palms with rat-guards, or in mangroves on small, rat-free offshore islets. Drainage of the freshwater wetlands has been the main cause of their decline, while predation by rats and brood-parasitism by the recently established Shiny Cowbird *Molothrus bonariensis* are contributory factors. Competition for nest-sites by Pearly-eyed Thrashers *Margarops fuscatus* may have restricted the breeding range of the blackbirds. The Puerto Rico Yellow-shouldered Blackbird is protected by law and by the US Endangered Species Act of 1973. The Mona Yellow-shouldered Blackbird *A. x. monensis* has a population of only 100–200 birds, which have

the same legal protection. This small island is threatened by proposals for development as a deep-water super-port and oil refinery, or as a US Navy bombing range, either of which would certainly exterminate the subspecies. The Shiny Cowbird has also recently begun to parasitise the nests of this race.

The long list of species known to be at risk in the Neotropical Region ends with the Endangered **Red Siskin** *Carduelis cucullata* (Plate XII) which is under intense pressure in Venezuela from trappers for the cage-bird market. Its range and population are rapidly diminishing and this trend is likely to continue until this beautiful little bird is exterminated. At present it is found in parts of the northern *cordilleras* of Venezuela, where 1981 estimates indicated only 600 to 800 individuals. It used also to exist in Colombia and in the north-western peninsula of Trinidad and the adjacent islands of Mona and Gaspares and in Puerto Rico. The Red Siskin is a semi-nomadic bird using many types of habitat including scrub wood and evergreen forest. The siskins used to form large flocks after breeding, which facilitated trapping, but no flocks are seen today and most records are of single birds. The reason for the demand for this species is its brilliant red plumage and the fact that it is easily hybridised with domestic canaries. Trappers were still getting $50 for males in 1974, while dealers in the United States and Japan could get three or four times this sum. The species is legally protected in Venezuela, but trapping is still rampant because it occurs in remote regions difficult to police.

91

ADDITIONAL CANDIDATE BIRDS OF THE NEOTROPICAL REGION

TINAMIDAE Tinamous
Solitary Tinamou *Tinamus solitarius* is scarce in the forests of eastern Brazil, Paraguay and Argentina.
Black Tinamou *Tinamus osgoodi* is known only from forests in southern Colombia and south-east Peru, and is very scarce in the latter.
Yellow-legged Tinamou *Crypturellus noctivagus* is scarce in the Atlantic forest of eastern Brazil.
Taczanowski's Tinamou *Nothoprocta taczanowskii* is confined to high grasslands in central and south-eastern Peru.
Kalinowski's Tinamou *Nothoprocta kalinowskii* is a species recorded in just two high-altitude grassland areas of Peru.
Lesser Nothura *Nothura minor* is found only in central Brazil.
Dwarf Tinamou *Taoniscus nanus* inhabits eastern Brazil and possibly Argentina, and is considered a threatened *campo* species.

SPHENISCIDAE Penguins
Peruvian Penguin *Spheniscus humboldti* has a much reduced population. It breeds along the coasts of Peru and northern Chile, and is threatened by predation and by off-shore over-fishing.

PROCELLARIIDAE Petrels, shearwaters
Defilippe's Petrel *Pterodroma defilippiana* occurs only on Isla Santa Clara in the Juan Fernandez archipelago of Chile.
Pink-footed Shearwater *Puffinus creatopus* breeds mainly on Juan Fernandez Islands of Chile, where it is decreasing. Its population is estimated at 2,000–3,000.

HYDROBATIDAE Storm-petrels
Markham's Storm-petrel *Oceanodroma markhami* occurs in waters off western South and Central America, Clipperton Island and Cocos Island, but its breeding grounds are unknown.
Ringed Storm-petrel *Oceanodroma hornbyi* occurs in waters off western South America, but its breeding grounds are unknown.

PELECANOIDIDAE Diving-petrels
Peruvian Diving-petrel *Pelecanoides garnoti* is threatened in Peru. It is common, though decreasing, in Chile.

PHOENICOPTERIDAE Flamingos
Andean Flamingo *Phoenicoparrus andinus* is the rarest of the Andean flamingos, with only one or two regular breeding sites. It occurs in Peru, Chile, Bolivia and Argentina.
Puna Flamingo *Phoenicoparrus jamesi* is restricted to a small number of lakes in the *puna* zone of the Andes.

ANHIMIDAE Screamers
Northern Screamer *Chauna chavaria* is restricted to lowland marshes in northern Colombia and north-western Venezuela where it is not numerous.

ACCIPITRIDAE Hawks, eagles, kites, old world vultures
Semicollared Sparrowhawk *Accipiter collaris* has a very restricted range in Colombia and Ecuador, with one record from Venezuela and one from Peru.
Gundlach's Hawk *Accipiter gundlachii* is a hawk of the lowland woods in Cuba. A maximum of about 200 are left.

Grey-bellied Hawk *Accipter poliogaster* is widely distributed in Guyana, Venezuela, Colombia, Ecuador, Peru, Brazil, Bolivia, Paraguay and Argentina, but is extremely scarce everywhere.

Plumbeous Hawk *Leucopternis plumbea* has a fairly restricted range in Panama, western Colombia and the extreme north-west of Peru.

White-necked Hawk *Leucopternis lacernulata* is found in Brazil and is almost wholly sympatric with its threatened congener the Mantled Hawk *L. polionata* (see p. 71).

Solitary Eagle *Harpyhaliaetus solitarius* is widely distributed in Mexico, Guatemala, Honduras, Costa Rica, Panama, Venezuela, Colombia, Ecuador and Peru, but is very scarce.

Crowned Eagle *Harpyhaliaetus coronatus* has a wide range in Brazil, Paraguay, Uruguay, Bolivia and Argentina, but is generally scarce.

Ridgway's Hawk *Buteo ridgwayi* is confined to Haiti and the Dominican Republic and surrounding islands. Much of its habitat has been destroyed.

Red-tailed Hawk *Buteo ventralis* inhabits the Andean region of central Chile and adjacent Argentina to the Straits of Magellan. It is apparently not at all common in Chile.

FALCONIDAE Falcons
Plumbeous Forest-falcon *Micrastur plumbeus* is restricted to the forests of south-west Colombia and north-west Ecuador, where it is nowhere numerous.

Traylor's Forest-falcon *Micrastur buckleyi* is known only from a dozen or so specimens taken in Amazonian Ecuador and north-east Peru.

Orange-breasted Falcon *Falco deiroleucus* has a huge range from southern Mexico to northern Argentina, but is everywhere regarded as very uncommon and patchily distributed.

CRACIDAE Guans, curassows
Rufous-headed Chachalaca *Ortalis erythroptera* occurs in arid scrub in western Ecuador southward to northern Peru.

Bearded Guan *Penelope barbata* occurs only in southern Ecuador and north-west Peru. It requires monitoring as little natural habitat remains and hunting pressure is intense.

Red-faced Guan *Penelope dabbenei* occurs in the forests of south-east Bolivia and north-west Argentina.

White-browed Guan *Penelope jacucaca* occurs in some densely populated areas of north-east Brazil.

Chestnut-bellied Guan *Penelope ochrogaster* occurs in central-north Brazil and requires monitoring.

Highland Guan *Penelopina nigra* is resident in the mountains of Mexico, Guatemala, El Salvador (at least formerly), Honduras and Nicaragua. It is severely at risk from hunting and deforestation.

Northern Helmeted Curassow *Pauxi pauxi* has a restricted range from north-west Venezuela to north-east Colombia.

Southern Helmeted Curassow *Pauxi unicornis* is known only from two specimens from central Peru and two from east-central Bolivia. Its forest habitat is being rapidly cleared.

Wattled Curassow *Crax globulosa* occurs in Colombia, Ecuador, Peru, Brazil and Bolivia. It inhabits river islands and riverine forest and is threatened throughout much of its range.

MELEAGRIDAE Turkeys
Ocellated Turkey *Agriocharis ocellata* is hunted in Mexico and Guatemala,

and declining in Belize possibly due to disease.

PHASIANIDAE Pheasants, quails, partridges
Chestnut Wood Quail *Odontophorus hyperythrus* is endemic to the subtropical forests of the Colombian Andes.

RALLIDAE Rails
Plain-flanked Rail *Rallus wetmorei* is restricted to mangrove swamps along part of Venezuelan coast. Mangrove destruction is probably affecting its survival.
Austral Rail *Rallus antarcticus* is apparently very scarce in southern Chile and Argentina, where there have been no sightings since 1950.
Dot-winged Crake *Porzana spiloptera* is known only from southern Uruguay and from central Argentina.
Horqueta or **Rufous-faced Crake** *Laterallus xenopterus* is extremely poorly known from Parguay and Brazil and, until recently, known only from the type-specimen.
Rusty-flanked Crake *Laterallus levraudi* occurs in lagoons and marshes in north-central Venezuela.

LARIDAE Gulls, terns
Olrog's Gull *Larus atlanticus* is known from a few Argentinian islets. The total population is estimated to be very small and vulnerable.
Lava Gull *Larus fuliginosus* is endemic to and widespread in the Galápagos Islands, but numbers only 300–400 pairs.

COLUMBIDAE Pigeons, doves
Ring-tailed Wood Pigeon *Columba caribaea* is restricted to the forested hills in Jamaica, where it is threatened by hunting.
Blue-eyed Ground Dove *Columbina cyanopis* occurs in central Brazil, where it is exceptionally rare.

Ochre-bellied Dove *Leptotila orchraceiventris* is confined to south-west Ecuador and Peru.
Grey-headed Quail Dove *Geotrygon caniceps* occurs in Cuba, where it is almost extinct, and in the Dominican Republic.
Blue-headed Quail Dove *Starnoenas cyanocephala* is restricted to Cuba, where it is now much less widespread than formerly owing to human persecution and loss of habitat.

PSITTACIDAE Lories, parrots, macaws
Red-fronted Macaw *Ara rubrogenys* is restricted to a small area of east-central Bolivia, where it is being heavily trapped for export.
Blue-winged Macaw *Ara maracana* occurs in eastern Brazil, eastern Paraguay and north-eastern Argentina. It has undergone a widespread decline owing to extensive loss of habitat.
Cuban Conure *Aratinga euops* is restricted to and increasingly rare in Cuba, and now extinct on the Isle of Pines.
Golden-capped Conure *Aratinga auricapilla* is endemic to south-east Brazil, and is uncommon and declining in the few sites it still occupies.
Pearly Conure *Pyrrhura perlata* is endemic to a small part of north-east Brazil. Numbers have declined substantially owing to forest destruction.
White-necked Conure *Pyrrhura albipectus* is restricted to a small region of south-east Ecuador, in which it is uncommon and perpetually vulnerable to habitat loss.
Brown-breasted Conure *Pyrrhura calliptera* is endemic to Colombia, where forest destruction has been extensive within its restricted range.
Slender-billed Conure *Enicognathus leptorhynchus* is endemic to central Chile, where it has decreased seriously

owing to hunting, habitat loss and Newcastle Disease.

Grey-cheeked Parakeet *Brotogeris pyrrhopterus* occurs in south-west Ecuador and north-west Peru, but has declined considerably owing to loss of habitat and trapping.

Spot-winged Parrotlet *Touit stictoptera* inhabits Colombia and Ecuador. It is threatened in the Andes part of its range in Colombia.

Pileated Parrot *Pionopsitta pileata* occurs in south-east Brazil, eastern Paraguay and north-east Argentina. It has declined in most of its range.

Yellow-faced Amazon *Amazona xanthops* inhabits eastern and central Brazil where its habitat is being cleared for agriculture.

Vinaceous Amazon *Amazona vinacea* occurs in south-east Brazil, south-east Paraguay and north-east Argentina, where it suffered a major decline through habitat loss.

Purple-bellied Parrot *Triclaria malachitacea* is endemic to south-east Brazil and is declining there.

CUCULIDAE Cuckoos
Cocos Cuckoo *Coccyzus ferrugineus* is the rarest of the Cocos Island endemics.

Banded Ground Cuckoo *Neomorphus radiolosus* is known only in the tropical forest zone of south-west Colombia southward to north-west Ecuador.

NYCTIBIIDAE Potoos
Long-tailed Potoo *Nyctibius aethereus* is scarce in Guyana, Venezuela, Colombia, Ecuador, Peru, Brazil and Paraguay.

White-winged Potoo *Nyctibius leucopterus* is known from two specimens, one from Bahía, province in Brazil.

Rufous Potoo *Nyctibius bracteatus* is an extremely rare species known from Colombia, Ecuador, Peru and Guyana.

CAPRIMULGIDAE Nightjars
White-winged Nightjar *Caprimulgus candicans* occurs in a very restricted range in south-eastern Brazil and in Paraguay.

Roraiman Nightjar *Caprimulgus whitelyi* is endemic to Mt. Roraima in Venezuela.

Pygmy Nightjar *Caprimulgus hirundinaceus* has two subspecies occurring only in eastern Brazil.

Long-trained Nightjar *Macropsalis creagra* occurs in south-east Brazil and perhaps also north-east Argentina.

Sickle-winged Nightjar *Eleothreptus anomalus* occurs in Brazil, Uruguay, Paraguay and Argentina. Extremely little is known about this species.

APODIDAE Swifts
White-chested Swift *Cypseloides lemosi* (Pl. X) is confined to the upper Cauca Valley in Colombia.

TROCHILIDAE Hummingbirds
Sooty Barbthroat *Threnetes niger* is confined to the forests of French Guiana.

Minute Hermit *Phaethornis idaliae* is endemic to south-east Brazil. Although apparently numerous in two forest areas, it is considered to be threatened due to its total small range.

White-tailed Sabrewing *Campylopterus ensipennis* is restricted to the forests of north-east Venezuela. Since the hurricane of 1963 it is now extinct or very scarce in Tobago where it was once common.

Napo Sabrewing *Campylopterus villaviscensio* is restricted to forest in one small part of eastern Ecuador.

Fiery-tailed Awlbill *Avocettula recurvirostris* occurs in Guyana, French Guiana, Venezuela and Brazil, and is little known.

Coppery Thorntail *Popelairia letitiae* is known only from two males collected in Bolivia.

Sapphire-bellied Hummingbird
Lepidopyga lilliae is known from near
the mouth of the Magdalena River and
one other site in Colombia. Its habitat
at the former is now destroyed by a
pipeline.

Honduran Emerald *Amazilia luciae* is
endemic to Honduras, where it is
extremely little known.

Tachira Emerald *Amazilia distans* is
known only from Tachira in
Venezuela.

Mangrove Hummingbird *Amazilia
boucardi* is confined to the Pacific slope
of Costa Rica.

Chesnut-bellied Hummingbird
Amazilia castaneiventris is restricted to
the western slope of the eastern Andes
of Colombia.

White-tailed Hummingbird
Eupherusa poliocerca is resident in
southern Mexico. Habitat destruction
has rendered it highly threatened.

Oaxaca or **Blue-capped Hummingbird**
Eupherusa cyanophrys is restricted to
the mountainous Pacific slope of
Oaxaca in Mexico. Its taxonomic status
is unclear.

Blossomcrown *Anthocephala floriceps*
is restricted to the Santa Marta
Mountains and, in the race *berlepschi*,
the central part of the east slope of the
central Andes in Colombia.

Ecuadorean Piedtail *Phlogophilus
hemileucurus* is found in forests around
the headwaters of the Rio Napo in east
Ecuador.

Peruvian Piedtail *Phlogophilus harterti*
is found in forests of central and
southern Peru. It is uncommon but
widespread. Its cloud-forest habitat is
threatened.

Pink-throated Brilliant *Heliodoxa
gularis* inhabits the tropical zone of east
Ecuador and north-east Peru. It has a
large range but is generally scarce.

Scissor-tailed Hummingbird
Hylonympha macrocerca is endemic to

the forests on the narrow 100 km long
Paria peninsula in north-east Venezuela.

Purple-backed Sunbeam *Aglaeactis
aliciae* has a small range in the northern
provinces of Peru.

Purple-throated Sunangel *Heliangelus
viola* lives in the subtropical and
temperate zones of west Ecuador and
the Marañón region of Peru. Its
montane forest habitat is threatened.

Royal Sunangel *Heliangelus regalis* is a
new species from Peru. It has a small
range, and requires protection.

Black-breasted Puffleg *Eriocnemis
nigrivestris* is endemic to north-west
Ecuador where it is regarded as
threatened.

Turquoise-throated Puffleg *Eriocnemis
godini* is endemic to Ecuador.

Colourful Puffleg *Eriocnemis mirabilis*
is known only from the western slopes
of the western Andes of Colombia,
where concern is expressed for its
future.

Black-thighed Puffleg *Eriocnemis
derbyi* is found in Colombia and
Ecuador.

Hoary Puffleg *Haplophaedia lugens* is
restricted to the forests of the Andes of
south-west Colombia and north-west
Ecuador.

Neblina Metaltail *Metallura odomae* is
a new species from the Piura
department in Peru.

Violet-throated Metaltail *Metallura
baroni* inhabits arid country in
south-west Ecuador.

Grey-bellied Comet *Taphrolesbia
griseiventris* occurs on both sides of the
western Andes and the western slope of
the central Andes in Peru.

Hyacinth Visorbearer *Augastes
scutatus* occurs in eastern Brazil where
it is considered threatened.

Hooded Visorbearer *Augastes luma-
chellus* is restricted to two mountain
ranges in Bahía province in Brazil.

Marvellous Spatuletail *Loddigesia*

mirabilis is known only from southern Amazonas in Peru.

Bee Hummingbird *Calypte helenae* is endemic to Cuba and the Isle of Pines where it is scarce.

Little Woodstar *Acestrura bombus* inhabits Ecuador and northern Peru. It used to be common but seems not to have been seen for years.

Esmeraldas Woodstar *Acestura berlepschi* occurs in the tropical zone of western Ecuador. It has not been seen in decades by anyone.

Glow-throated Hummingbird *Selasphorus ardens* is restricted to the highlands of western Panama.

TROGONIDAE Trogons

Baird's Trogon *Trogon bairdii* is a tropical zone species of south-west Costa Rica and west Panama. It is exceedingly scarce in the latter.

MOMOTIDAE Motmots

Keel-billed Motmot *Electron carinatum* (Pl. IX) is very scarce in Mexico, Guatemala, Honduras, Nicaragua, Costa Rica, Belize and perhaps also El Salvador. This is the rarest of the motmots.

GALBULIDAE Jacamars

Three-toed Jacamar *Jacamaralcyon tridactyla* is restricted to south-east Brazil.

CAPITONIDAE Barbets

White-mantled Barbet *Capito hypoleucus* (Pl. X) occurs in the forest in central Colombia, where it is scarce and local.

RAMPHASTIDAE Toucans

Yellow-browed Toucanet *Aulacorhynchus huallagae* is restricted to the forest in one department of north-east Peru.

PICIDAE Woodpeckers, piculets

Speckle-chested Piculet *Picumnus steindachneri* is restricted to the

drainage area of the Rio Huallaga in Peru, where its habitat is threatened.

Black-bodied Woodpecker *Dryocopus schulzi* is found in Argentina and was recorded once from Paraguay.

Robust Woodpecker *Campephilus robustus* occurs in south-east Brazil, eastern Paraguay and north-east Argentina.

DENDROCOLAPTIDAE Woodcreepers

Snethlage's Woodcreeper *Xiphocolaptes franciscanus* is known only from the west bank of the Rio São Francisco in Minas Gerais Province of Brazil.

FURNARIIDAE Ovenbirds, spinetails

White-bellied Cinclodes *Cinclodes palliatus* has a fairly wide range in western Peru. It is seldom encountered and therefore its status will be difficult to determine.

Stout-billed Cinclodes *Cinclodes aricomae* may prove to be a separate species and may be acutely threatened. It is known only from the type-locality of the Aricoma Pass in Peru.

Masafuera Rayadito *Aphrastura masafuerae* has a population of a few hundred living on Isla Alejandro Selkirk in the Juan Fernandez Islands of Chile.

White-browed Tit Spinetail *Leptasthenura xenothorax* is endemic to *Polylepis* woodland in the Urubamba drainage in Cuzco department of Peru.

Plain Spinetail *Synallaxis infuscata* is restricted to a small region near the coast of north-east Brazil, and known from fewer than ten specimens.

Apurimac Spinetail *Synallaxis courseni* is known only from the mountains immediately north-west of Abancay in south Peru. The felling of humid forest in the area is drastic.

Chestnut-throated Spinetail *Synallaxis cherriei* occurs very locally in

Ecuador, Peru and Brazil. In Peru its low-land habitat is rapidly being destroyed.

Russet-bellied Spinetail *Synallaxis zimmeri* is endemic to montane scrub on the western slope of the Andes in Ancash department of Peru.

Austral Canastero *Thripophaga anthoides* has a range in Chile and Argentina. It is extremely scarce due to grazing and vegetation changes.

Line-fronted Canastero *Asthenes urubambensis* lives in small patches of humid *Polylepis* wood in Peru. It is known from very few places.

Orinoco Softtail *Thripophaga cherriei* is known only from the type-locality in south-west Venezuela.

Striated Softtail *Thripophaga macroura* is restricted to forest in south-east Brazil.

Chestnut-backed Thornbird *Phacellodomus dorsalis* is apparently restricted to the Marañón watershed in northern Peru.

Canebrake Groundcreeper *Phacellodomus dendrocolaptoides* is endemic to south-east Brazil, eastern Paraguay and north-east Argentina. It is very scarce in the last-mentioned area.

White-throated Barbtail *Margarornis tatei* occurs in wet cloud-forest of the Paria peninsula of Venezuela. Its very limited habitat is disappearing.

White-browed Foliage-gleaner *Philydor amaurotis* occurs in south-east Brazil and Argentina. It is the scarcest of the region's foliage-gleaners.

Alagoas Foliage-gleaner *Philydor novaesi* is a new species from north-east Brazil.

Russet-mantled Foliage-gleaner *Philydor dimidiatus* occurs in Brazil and Paraguay. It is likely to decline with the clearance of its riparian woodland habitat.

Rufous-necked Foliage-gleaner *Automolus ruficollis* occurs in Ecuador

and Peru. Its montane forest habitat is being cleared and degraded by cattle.

Chestnut-capped Foliage-gleaner *Automolus rectirostris* occurs in central Brazil where it must be suffering from clearance of its riverine forest habitat.

Henna-hooded Foliage-gleaner *Automolus erythrocephalus* is restricted to south-west Ecuador and north-west Peru.

Great Xenops *Megaxenops parnaguae* is extremely local and little known in eastern Brazil.

FORMICARIIDAE Antbirds
White-bearded Antshrike *Biatas nigropectus* is restricted to south-east Brazil and north-east Argentina. It was not seen during recent fieldwork in its Brazilian range.

Cocha Antshrike *Thamnophilus praecox* is known only from the upper Rio Napo in Ecuador on the Peruvian border. The female is unknown, and its taxonomic status is questionable.

Recurve-billed Bushbird *Clytoctantes alixii* (Pl. X) occurs from extreme north-west Venezuela westward across northern Colombia to the lower Cauca valley, which is vulnerable, but it favours secondary growth so may survive.

Plumbeous Antshrike *Thamnomanes plumbeus*, from south-east Brazil, was recently revised to become a full species.

Klages's Antwren *Myrmotherula klagesi* is known from only a few localities on both banks of the lower Amazon region in Brazil.

Salvadori's Antwren *Myrmotherula minor* has a small range in south-east Brazil.

Ashy Antwren *Myrmotherula grisea* is known only from the type-locality in La Paz in Bolivia.

Black-capped Antwren *Herpsilochmus pileatus* is now considered restricted to two localities in the Bahía province of Brazil.

Ash-throated Antwren *Herpsilochmus parkeri* is a recently discovered species from northern Peru, known from one ridge east of Tarapato.

Rufous-tailed Antbird *Drymophila genei* is threatened in Brazil in the states of Minais Gerais and Rio de Janeiro.

Yellow-rumped Antwren *Terenura sharpei* is known only in south-east Peru and northern Bolivia. Its *Yungas* forest habitat is being cleared rapidly.

Orange-bellied Antwren *Terenura sicki* is a new species from north-east Brazil.

Rio de Janeiro Antbird *Cercomacro brasiliana* is endemic to south-east Brazil. It is declining and threatened by deforestation.

Rio Branco Antbird *Cercomacra carbonaria* is known only from the upper Rio Branco in northern Brazil.

Scalloped Antbird *Myrmeciza ruficauda* occurs in eastern and south-eastern Brazil, but was found in only one of five forests recently surveyed.

Grey-headed Antibird *Myrmeciza griseiceps* is restricted to the forests of the subtropical zone in south-west Ecuador and north-west Peru. Its habitat is threatened.

Spot-breasted Antbird *Myrmeciza stictothorax* is known only from the type-locality on the Rio Tapajóz in Brazil. It was not found during a survey in 1985, although much forest remains.

Bare-eyed Antbird *Rhegmatorhina gymnops* is apparently restricted to the region between the Rio Tapajóz and the Rio Xingú in central Brazil. The area is scheduled for development in the 1990s.

Rufous-fronted Antthrush *Formicarius rufifrons* is known only from two females from Madre de Dios in south-east Peru.

Giant Antpitta *Grallaria gigantea* occurs in the Andes in Colombia and Ecuador. It has a small distribution, and the population in north-east Ecuador is especially threatened.

Great Antpitta *Grallaria excelsa* is a subtropical zone species of western and northern Venezuela. Little is known about this species.

Tachira Antpitta *Grallaria chthonia* occurs in the subtropical zone around north-west Tachira in Venezuela.

Scallop-breasted Antpitta *Grallaricula loricata* has a very restricted distribution west of Caracas in northern Venezuela.

Hooded Antpitta *Grallaricula cucullata* is recorded from the subtropical zone of the western and central Andes in Colombia. It is known from a few localities in Venezuela.

CONOPOPHAGIDAE Gnateaters
Hooded Gnateater *Conopophaga roberti* occurs in eastern Brazil where it is losing its habitat.

COTINGIDAE Cotingas
Shrike-like Cotinga *Laniisoma elegans* is a little-known species from Peru, Venezuela, Colombia, Ecuador, Bolivia and Brazil.

Grey-winged Cotinga *Tijuca condita* is a new species, restricted to and scarce in the Serra dos Orgãos and Serra da Tingua near Rio de Janeiro in Brazil.

Black-headed Berryeater *Carpornis melanocephalus* is endemic to coastal south-east Brazil. It is now regarded as declining.

White-cheeked Cotinga *Ampelion stresemanni* is confined to *Polylepis* woodland at seven localities in Peru.

Buff-throated Purpletuft *Iodopleura pipra* is endemic to south-east Brazil, where it is extremely rare.

Cinnamon-vented Piha *Lipaugus lanioides* is endemic to south-east Brazil. It was found in only one of five forests during a recent survey.

Turquoise Cotinga *Cotinga ridgwayi*

is endemic to Costa Rica and western Panama.

Yellow-billed Cotinga *Carpodectes antoniae* is endemic to Costa Rica and western Panama. Its very small population is threatened by destruction of coastal mangroves.

White Cotinga *Carpodectes hopkei* is a tropical zone species of eastern Panama, western Colombia and north-eastern Ecuador.

PIPRIDAE Manakins
Black-capped Manakin *Piprites pileatus* is endemic to south-east Brazil and north-east Argentina. It was not seen on a recent survey in the former region.

Golden-crowned Manakin *Pipra vila-sboasi* is known only from the head-waters of the Rio Tapajóz in Brazil.

TYRANNIDAE Tyrant flycatchers
White-tailed Shrike Tyrant *Agriornis albicauda* is scarce and local in open scrub in Ecuador, Peru, Bolivia, Argentina and Chile.

Cock-tailed Tyrant *Alectrurus tricolor* occurs in brush and woodland in Bolivia, Brazil, Paraguay and Argentina. It is becoming scarce everywhere.

Strange-tailed Tyrant *Yetapa risoria* occurs in Brazil, Parguay, Uruguay and Argentina.

Grey-breasted Flycatcher *Empidonax griseipectus* is one of the least common of the north-western Peru and south-western Ecuador endemic birds.

Belted Flytchatcher *Xenotriccus callizonus* is scarce and local in south-east Mexico and Guatemala.

Tawny-chested Flycatcher *Aphanotriccus capitalis* occurs in south-east Nicaragua and central Costa Rica.

Russet-winged Spadebill *Platyrinchus leucoryphus* is endemic to south-east Brazil and eastern Paraguay. It may be in real danger.

Short-tailed Tody-flycatcher *Todirostrum viridanum* occurs in

north-west Venezuela.

Fork-tailed Pygmy Tyrant *Ceratotriccus furcatus* is endemic to south-east Brazil.

Kaempfer's Tody Tyrant *Idioptilon kaempferi* is known only from the type-specimen collected in eastern Brazil.

Southern Bristle Tyrant *Pogonotriccus eximius* inhabits south-east Brazil, eastern Paraguay and north-east Argentina. It was not seen in a recent survey in Brazil.

Venezuelan Bristle Tyrant *Pogonotriccus venezuelanus* is restricted to a heavily populated region of northern Venezuela.

Minas Gerais Tyrannulet *Phylloscartes roquettei* is known only from the type-specimen collected in Minas Gerais, Brazil.

São Paulo Tyrannulet *Phylloscartes paulistus* occurs in south-east Brazil and eastern Paraguay. It was found in only one of five forests recently studied in Brazil.

Long-tailed Tyrannulet *Phylloscartes ceciliae* is a recently discovered species confined to north-east Brazil.

Bearded Tachuri *Polystictus pectoralis* occurs in Guyana, Suriname, Venezuela, Brazil, Colombia, Paraguay, Bolivia and Argentina.

Grey-backed Tachuri *Polystictus superciliaris* is restricted to the border of Minas Gerais and Bahía provinces of Brazil.

Sharp-tailed Tyrant *Culicivora caudacuta* occurs in Brazil, Paraguay, Bolivia and Argentina. Its *campos* habitat is disappearing.

Ash-breasted Tit Tyrant *Anairetes alpinus* is endemic to the *Polylepis* woodlands, with three populations in Peru and Bolivia, but is scarce.

PHYTOTOMIDAE Plantcutters
Peruvian Plantcutter *Phytotoma raimondii* inhabits the tropical zone of

coastal Peru. It has a small range in desert oases, and faces a lot of population pressure.

HIRUNDINIDAE Swallows
Bahama Swallow *Callichelidon cyaneoviridis* has become an uncommon species nesting on only a few Bahaman islands.

MOTACILLIDAE Pipits
Chaco Pipit *Anthus chacoensis* is known only from the type-locality in northern Argentina and one in Paraguay. Both specimens were non-breeding birds.
Ochre-breasted Pipit *Anthus nattereri* occurs in south-east Brazil, Paraguay and Argentina.

TROGLODYTIDAE Wrens
Slender-billed Wren *Hylorchilus sumichrasti* is restricted to south-east Mexico, where it is now local.
Niceforo's Wren *Thryothorus nicefori* is known only from the type-locality on the western slope of the eastern Andes in Santander Province in Colombia.

(MUSCICAPIDAE) TURDINAE Thrushes
Rufous-brown Solitaire *Myadestes leucogenys* inhabitats Guyana, Venezuela, Ecuador, Peru and Brazil. It is very local.

(MUSCICAPIDAE) POLIOPTILINAE Gnatcatchers
Cuban Gnatcatcher *Polioptila lembeyei* has a somewhat restricted range on Cuba.

(EMBERIZIDAE) EMBERIZINAE Buntings
Black-throated Finch *Melanodera melanodera* occurs in Argentina from Santa Cruz southward to Tierra del Fuego in Chile. Little is known about this species but it is expected to be extremely scarce due to grazing and vegetation changes.

Slender-billed Finch *Xenospingus concolor* occurs on Pacific slopes up to 2,400 m in south Peru and north Chile. Its riparian habitat is rapidly disappearing.
Grey-winged Inca Finch *Incaspiza ortizi* is only known from one female from northern Peru.
Rufous-breasted Warbling Finch *Poospiza rubecula* occurs in woodland and brush on both slopes of the western cordilleras of Peru. It has a small range and its habitat is threatened.
Cochabamba Mountain Finch *Poospiza garleppi* is restricted to *Polylepis* woodlands and adjacent cultivation in Cochabamba in Boliva.
Tucuman Mountain Finch *Poospiza baeri* is restricted to Tucuman province in north-west Argentina. It is more abundant than once thought, but not common.
Buffy-throated Seedeater *Sporophila frontalis* is endemic to south-east Brazil, eastern Paraguay and north-east Argentina. It was not seen during a recent survey in Brazil.
Temminck's Seedeater *Sporophila falcirostris* is endemic to eastern Brazil, but was not seen during a recent survey. There are unconfirmed records from Argentina.
Rufous-rumped Seedeater *Sporophila hypochroma* occurs in Bolivia and Argentina.
Dark-throated Seedeater *Sporophila ruficollis* occurs in Brazil, Uruguay, Paraguay, Bolivia and Argentina. It is threatened by habitat loss and trappers.
Chestnut Seedeater *Sporophila cinnamomea* has a restricted distribution in Brazil, east of Villarica in eastern Paraguay and Argentina.
Black-bellied Seedeater *Sporophila melanogaster* is a scarce endemic of south-east Brazil.
Blackish-blue Seedeater *Amaurospiza moesta* is a local species of south-east

Brazil and north-east Argentina. It was not seen during a recent survey in Brazil.

Floreana Tree Finch *Camarhynchus pauper* is endemic to Floreana Island in the Galápagos Islands. It may be extinct.

Pale-headed Brush Finch *Atlapetes pallidiceps* is restricted to arid tropical and subtropical scrub in south-western Ecuador.

Black-masked Finch *Coryphaspiza melanotis* occurs in Brazil, Bolivia, Paraguay and Argentina. It is apparently restricted to near-virgin grassland, a threatened ecosystem.

Yellow Cardinal *Gubernatrix cristata* (Pl. XII) occurs in Argentina, Uruguay and southern Brazil, where it has been much affected by trade and habitat conversion.

(EMBERIZIDAE) CARDINALINAE
Cardinal grosbeaks

Black-cowled Saltator *Saltator nigriceps* ranges from south Ecuador to north-west Peru. Its montane forest habitat is being cleared and degraded by cattle.

Masked Saltator *Saltator cinctus* is known from eastern Ecuador. It is a strange species that may be nomadic.

(EMBERIZIDAE) THRAUPINAE
Tanagers

Cone-billed Tanager *Conothraupis mesoleuca* is still only known from the type-specimen from Mato Grosso in Brazil.

Yellow-green Bush Tanager *Chlorospingus flavovirens* is recorded from north-west Ecuador and in west-central Colombia.

Black-cheeked Ant Tanager *Habia atrimaxillaris* is known only from south-west Costa Rica.

Sooty Ant Tanager *Habia gutturalis* has a restricted range in dense forest in north-central Colombia.

Black-and-gold Tanager *Buthraupis melanochlamys* has a restricted range in the forests on the western slope of the Andes near the source of the Rio San Juan in Colombia. It is threatened by deforestation.

Gold-ringed Tanager *Buthraupis aureocincta* is known only from the source of the Rio San Juan in Colombia.

Golden-backed Mountain Tanager *Buthraupis aureodorsalis* is known only from Huanaco department of Peru. It is fairly common but restricted to a few localities.

Green-throated Euphonia *Euphonia chalybea* is endemic to south-east Brazil, eastern Paraguay, and north-east Argentina.

Multicoloured Tanager *Chlorochrysa nitidissima* is endemic to Colombia from the western slope of the central Andes and to the western slope of the western Andes. Its population is very fragmented.

Black-backed Tanager *Tangara peruviana* is known from south-east Brazil. It is considered to be probably in real danger.

Green-capped Tanager *Tangara meyer-deschauenseei* is a recently discovered species of semi-arid montane scrub in one valley in south Peru.

White-bellied Dacnis *Dacnis albiventris* occurs in eastern Colombia, southern Venezuela, central Brazil, eastern Ecuador and north-east Peru. It is an extremely and inexplicably scarce bird despite its large range.

Turquoise Dacnis *Dacnis hartlaubi* is restricted to the western slope of the western Andes in Colombia, where it has a fragmented range.

Black-legged Dacnis *Dacnis nigripes* occurs in low numbers in the forests of eastern Brazil.

Scarlet-breasted Dacnis *Dacnis berlepschi* is a very scarce species known from south-west Colombia and north-west Ecuador.

Venezuelan Flowerpiercer *Diglossa venezuelensis* is restricted to the mountains in north-east Venezuela.

PARULIDAE Wood warblers
Whistling Warbler *Catharopeza bishopi* is a rare bird restricted to St. Vincent.

Black-polled Yellowthroat *Geothlypis speciosa* is resident in the marshes of south-central Mexico and is at serious risk from drainage.

Yellow-faced Redstart *Myioborus pariae* is endemic to the Paria peninsula in north-east Venezuela.

Grey-throated Warbler *Basileuterus cinereicollis* occurs in Venezuela and Colombia. There is practically no recent information on this bird.

Pirre Warbler *Basileuterus ignotus* is known only from the unique type from Mount Pirre in Panama.

Grey-headed Warbler *Basileuterus griseiceps* is a forest species with a restricted distribution in Venezuela.

White-striped Warbler *Basileuterus leucophrys* occurs in central Brazil. It will decline rapidly as its riparian woodland habitat is cleared.

White-winged Ground Warbler *Xenoligea montana* is restricted to the forested mountains of Haiti and the Dominican Republic.

Pearly-breasted Conebill *Conirostrum margaritae* occurs in Peru and western Brazil. It is threatened by the expansion of the timber and pulp industries.

VIREONIDAE Vireos
San Andres Vireo *Vireo caribaeus* is restricted to San Andres Island, off Colombia. Its population is small.

ICTERIDAE American blackbirds
Chestnut-mantled Oropendola *Psarocolius cassini* occurs in north-west Colombia.

Selva Cacique *Cacicus koepckeae* appears to be known only from the type-specimen locality in eastern Peru.

Martinique Oriole *Icterus bonana* is endemic to Martinique and reported to be in serious decline.

Monserrat Oriole *Icterus oberi* is endemic to Monserrat.

Saffron-cowled Blackbird *Agelaius flavus* occurs in southern Brazil, Uruguay, Paraguay, Bolivia and Argentina where it is seriously declining.

Lesser Red-breasted Meadowlark *Sturnella defilippi* occurs in south-east Brazil, Uruguay and Argentina where it is declining.

Red-bellied Grackle *Hypopyrrhus pyrohypogaster* has a widespread but local distribution in Colombia.

Forbes's Blackbird *Curaeus forbesi* is restricted to and rare in north-eastern Brazil.

FRINGILLIDAE Finches
Yellow-faced Siskin *Carduelis yarrellii* occurs in northern Venezuela and eastern Brazil. It is scarce in the former and very restricted in the latter and is trapped in both countries for the cage-bird trade.

Saffron Siskin *Carduelis siemiradzkii* has a very restricted range in arid scrub in south-west Ecuador.

CORVIDAE Crows
Beautiful Jay *Cyanolyca pulchra* occurs from Pacific Colombia southward to north-west Ecuador.

Dwarf Jay *Cyanolyca nana* is a scarce species restricted to three provinces of southern Mexico. Its habitat is disappearing.

White-throated Jay *Cyanolyca mirabilis* is local in the mountains of southern Mexico, where the habitat is being cleared and grazed.

Azure Jay *Cyanocorax caeruleus* occurs in south-east Brazil and northern Argentina, and is in steep decline.

Chapter 5
The Afrotropical Region

MAINLAND AFRICA

The Afrotropical Region includes all of Africa except the Mediterranean zone roughly as far south as 19°N, which in zoogeographical terms belongs to the Palaearctic region. For present purposes it also includes Madagascar and related islands in the Atlantic and Indian Oceans. The region is largely tropical and although a large part of it is desert it is not only rich in bird species, but also benefits from a massive annual influx of migrants from Europe and the Middle East and even a few from Asia.

The African continent provides an extensive variety of habitats, ranging from totally arid deserts to vast swamps, humid rain-forests, open savanna, snow-capped mountains, alpine meadows, huge freshwater and soda lakes and some of the world's biggest rivers, such as the Nile, the Zaire, the Niger and the Zambezi. The vegetational zones radiate from the Zaire Basin. Along parts of the West African coast and the Gulf of Guinea there are narrow strips of tall mangroves, giving way inland to heavily exploited lowland rain-forest, with here and there patches of montane forest such as those on Mount Cameroon and Mount Oku. On the north-east edge of the rain-forest is a broad band of fairly open forest–savanna mosaic and then a narrower belt of what is known as moist Guinean woodlands. Between 10°N and 15°N these are replaced by the huge expanse of the dry Sudanian and Sahelian belts, with much reduced and erratic rainfall and sparse, over-grazed and severely stripped vegetation such as patches of acacia in the waterways and palms in the oases. Finally come the sub-desert and the vast, extremely hot Sahara, stretching right across Africa. A similar southward succession of zones culminates in the hostile deserts of the Kalahari and the Namib in the far south-west. There is urgent need for further exploration and research, particularly in the surviving rain-forests in the west, which, though less rich in birds than the Amazon forests, contain a number of little-known species. The montane forests in the east of equatorial Africa also need more study before the timber exploiters complete their ravages. Both contain threatened species which may vanish before the end of the century if the destruction continues. Africa has been called a dying continent. The rapidity with which it is losing its vegetation and soil fertility indicates that the term is not an exaggeration.

The regions of lightly wooded savanna and open grasslands to the north, east and south of the rain-forests attract more than one thousand species of birds, either as residents or during the great migratory influx in the winter. During this season the mixture of Palaearctic and Afrotropical species feeding on the abundant equatorial insect life becomes bewildering in its complexity. It has been estimated that migrants from Europe alone swell the African bird population by at least 1,500 million every year.

The soda lakes of the Rift Valley and the great papyrus swamps of the Sudd in Sudan and of the Okavango in Botswana are famous for their huge concentrations of aquatic birds. To see a million flamingos feeding on Lake Nakuru, or breeding on Lake Natron, is an experience never to be forgotten. There are many large national parks and wildlife reserves throughout Africa and the conservation of wildlife is making good progress in some countries, though still backward in others. The majority of governments are cooperating with ICBP, IUCN and WWF and have signed the CITES convention. Sadly, recurrent revolutions have destroyed many years' work in some countries, but as soon as these die down the conservationists re-establish contact and begin their devoted work again.

Madagascar and its endemic birds are treated separately. It is an immense island, 1,700 km long from north to south, with a range of mountains about 2,500 m high along the eastern side. Like Africa, it has well defined vegetational zones. Down the east coast is a narrow belt of rain-forest and open grassland, with a band of semi-arid vegetation in the south-west. However, the massive deforestation and land clearance which has taken place since the island was colonised by the French has left only remnants of its earlier vegetational richness. Most of what remains is secondary growth and much of that is now threatened. The island bears little resemblance to its original state when its tropical forests were extensive and many of its endemic mammals and birds are now very close to extinction.

At the head of the Mozambique Channel between Madagascar and the African mainland lie the Aldabra and Comoro Islands and further east the Mascarenes—Réunion, Mauritius and Rodrigues, each famous for its lost or vanishing birds and each now the subject of vigorous conservation programmes. And to the north-east lie the Seychelles, where a number of important projects organized by ICBP and funded by the WWF and others are producing encouraging results including the island of Cousin, which is wholly owned and run by the ICBP.

Off the west coast of Africa are many other islands, such as the Canaries, Madeira, Azores and Cape Verde. For the purpose of this book they, and others as far south as Tristan da Cunha in the Mid-Atlantic, are included in the Afrotropical Region, as are all the Indian Ocean islands west of 80°E.

For the sake of convenience the threatened bird species of the Afrotropical Region are divided into three parts, the first referring to the African mainland as far north as the Saharan belt where it meets the Palaearctic, the second to Madagascar and the third to the related islands in the Indian and South Atlantic oceans.

The only penguin species breeding in the Afrotropical Region is the **Jackass Penguin** *Spheniscus demersus*. It once had a very large population, but is now restricted to about 25 small islands off the coasts of Namibia and South Africa, smaller numbers occasionally also breeding on the mainland coast. Outside the breeding season its range extends in coastal waters as far as southern Angola, the Transkei and southern Mozambique. Its population has been seriously threatened by excessive egg-cropping, 14 million eggs being taken between 1900 and 1930. Other threats have been the decline in the pilchard population, on which it depends for food, and the disturbance caused by the exploitation of guano and seals on its breeding islands. Marine pollution, notably from major oil-spills, has also contributed to its decline. The species is subject to constant monitoring and its present population is estimated as 171,000, representing a 90% decline this century. While the species is not yet regarded as threatened, the Jackass Penguin is so vulnerable that it has been classified by ICBP as a Species of Special Concern. Recommendations have been made to ban all shoal-fishing within 25 km of the breeding colonies and to enforce the ban on the remaining egg-cropping and guano-collecting.

The ornithologically famous Okavan-go delta of Botswana, the wetlands of Kafue, Liuwa and Bangweulu in Zambia and the Caprivi Strip in Namibia are the only areas where the rare **Slaty Egret** *Egretta vinaceigula* is known to occur. It used to be regarded as a variant of the Black Egret *E. ardesiaca*, but is now recognised as a separate species. Although its total population may still exceed one thousand, it is believed to be drifting towards extinction for no very apparent reason. It is certainly threatened by the drainage or damming of its floodplain habitat and to some extent by the taking of its nestlings for food. If any of the various current proposals to utilise the Okavango delta to improve Botswana's economy are carried out, the Slaty Egret and many other aquatic birds would suffer severely. All egrets are protected by law in Zambia and they benefit from the many national parks and wildlife reserves in the areas they occupy, but the future of the Slaty Egret is by no means assured. The status accorded it by ICBP is Indeterminate because more needs to be learnt about it.

Another declining bird of the African swamplands is the rather grotesque **Shoebill** *Balaeniceps rex*, a huge, dull-coloured species with a massive bill, and the sole member of its family. It is found in the marshy areas of Sudan, Uganda and parts of Zaire and Zambia, occa-

Jackass Penguins

sionally also elsewhere. No detailed census has yet been made, but its total population is probably about 15,000. Its numbers are declining because of land drainage and the increase in cattle grazing. As it nests in the dry season its eggs and young are frequently lost to bushfires. It is protected by law in Sudan and other countries, but if it is to have a secure future more areas of Papyrus swampland must be put under protection. It is listed by ICBP as a Species of Special Concern.

Shoebill

The **Southern Bald Ibis** *Geronticus calvus* (Plate XV) is closely related to the Waldrapp or Northern Bald Ibis *G. eremita* of Morocco and Turkey (see page 35) and has a similar habit of nesting on cliff ledges. It inhabits the grassy highlands of South Africa, but much of its habitat is being lost to forestry and its cliff-nesting colonies suffer considerable human disturbance. Its total population has been reduced to about 8,000 birds, of which 2,250 are in Transvaal. It is now classified by ICBP as Rare. A captive-beeding project has been started.

The present population of the **Cape Vulture** *Gyps coprotheres* (Plate XV) is believed to be in the order of 10,000 birds and the species is listed as Rare. The vulture is restricted to southern Africa and has declined markedly in certain parts of its range. It was formerly dependent on large migratory mammals for food but now feeds mostly on the carcasses of domestic stock. The species's initial decline coincided with the 1898–1903 rinderpest epidemic in which millions of cattle were lost. There is little evidence that food supply presents a serious problem today, although intensive farming practices in which dead animals are found and quickly disposed of may change this. The problem is not quantity of food but quality. The dis-

appearance of large mammalian carnivores which crunch up bones in carcasses means that the vultures are no longer able to feed bone flakes to their chicks. They in turn suffer from severe calcium shortage and consequently broken bones. Hunting, poisoning, disturbance from industrial development and electrocution from pylons all add to early mortality. The Vulture Study Group, in conjunction with appropriate national and provincial nature conservation bodies, is approaching owners of breeding and roosting sites to try to effect local conservation measures. For instance, vulture "restaurants" have been established where carcasses, whose bones have been smashed, are put out. These efforts appear to be giving positive results.

One of the most threatened birds of north-east Africa is the **Djibouti Francolin** *Francolinus ochropectus*, which is found only in the small relict Forêt du Day in the Djibouti area of the Goda massif and in Mabla, 100 km east of Day. Almost none of the primary forest on which the species depends now survives and more than half of it has been lost in the past seven years. At the present rate of destruction the forest will be entirely degraded by 1995. The Djibouti Francolin is gravely threatened, not only by the loss of habitat, but also by the overgrazing and trampling of countless cattle, sheep, goats, camels and donkeys

Congo Peacock

and by frequent bush-fires. The Forêt du Day, where it occurs, is part of the Day National Park, which, in theory, should provide some protection. In 1984 its population in the two localities was recorded as 1,500 birds, but unless the remnant of forest is given immediate and effective protection this species seems doomed to extinction. It is classified by ICBP as Endangered.

Three other francolins in Africa are threatened: the **Mount Cameroon Francolin** *Francolinus camerunensis*, listed as Rare and known only from the forests of Mount Cameroon; **Swierstra's Francolin** *F. swierstrai*, which is restricted to forest patches and adjacent areas in the mountains of western Angola and considered Indeterminate; and **Nahan's Francolin** *F. nahani* which occurs only in a few localities of the lowland rain-forest of eastern Zaire and central and western Uganda, and which is classified as Rare. All three of these elusive and rather partridge-like species are threatened by the loss of their forest habitat and by hunting.

In 1936 a new African bird, which was also the first (and only) true pheasant species in the continent, was discovered. This was the **Congo Peacock** *Afropavo congensis*, hitherto known only from a single feather worn by a native in the Ituri Forest of eastern Zaire in 1913. This highly secretive, ground-haunting bird which, although quite large, had escaped

detection for so long, is now known to occur quite widely over a fairly large area of equatorial rain-forest. It is hunted by the forest tribes but is apparently not in danger so long as the forests survive. The threat to the forests is, however, very real. As the total population of the species is evidently not large, it could easily be wiped out. About 40 Congo Peacocks are held in various zoos and an organised captive-breeding programme might become necessary. Meanwhile they are protected in Zaire and classified by ICBP as a Species of Special Concern.

Among the most seriously threatened birds in Africa is the handsome **White-breasted Guineafowl** *Agelastes meleagrides*, classified as Endangered. It has become extinct through most of its former range as a result of excessive hunting and the destruction or alteration of its primary rain-forest habitat. It apparently now survives only in one or two areas of Liberia, Ivory Coast and easternmost Sierra Leone, and may already be extinct in Ghana, where it once occurred. The rate of forest destruction in West Africa is now so high that any endemic species dependent on a primary forest habitat and unable to adapt to secondary growth must inevitably be gravely threatened. The White-breasted Guineafowl is still hunted even in the Tai National Park in Ivory Coast, and neither the Sapo National Park nor the Grebo National

Forest in Liberia are sufficiently protected to be of real value to the species. No specific measures have yet been taken to protect it.

Many of the cranes of the world are now at risk. In Africa the **Wattled Crane** *Bugeranus carunculatus* may soon be classified as a threatened species unless urgent steps are taken to protect its habitat, even though its present population is still probably between 6,000 and 7,500. It is a shy, mainly vegetarian bird, which occurs in the marshes and floodplains of Ethiopia and parts of central and southern Africa. In most of its range its population has declined and it faces a variety of threats, chiefly to its habitat through drainage, damming and human disturbance. In southern Africa it is much persecuted for food. Like all the cranes it requires large areas of undisturbed open habitat and it has a very low rate of reproduction. The many national parks it frequents provide some measure of protection, but it suffers from the continuing loss of natural habitat and persecution. Although difficult to breed in captivity, efforts are now being made by the International Crane Foundation and several zoos to rear captive stocks. Meanwhile it is listed by ICBP as a Species of Special Concern.

A tiny, nomadic rail, called the **White-winged Flufftail** *Sarothrura ayresi*, was known until the 1950s to inhabit the Ethiopian highlands. During the last century it also occurred in South Africa and then disappeared. In 1982 it was rediscovered there. The only records of the species between Ethiopia and South Africa are two from Zambia and three from Zimbabwe. Very little is known about this elusive bird and no estimate of its population has been possible. Like the Wattled Crane, it would presumably benefit from those marshy areas which are now under protection within its apparently discontinuous range. In Ethiopia, however, after years of drought, very little marshland survives. Because of the lack of information about its status, the species is listed by ICBP as Indeterminate.

The **Damara Tern** *Sterna balaenarum* has been listed as one of the 20 bird species requiring highest conservation action in South Africa. It has widely dispersed colonies in Namibia, South Africa and probably Angola, with a total population estimated at only 1,000–2,000 pairs, although recent work suggests that this figure is too low. The birds are particularly vulnerable throughout their range to disturbance by tourists. Dune buggies now enable the public to reach previously inaccessible places where the Damara Tern breeds. In addition military developments along the coast undoubtedly cause disturbance, and dune stabilisation policies encourage the growth of vegetation which makes the habitat unsuitable for nesting. Although there is no clear evidence of a decline in this species, its generally low numbers and the wide range of threats that it faces gives grounds for ICBP to treat it as Rare.

The **Somali Pigeon** *Columba oliviae* is an extremely poorly known rock-dwelling species, endemic to the arid coastal regions of north-east Somalia. The total numbers of this species are unknown, but on existing evidence are likely to be small. No threats appear to exist, other than that the range is somewhat restricted and this may be due to its inability to compete with the Speckled Pigeon *C. guinea* under less extreme conditions. ICBP considers the Somali Pigeon as Rare.

Another bird with a very restricted distribution and also classified as Rare is the **Black-cheeked Lovebird** *Agapornis nigrigenis*. It appears to be very local in southern Zambia, although formerly it was far more numerous with as many as 16,000 captured in four weeks during 1929, all for the cage-bird market. Despite being completely protected by law in Zambia, the Black-cheeked Lovebird is still common as a cage-bird and subject to illegal trapping.

Several of Africa's colourful turacos are threatened by forest clearance. The most threatened is **Bannerman's Turaco** *Tauraco bannermani* of the Bamenda–Banso Highlands in western Cameroon, where it is under very serious threat from forest destruction and over-grazing. Its population is very restricted. ICBP list the species as Endangered and has recommended that the Cameroon Government gives the montane forest on Mount Oku total protection for the sake of this handsome species and also in order to protect the threatened Banded Wattle-eye *Platysteira laticincta*, the Green-breasted Bush-shrike *Malaconotus gladiator* and Bannerman's Weaver *Ploceus bannermani*, which also occur in these highlands (see p. 122, 114 & 124).

Prince Ruspoli's Turaco *Tauraco ruspolii* of juniper and acacia woodland in southern Ethiopia is also presumed to be at risk from habitat loss, although it has been suggested that it may be a relict species and declining from natural causes. It is listed as Rare.

A not inconsiderable number of the world's birds are known only from a single museum skin and in spite of repeated searches nothing more has been learned about them. Some are now probably extinct, though a few may be rediscovered, as has happened on several occasions. One such extreme rarity is the **Itombwe Owl** *Phodilus prigoginei*. It is at present known only from the type-specimen collected in 1951 while sleeping in long grass high in the Itombwe Mountains of eastern Zaire. There was

Prince Ruspoli's Turaco

one probable, but unconfirmed, sighting of this species in the 1970s, on a tea estate in Burundi, but otherwise the bird remains a total mystery. A conservation plan for the valuable area of the Itombwe Forest has been prepared for the Zaire Government. Six other threatened species occur in the region: the Albertine Owlet *Glaucidium albertinum*, Schouteden's Swift *Schoutedenapus schoutedeni*, the African Green Broadbill *Pseudocalyptomena graueri*, the Forest Ground-thrush *Turdus oberlaenderi*, Chapin's Flycatcher *Muscicapa lendu* and Rockefeller's Sunbird *Nectarinia rockefelleri* (see p. 123). For lack of information on its status the Itombwe Owl is listed by ICBP as Indeterminate.

The **Albertine Owlet** *Glaucidium albertinum* is known from five specimens, four from eastern Zaire and one from Rwanda. It is classified as Rare.

Another very scarce owl of the African mainland is the **Sokoke Scops Owl** *Otus* *ireneae* (Plate XIII), listed by ICBP as Endangered. Discovered only in 1965, it has a population of about 2,000 pairs confined to a single patch of lowland forest, the Sokoke, in coastal Kenya. This miniature owl has thus far successfully withstood the logging which takes place in the forest, but is likely to become extinct if it continues. It is protected by Kenyan law, but the illegal extraction of timber from the small wildlife reserve which has been created within the forest is still continuing despite the area being regarded by ornithologists as one of the most important in Africa. Five other threatened species occur there: the Sokoke Pipit *Anthus sokokensis*, the East Coast Akalat *Sheppardia gunningi*, the Spotted Ground-thrush *Turdus fischeri*, the Amani Sunbird *Anthreptes pallidigaster* and Clarke's Weaver *Ploceus golandi* (see pp. 113–115, 123 & 124).

The **Usambara Eagle Owl** *Bubo vosseleri* is a large forest owl known from the Usambara Mountains of northeastern Tanzania, with a total population of 200–1,000 birds. The forests of Usambara have suffered considerably from clearance for subsistence farming and for tea and cardamon cultivation. The latter may not present problems as several young birds have been found in areas cleared for cardamon which is generally grown under an intact forest canopy. The Usambara Eagle Owl is classified as Rare.

The **Rufous Fishing Owl** *Scotopelia ussheri* (Plate XIV) is a little-known species restricted to the rain-forest zone of West Africa between Ghana and Sierra Leone. It is an elusive bird and consequently its numerical status is unclear, although it is presumed to be declining due to forest and mangrove clearance, and pollution from iron ore mining of its riverine habitat. ICBP lists this owl as Rare.

The Itombwe Mountains in Zaire are the home of another only recently discovered and little-known species, **Schouteden's Swift** *Schoutedenapus schoutedeni*. Two specimens were collected in 1959 and it has since been recorded only three times, though possibly overlooked among other swifts. If, as is suspected, it is a forest-dependent species, it will be threatened by the increased felling in the Itombwe Forest, which is also becoming an important mining centre. No conservation measures have yet been planned for this rare species, whose status, for lack of information, is given by ICBP as Indeterminate.

Another species, the **Fernando Po Swift** *Apus sladeniae*, is similarly enigmatic and is indeed classified as Insufficiently Known. It was first identified from six specimens collected on the island of Fernando Po off Equatorial Guinea in 1903–1904. It has never been seen again on the island, but specimens have subsequently been collected in Cameroon, Nigeria and Angola. Nothing is known of its population size or breeding behaviour, although it is believed that a few may nest on Mount Môco in Angola.

Even less is known about the **White-chested Tinkerbird** *Pogoniulus makawai*, of which, like the Itombwe Owl, only a single skin exists. This was collected in 1964 in a dense evergreen thicket in north-western Zambia. Repeated searches have failed to find it again, and ICBP therefore list it as Indeterminate.

The **Yellow-footed Honeyguide** *Melignomon eisentrauti* has been definitely identified only in the forests of Cameroon and Liberia, but may also occur in Ghana, Ivory Coast and Sierra Leone. It appears to be rare (although honeyguides are notoriously unobtrusive) and to suffer from the extensive

Ash's Lark

forest clearance within its range. Very little is known about it and its status is given as Insufficiently Known.

The **African Green Broadbill** *Pseudocalyptomena graueri* is known from only three mountain ranges; two in eastern Zaire (the Itombwe Mountains and the mountains west of Lake Kivu) and one in south-western Uganda (the Impenetrable Forest). It is listed as Rare. There is little recent information on status and numbers, but forest destruction is presumed to be detrimental to this species.

Six species of lark in Africa are now regarded as threatened. One of these, **Ash's Lark** *Mirafra ashi*, was discovered only as recently as 1981 in a single area of over-grazed plain in southern coastal Somalia. It is known by visiting ornithologists that nine other species of lark frequent the same general area and it is surprising that this one was overlooked for so long, for once identified it was found to be quite numerous. Pending further study it is classified as Insufficiently Known.

A related species, the **Degodi Lark** *M. degodiensis* was described from two specimens collected in the Degodi region of eastern Sidamo Province in southern Ethiopia. These two birds were so similar to another kind of lark that their status as new to science was not recognised until comparisons were made back in the Paris museum. Nothing whatever

is yet known about the Degodi Lark, beyond the fact that it is possibly very local. It is also classified as Insufficiently Known.

A rather similar case is that of the **Sidamo Long-clawed Lark** *Heteromirafra sidamoensis*, the only two specimens of which have been collected near Neghelli in central Sidamo Province. Again, nothing is known about the status of the species, which has been classified as Indeterminate.

There are two other Long-clawed Larks of the genus *Heteromirafra*, and both have been given an Indeterminate status. One is the obviously rare **South African Long-clawed Lark** *H. ruddi* (Plate XV), which occurs in the high-altitude grasslands of Transvaal, Orange Free State, Natal, Lesotho and perhaps Swaziland. It now seems to have disappeared from much of the southern part of its range because of over-grazing and excessive burning of the grasslands.

The other species is the **Somali Long-clawed Lark** *H. archeri*, which occupies an extremely restricted area of grassland in the Hargeisa–Buramo region of north-west Somalia. With such a limited range and an obviously small population it is particularly vulnerable as the area is under cultivation for a refugee settlement.

Finally, **Botha's Lark** *Spizocorys fringillaris* (Plate XV), endemic to South Africa, is known only from a small area of high grassland in northern Orange Free State and south-eastern Transvaal. Like the preceding species it is very little known and rarely seen. It is assumed to be rare and is protected by South African law. It too is classified as Indeterminate.

The **White-tailed Swallow** *Hirundo megaensis* has a restricted range in southern Ethiopia. It inhabits arid, short-grass country with scattered thorn bushes and is suspected of nesting in holes in chimney-stack termitaria. Within its small range it is considered fairly common, but the limiting factors are not well understood since apparently suitable habitat occurs elsewhere, and so the White-tailed Swallow is considered at risk and listed as Rare.

A threatened, forest-dwelling pipit, found in only three coastal forest sites, one in Kenya and two in Tanzania is the **Sokoke Pipit** *Anthus sokokensis* (Plate XIII), which ICBP lists as Vulnerable, and for good reason. In the 1970s its population in the Sokoke Forest Reserve was estimated at between 3,000 and 5,000 pairs, but following the felling of a large part of the forest only 2,000 pairs are now judged to remain. In Tanzania the species was recorded over 50 years ago near Moa in the north-east, but it is not known if forest still survives there; otherwise it is known only from in and around the Pugu Hills, behind Dar es Salaam. Its numbers in the Pugu Hills are now very small and it is threatened there, since the area is a rich source of kaolin and mining involves deforestation.

The **Western Wattled Cuckoo-shrike** *Campephaga lobata* probably once occurred in suitable habitat throughout the Upper Guinea forests, between Sierra Leone and Ghana. This handsome red, black and yellow bird is now scarce and seriously threatened by the continuous destruction of forests. The species is listed as Vulnerable, but this is likely soon to be changed to Endangered.

Two of Africa's bulbul species are threatened. One is the **Yellow-throated Olive Greenbul** *Criniger olivaceus* (Plate XIV), which like the preceding species is restricted to surviving areas of primary rain-forest in the Upper Guinea forest block. The other is **Prigogine's Greenbul** *Chlorocichla prigoginei*, which occurs only in the forests and thickets at medium elevation to the

north-west of Lake Edward and on the Lendu Plateau west of Lake Albert in eastern Zaire. Both are threatened by forest destruction. Not much is known about either species and no measures have yet been taken to protect them. Both are listed as Vulnerable.

The **Gabela Helmet-shrike** *Prionops gabela*, which is listed as Indeterminate, is known only from secondary forest in a very small part of western Angola. In 1962 it was described as not uncommon in the Amboim Forest near Gabela, which indicates that it is able to survive in forest which has been underplanted with coffee; but it is unlikely to survive the total destruction which is believed to be occurring in many such forests. It is one of four threatened species which are endemic to the escarpment zone of western Angola, two others being the Gabela Akalat *Sheppardia gabela* and the Pulitzer's Longbill *Macrosphenus pulitzeri* (see p. 114 & 122).

The fourth is **Monteiro's Bush-shrike** *Malaconotus monteiri*, which is one of the least-known of Africa's birds and listed as Indeterminate. It has been recorded only a very few times in the evergreen or gallery forests of the escarpment of western Angola and once, anomalously, on Mount Cameroon.

The related **Mount Kupe Bush-shrike** *M. kupeensis* is perhaps even more scarce. It has been recorded only in the tiny rain-forest area of Mount Kupe in

Gabela Helmet-shrike

Cameroon, where there have been no sightings since 1951. The forest is locally held in superstitious dread and has therefore survived, which suggests that this species may be declining for natural reasons. Like the Monteiro's Bush-shrike, the Mount Kupe species is listed as Indeterminate.

The **Green-breasted Bush-shrike** *Malaconotus gladiator*, listed as Rare, occurs in western Cameroon, including Mount Kupe, and eastern Nigeria. It is known from only five specimens and a few sight records, and is presumed to be at risk from potential forest clearance.

The **Uluguru Bush-shrike** *Malaconotus alius* has been recorded only from Tanzania in the Uluguru Mountain forests. It was rediscovered in 1981 after an absence of records for nearly 20 years. There is very little cutting of the forest at the moment within the altitudinal range of this species; however, because of its low numbers even minor changes in habitat might adversely affect it and for this reason it is listed as Rare.

Swynnerton's Forest Robin *Swynnertonia swynnertoni* is a ground-haunting robin with three subspecies found in middle altitude and montane forest in Zimbabwe, Mozambique and Tanzania. Although not uncommon within each small geographical range at present, this is yet another species threatened by forest clearance. Part of its habitat is protected but meanwhile it is classified as Rare.

The **Gabela Akalat** *Sheppardia gabela* mentioned above is known only in the dense understorey of the primary and secondary forest patches near Gabela, on the escarpment of western Angola. Much of this habitat has now been converted to coffee plantations, in which it is unlikely to survive. No information is available about its present status and it is therefore listed as Indeterminate.

Green-breasted Bush-shrike

The related **East Coast Akalat** *Sheppardia gunningi* (Plate XIII) from Kenya, Tanzania, Mozambique and Malawi is an extremely local bird also threatened by forest destruction. Numbers are not known, but there are a few localities where this skulking species has been found to be fairly common. However its habitat is under pressure throughout its range, even within forest reserves, and the species is consequently given Rare status.

The scarcity of records for the beautiful red, black and white **White-headed Robin-chat** *Cossypha heinrichi* suggest that it must be very rare. It is a skulking bird which apparently haunts the dense undergrowth in a single locality in northern Angola and a few forest patches in western Zaire. The size of its population is not known. The only potential threat to its survival would be the destruction of its habitat. Its ICBP classification is Indeterminate.

The **Dappled Mountain Robin** *Modulatrix orostruthus* is a highly elusive, very low-density species. Its known range consists of several small well-separated patches of montane forest in Mozambique and Tanzania. Virtually nothing is known about this species and it is rarely observed in the field. ICBP lists it as Rare.

The **Usambara Ground Robin**

Dryocichloides montanus is restricted to a single mountain range, the West Usambaras, in Tanzania. The forests here are slowly being replaced by softwood plantations, and are also being degraded by excessive harvesting of camphor trees. A conservative estimate of the total population has suggested 28,000 birds; although this species may be numerically strong, it has to be considered at risk given its tiny distribution and ICBP gives it Rare status.

The **Iringa Ground Robin** *Dryocichloides lowei* is a seldom-recorded species known from only six forest patches in southern Tanzania. The area of dry forest patches it inhabits is probably not very great, and being reduced as a result of both fires and human exploitation, and so the population of this species is assumed to be small. It is listed as Rare.

Another elusive, ground-haunting species is the curiously named **Thyolo Alethe** *Alethe choloensis*, which is related to the robin-chats. It is known only in 13 small areas of highland forest in southern Malawi and adjacent Mozambique east of the Shire Valley. Several such forest patches have recently been destroyed and the species is threatened by this continuing process within its range, as are several other rare species. The population in Mozambique is not known, but in Malawi it is thought to be about 1,500 pairs in small scattered

Taita Thrush

groups. Although now listed as Endangered, no steps have yet been taken to protect it.

A species known only from two males collected in 1966 and not seen since is the **Kibale Ground-thrush** *Turdus kibalensis*, from the Kibale Forest in western Uganda. This area has since been carefully searched by ornithologists without result. Of the forest where these birds were found, the northern third has been selectively felled and the southern third lost to agriculture. Only 185 sq km are now protected and are being carefully surveyed. Meanwhile, the status of the Kibale Ground-thrush is listed as Indeterminate.

Another almost wholly unknown related species is the **Taita Thrush** *Turdus helleri*. It is a ground-dwelling species and apparently confined to the Taita Hills and Mount Kasigau in south-east Kenya. Its available habitat is under serious threat by an ever-increasing human population. The Taita Hills are particularly rich in unusual species of wildlife and efforts are being made to put what remains of the natural vegetation under protection. This species is listed as Endangered.

The **Forest Ground-thrush** *Turdus oberlaenderi* appears to be restricted to a few places in eastern Zaire. Numbers are not known and the small number of specimens collected justify its Rare status. It used to occur in western Uganda, but the Bwamba Forest it inhabited has suffered much disturbance and it could be extinct there. The remaining population in Zaire could easily follow suit.

The **Spotted Ground-thrush** *Turdus fischeri* (Plate XIII) is another elusive and poorly known bird. It is evidently a relict species, having one of the most extraordinary distributions of any African bird: two migratory coastal subspecies in East and South Africa and three resident inland subspecies in Malawi, Sudan and Zaire. The forest habitats of all the populations are threatened and the species is classified as Rare.

Although Kenya has for so long been studied by competent observers it is surprising how many endemic species of bird have escaped observation. **Hinde's Pied Babbler** *Turdoides hindei* is an example of this, for although usually skulking in behaviour it is not inconspicuous. It is said to have been fairly common until the 1950s, but now apparently has a very restricted range and a very small population south and east of Mount Kenya. It is listed as Vulnerable but it may, however, be more numerous than it seems. Its habitat is secondary vegetation and open woodlands in steep-sided valleys. Its decline is probably due to the conversion of much of its former range to the growing of rice and maize and perhaps also to the too frequent collection of museum specimens.

The **White-throated Mountain Babbler** *Lioptilus gilberti* has been found only in a few montane localities in western Cameroon and eastern Nigeria. The species is common where it occurs but as

it is dependent on primary forest and has a restricted distribution it is classified as Rare.

The two remarkable colonial cave-nesting picathartes (or rockfowl) species, the **White-necked Picathartes** *Picathartes gymnocephalus* and the **Grey-necked Picathartes** *P. oreas*, are both threatened by forest clearance. The White-necked Picathartes, listed as Vulnerable, was first discovered in Guinea in 1825. Specimens were later collected in the forests of Ghana, Liberia, Togo, Sierra Leone and Ivory Coast. Nearly all these were in small breeding colonies. The species is now threatened not only by the destruction of its rainforest habitat, which is very extensive everywhere west of the Dahomey Gap, but also by hunting and excessive collecting for zoos. No estimate has yet been made of its total population, but because of its highly specialised habitat and cave-nesting requirements it is clearly both localised and very small. In Ghana it is now protected by law. If it is to survive, Guinea, Ivory Coast, Liberia, Sierra Leone and Togo must follow Ghana's lead and give this unique species the fullest protection. Probably because of

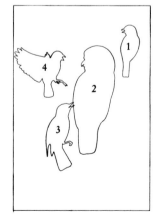

PLATE XIII Sokoke Forest.
1 Clarke's Weaver (p. 124),
2 East Coast Akalat (p. 114),
3 Sokoke Pipit (p. 113),
4 Spotted Ground-thrush (p. 115), 5 Amani Sunbird (p. 123), 6 Sokoke Scops Owl (p. 110).

PLATE XIV Tai Forest.
1 Nimba Flycatcher (p. 122),
2 Rufous Fishing Owl (p. 111),
3 Yellow-throated Olive Greenbul (p. 113), 4 Gola Malimbe (p. 124).

Norman Arlott '86

Norman Arlott '84

Norman Arlott 87

Norman Arlott 87

its unusual, almost bald-headed appearance, it has been in great demand by zoos and at least 130 have been taken by them. Nearly all have died within a year or two and captive-breeding results have been minimal. Much the same remarks apply to the Grey-necked Picathartes, which has a similar breeding biology and is similarly restricted to rocky areas of rain-forest in southern Cameroon, north-east Gabon and perhaps Equatorial Guinea, and in 1987 it was found to occur in eastern Nigeria. It is listed as Rare. Part of its population is in the new Korup National Park, for which a special fund-raising campaign was organised by the United Kingdom section of WWF, and another part in the area of the proposed Dja National Park in southern Cameroon. The number in zoos is relatively small and it seems that captive-breeding will not be any more successful than with its relative.

We now come to the many species of small African warblers of the sub-family Sylviinae which are regarded as threatened or so little-known that their status cannot yet be established. Many are simply described as Rare. This may reflect the natural tendency of many

collectors and ornithologists to concentrate on the larger and more colourful birds in areas where observation is often extremely difficult.

Grauer's Swamp Warbler *Bradypterus graueri* is known only in a few highland swamps in eastern Zaire, south-western Uganda, Rwanda and northern Burundi, but seems to be fairly common in these regions. It is, however, severely threatened by widespread drainage schemes and is therefore classified as Vulnerable.

The related **Dja River Warbler** *B. grandis*, known only in a few localities in southern Cameroon and Gabon, does not appear to be particularly threatened except by its obviously small numbers. A proper survey is needed to provide an explanation for its scarcity. Meanwhile it is listed as Insufficiently Known.

The **Papyrus Yellow Warbler** *Chloropeta gracilirostris* is a Rare status warbler, known chiefly from papyrus swamps, but occasionally other marshy habitats, in areas of high rainfall in Burundi, Kenya, Rwanda, Uganda, Zaire and Zambia. It is threatened by the draining of swamps and the cutting of papyrus. If papyrus-cutting schemes are subject to

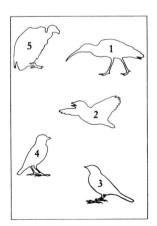

PLATE XV South African Grasslands. **1** Southern Bald Ibis (p. 107), **2** South African Long-clawed Lark (p. 112), **3** Yellow-breasted Pipit (p. 125), **4** Botha's Lark (p. 112), **5** Cape Vulture (p. 107).

PLATE XVI São Tomé. **1** Maroon Wood-pigeon (p. 142), **2** São Tomé Short Tail (p. 142), **3** Dwarf Olive Ibis (p. 141), **4** São Tomé Fiscal Shrike (p. 142), **5** Grosbeak Bunting (p. 142), **6** São Tomé Scops Owl (p. 142).

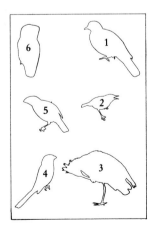

careful guidelines that limit ecological damage, the species may be able to survive in managed habitat.

Three other warblers with an Insufficiently Known status are the **Tana River Cisticola** *Cisticola restricta*, of which a few specimens have been collected in the lower Tana River basin in eastern Kenya; the **River Prinia** *Prina fluviatilis*, found in a few localities between Niger, Chad and northern Cameroon; and the **Karamoja Apalis** *Apalis karamojae*, which has been recorded a few times in north-east Uganda and northern Tanzania. Almost nothing is known of these three species beyond their original identification from collected specimens and a few subsequent sightings.

A further five warblers at risk, all from East Africa, all threatened by forest clearance and all with Rare status, are the **Kungwe Apalis** *Apalis argentea* from western Tanzania, eastern Zaire, Rwanda and Burundi; the **Kabobo Apalis** *A. kaboboensis* from eastern Zaire; the **Long-billed Apalis** *A. moreaui* from Tanzania and Mozambique; **Mrs Moreau's Warbler** *Bathmocercus winifredae* from eastern Tanzania; and **Turner's Eremomela** *Eremomela turneri* from western Kenya, south-western Uganda and eastern Zaire.

Pulitzer's Longbill *Macrosphenus pulitzeri* is another threatened species of warbler. It occurs in two localities in dry

Long-billed Apalis

evergreen forest on the escarpment of western Angola, where in the 1960s it was described as very rare and difficult to observe. Little has been learned about it since then and ICBP give it the status of Indeterminate.

There are a number of threatened members of the flycatcher family. One is the little-known **Nimba Flycatcher** *Melaenornis annamarulae* (Plate XIV), listed as Indeterminate and found only in primary rain-forest at the foot of Mount Nimba in Liberia and in the Tai National Park of south-western Ivory Coast; the former area is being rapidly cleared for mining and farming, while the latter suffers from much illegal encroachment.

Chapin's Flycatcher *Muscicapa lendu* is known with certainty from only two mountain ranges in eastern Zaire, one forest in south-western Uganda and one small area in western Kenya. It might occur more widely, but is uncommon throughout its known range and so is given Rare status. The species is probably suffering as a result of forest clearance, which is known to be taking place in these areas.

Another threatened flycatcher is the **Banded Wattle-eye** *Platysteira laticincta*, which is already listed as Endangered. It is known only from the high montane forest in the Bamenda Highlands of western Cameroon, where it was recently reported to be still fairly numerous, but where it is now seriously threatened by the rapid destruction of its habitat. Unless the forests on Mount Oku can be fully protected, as ICBP have recommended, there is little hope for this species.

Some of Africa's colourful nectar-feeding sunbirds are becoming rare because of loss of habitat. One, the **Marungu Sunbird** *Nectarinia prigoginei* of Zaire, occurs only in a few parts of the Marungu Highlands and is now on the

Endangered list because of the accelerating destruction of the riparian forest it inhabits. No measures have yet been taken to protect it.

The other four threatened sunbirds are all from East Africa and all are given Rare status. The **Amani Sunbird** *Anthreptes pallidigaster* (Plate XIII) is confined to two small areas of forest in Kenya and Tanzania, where habitat destruction constitutes the principal threat to the species. The **Banded Green Sunbird** *A. rubritorques* is known from four forest areas in eastern Tanzania. In only one of these localities is it at all common and this is the area where it is most threatened by forest destruction. The **Rufous-winged Sunbird** *N. rufipennis*, only discovered in 1981, is known from only one mountain forest area in eastern Tanzania. It is a bird of the forest interior and would decline if forest clearance started there. Lastly **Rockefeller's Sunbird** *Nectarinia rockefelleri* is restricted to high montane forest and afro-alpine moorland in three mountain ranges in eastern Zaire. The bird is considered threatened because its distribution covers such a tiny area, even though forest destruction is unlikely given the high altitudes involved.

One of the small finches which may already be extinct is the **Yellow-throated Serin** *Serinus flavigula*. It is known only from three specimens collected in the 1880s on the eastern escarpment of the West Highlands in the Shoa Province of Ethiopia. Not having been seen for nearly 100 years it should perhaps now be regarded as finally extinct, but ICBP, hoping it may yet be rediscovered, lists it as Indeterminate.

Another finch from the same region in Ethiopia is the **Ankober Serin** *Serinus ankoberensis*. This is a small, cliff-frequenting species first discovered in 1976. No threats are known, but the

Black-lored Waxbill

apparent restriction of the species's range is a general cause for concern and it is classified as Rare.

The **Warsangli Linnet** *Acanthis johannis*, classified as Rare, is endemic to the main mountainous range bordering the Gulf of Aden in northern Somalia. It occurs in both open country and juniper forest which is declining, but it would appear that the density of the species increases with the amount and proximity of forest. Thus although partial forest destruction does not seem to have been harmful, total destruction would seem likely to be highly detrimental.

Two waxbills are classified as Insufficiently Known. It is possible that neither is seriously threatened, but so little information about them is available, apart from the knowledge that their distribution is very restricted, that their future remains uncertain. One is the **Anambra Waxbill** *Estrilda poliopareia* reported from a few riverine grasslands in southern Nigeria, the other is the **Black-lored Waxbill** *E. nigriloris*, which is known only in a restricted area around the Lualaba River and Lake Upemba in southern Zaire; part of its range is within the Upemba National Park, which provides some protection. However, there have been no confirmed reports of this species since 1950.

Weavers are among the most typical and obviously successful of Africa's birds, yet no fewer than 12 of the lesser-known species are now classified as threatened to greater or lesser degree. **Bannerman's Weaver** *Ploceus bannermani* is disappearing because of the destruction of its habitat in a few montane areas of western Cameroon and eastern Nigeria. It is classified as Vulnerable. **Bates's Weaver** *P. batesi* of the lowland rain-forest in Cameroon is classified as Rare and is also threatened by habitat destruction. The **Black-chinned Weaver** *P. nigrimentum* has been recorded only in two widely separated areas, one in Angola and one in Zaire; almost nothing is known about it and it is therefore listed as Insufficiently Known. The same applies to the **Loango Slender-billed Weaver** *P. subpersonatus*, which is known only from the coastal strip from Gabon to the mouth of the Zaire River (although it has recently been found to be reasonably common in Gabon), and the even less-known **Lake Lufira Weaver** *P. ruweti* which is confined to the swamps surrounding Lake Lufira in southern Zaire. The **Golden-naped Weaver** *P. aureonucha* has been recorded only from a very small part of the Ituri Forest in eastern Zaire; nothing was learned about it between 1926 and 1986, when researchers rediscovered it in forest-edge habitat, so that ICBP now

judges it as Rare. Also in the Ituri Forest is the **Yellow-legged Weaver** *P. flavipes*, about which nothing was heard from 1953, when it was reported to be still found in the lowland forest region, until 1986 when again researchers relocated it and provided ICBP with enough data to modify its status from Indeterminate to Rare. **Clarke's Weaver** *P. golandi* (Plate XIII) is better documented than the Yellow-legged. It is an elusive species known only from the Sokoke Forest on the Kenya coast, which is now seriously threatened by logging. Its population is estimated at between 1,000 and 2,000 pairs. Part of the Sokoke Forest is protected, but this species is nevertheless listed as Endangered. The **Tanzanian Mountain Weaver** *Ploceus nicolli*, classified as Rare, is restricted to three Tanzanian mountain ranges, where it is elusive and occurs at low densities, and is under some threat from forest destruction.

Two closely related weavers, the **Ibadan Malimbe** *Malimbus ibadanensis* and the **Gola Malimbe** *M. ballmanni* (Plate XIV) appear to be now gravely threatened. The former has a very restricted distribution in south-western Nigeria, mainly between the forest edge and open savanna, where it is constantly threatened by the increasing clearance for agriculture; it is listed as Endangered. The Gola Malimbe of Sierra Leone, Liberia and the Ivory Coast is also thought to be in severe danger from forest destruction. Its exact status cannot yet be defined, however, and it is listed as Indeterminate.

Although only listed as Rare and as yet apparently not seriously threatened, the **Ethiopian Bush Crow** *Zavattariornis stresemanni*, which is found in the thornbush savanna of southern Ethiopia, deserves special mention. Like the Congo Peacock (see p. 108) it is one of the most

Ethiopian Bush Crow

remarkable ornithological discoveries made in Africa this century. Discovered only in 1942, it has generated considerable debate about its affinities, or lack of them, to the crows and starlings. Its very restricted range and apparent habit of cooperative breeding are as yet unexplained.

ADDITIONAL CANDIDATE BIRDS OF MAINLAND AFRICA

HIRUNDINIDAE Swallows
Red Sea Cliff Swallow *Hirundo perdita* is a recently discovered species. A dead specimen was picked up on an islet off Port Sudan in 1984. Nothing more has been discovered about the species.

MOTACILLIDAE Pipits
Yellow-breasted Pipit *Anthus chloris* (Pl. XV) is an endemic of high altitude grasslands in South Africa. Burning and grazing diminish its habitat and fewer migrants are now seen in winter at lower altitudes.

PYCNONOTIDAE Bulbuls
Spot-winged Bulbul *Pycnonotus leucolepis* is a new species recently described from primary forest in southeast Liberia. Its status and range are unknown.

(MUSCIPAIDAE) SYLVIINAE Old World warblers
White-winged Apalis *Apalis chariessa* from Kenya, Malawi, Mozambique and Tanzania is threatened by forest destruction.

PLOCEIDAE Weavers
Entebbe Weaver *Ploceus victoriae* is a recently described species known only from the type-locality in Entebbe, Uganda.

STURNIDAE Starlings
Abbott's Starling *Cinnyricinclus femoralis* is known from a few mountain forests in Kenya and Tanzania. Although partly protected by National Parks the species is threatened by forest destruction.

MADAGASCAR

Madagascar has the unenviable distinction of having suffered a greater degree of environmental destruction than almost any other country. No less than 80% of its once rich and extensive forests have disappeared and many of its unique endemic forms of wildlife, including several species of birds, are now extinct. About one quarter of its surviving birds are severely threatened by loss of habitat and insufficiently controlled hunting. Four species have not been seen for the past 50 years or more. Nevertheless, some efforts have now been made to improve the protection of vulnerable habitats and species. Cooperation between the Malagasy Government and international conservation organisations such as WWF, IUCN and ICBP is encouraging, and a number of important projects have resulted.

According to the latest information, 28 species of Madagascar's birds are currently listed as threatened. Of these, four are known to be definitely Endangered and several others would probably be put in this category if more were known about them. At the present rate of forest destruction on the island, and unless the alterations to and drainage of swamplands can be halted and hunting more strictly controlled, there will be many inevitable losses in the near future. All further collecting should also be prohibited.

One of the endemic species under multiple threats is the once common and widespread **Madagascar Little Grebe** *Tachybaptus pelzelni* (Plate XVII). It inhabits lakes, pools and slow-flowing rivers, which it shares with two related species, the Little Grebe *T. ruficollis* and the Alaotra Grebe *T. rufolavatus*. The former has spread rapidly in Madagascar and is now hybridising with *T. pelzelnii* which it is threatening genetically to swamp, as is already happening to the scarce Alaotra Grebe. Related to this problem has been the introduction of herbivorous tilapia fish into many of the waters occupied by grebes, thus causing a serious reduction in the aquatic vegetation on which both *T. pelzelnii* and *T. rufolavatus* depend for food. The Little Grebe is more of a fish-eating species, which can thrive in open water from which the other two are usually excluded. In addition, introduced predatory Black Bass are now preying on the chicks of the Madagascar Little Grebe and of other aquatic species. There has been a great reduction of lakes available to water-birds, most of them having been converted to rice-fields or fish-farms, and there is serious pollution in the waters around Antananarivo. No measures have yet been taken to protect this species, which is listed by ICBP as Insufficiently Known.

The related **Alaotra Grebe** *T. rufolavatus* is known chiefly from the region of Lake Alaotra, where it is in the irreversible process of disappearing through hybridisation with the dominant Little Grebe *T. ruficollis*. The population of pure-strain birds is now extremely small and their disappearance has probably been accelerated by the collection of museum specimens. No fewer than 13 were shot in 1960 when the total seen on the lake was only 50. In 1982 only 12 were seen. It may now be too late even to attempt a captive-breeding effort to save the species. Meanwhile it is listed as Endangered.

Another species threatened by the deterioration of wetlands is the **Madagascar Heron** *Ardea humbloti* (Plate XVII). Its population was reported in 1973 to have declined alarmingly, although apparently still fairly safe in some parts of the west coast. The species may suffer competition from the more numerous Grey Heron *A. cinerea* and Purple Heron *A. purpurea*, both of which are represented in Madagascar by endemic subspecies. Its large size and relative tameness make it vulnerable to native hunters, who also take its eggs. In 1961 both the Grey and the Purple Herons were officially classified by the Malagasy Government as harmful to fishing interests, and the Madagascar Heron undoubtedly suffered from the persecution of all herons which followed. At present the only safety it finds is in a small nesting colony on Nosy Manitra, which is protected by a local taboo. There is an urgent need for a joint study of this species, the Madagascar Pond Heron *Ardeola idae* and the Madagascar Fish Eagle *Haliaeetus vociferoides* and for a fully protected reserve for all three species in the Antsalova region. The Madagascar Heron is listed as Insufficiently Known.

Two of Madagascar's endemic duck species are gravely threatened by excessive and uncontrolled hunting as well as by loss of suitable habitat. The **Madagascar Teal** *Anas bernieri* (Plate XVII), listed as Vulnerable, was reported in the nineteenth century as occurring in small flocks on many estuaries, marshes and pools, but by 1930 it was rare and is now restricted to a few sites along the west coast, where its numbers are very low. Hunting is supposed to be banned on several lakes where it might appear, but there is still plenty of poaching and egg-collecting. No specific measures have been taken to save this species and only one specimen has ever been kept in captivity.

The situation of the **Madagascar Pochard** *Aythya innotata* is much worse. This freshwater diving duck is extremely poorly documented and since 1970 has become increasingly rare. Nothing has yet been done to save it. Around 1930 it was common and bred on Lake Alaotra, where 27 were collected that year by a Franco–Anglo–American expedition. Two independent observers during the 1970s and 1980s reported the species to be on the brink of extinction. Uncontrolled hunting has been the main cause, but the introduction of predatory Black Bass, gill-net fishing and the conversion of lakes to rice-growing have probably also contributed. No conservation measures have yet been introduced, though legal protection for the species was urged on the Malagasy Government ten years ago. It is listed by ICBP as Endangered.

Another species which appears to be heading for extinction is the handsome

Madagascar Serpent Eagle

Madagascar Fish Eagle *Haliaeetus vociferoides* (Plate XVII), listed as Endangered. Although obviously rare and now confined to the shoreline of the west coast near Morondava north to Diégo Suarez, a proposal made in 1970 to examine its status has only just been funded. Its total population is now approximately 40 pairs and many of these are vulnerable to amateur sportsmen. However, a leaflet drawing attention to its plight has been recently issued.

Probably even nearer to extinction is the strikingly hooded **Madagascar Serpent Eagle** *Eutriorchis astur*, also given Endangered status. It is the only one of its genus and therefore particularly valuable to science. It is very little known, only having definitely been seen alive more than 50 years ago. Hopes for its survival are largely pinned on the conservation of adequate areas of primary rain-forest, very little of which now remains in Madagascar. There have been a few unconfirmed sightings which sustain speculation that this enigmatic bird may still exist, the last being in the north-east of the island in 1977. Meanwhile it is calculated that all the rich lowland forests of the island will have been destroyed within the next few years unless plans for immediate action can be implemented to save a few patches. The Madagascar Serpent Eagle is regarded as among the six rarest birds of prey in the entire world. Proposals have been made for the complete protection of the "Sihanaka Forest", which at present is believed to harbour many of the endangered species of rain-forest birds of Madagascar, and to conduct a full survey of their status and needs. Another project was proposed by ICBP's Bird of Prey specialist group to conduct a thorough search for the Madagascar Serpent Eagle in the Marojejy Nature Reserve and the Masoala Peninsula, but neither project has yet been carried out.

The mesite family is endemic to Madagascar and consists of three species, all of which are threatened. They are shy, terrestrial birds which fly reluctantly and somewhat resemble large, long-legged pigeons, though their behaviour is more like that of a rail. The **White-breasted Mesite** *Mesitornis variegata* was until recently known only from two sites in dry forest in north-west Madagascar, but

has now been recorded at several other localities near the west coast. It is listed by ICBP as Rare.

The **Subdesert Mesite** *Monias benschi*, also listed as Rare, is restricted to a sub-desert coastal strip between the Mangoky and Fierenana Rivers in southwest Madagascar. It is of particular biological interest as it has unusual breeding behaviour which may include polyandry, but observation is difficult as it inhabits dense cover in sandy regions.

The third species, the **Brown Mesite** *Mesitornis unicolor* (Plate XVIII), apparently has a wider distribution but may be at risk from both forest destruction and introduced mammalian predators such as the Brown Rat *Rattus norvegicus*. It is a rain-forest species, scuttling through the undergrowth very inconspicuously but nesting one or two metres above ground. It may occur throughout eastern Madagascar, but its exact range and population size are not yet known. It is therefore listed as Insufficiently Known.

The **Slender-billed Flufftail** *Sarothrura watersi* is a small marsh rail known only from five well separated areas of central and eastern Madagascar. It may be more at risk from natural causes than from man. Very little is known about it and it was not seen in the wild with absolute certainty for more than 50 years before one was netted late in 1987. There is speculation that a few may still breed in the region of Antananarivo but no confirmation has been obtained. ICBP list it as Indeterminate.

The marsh-dwelling **Sakalava Rail** *Amaurornis olivieri* (Plate XVII) is another almost unknown species which has been recorded from three widely separated areas in the Sakalava country of western Madagascar. Rice-growing has overrun some of its original habitat and it is possible that it has suffered from

Slender-billed Flufftail

systematic exploitation for food by local natives. It appears not to have been recorded since 1962 and is listed by ICBP as Insufficiently Known.

The **Madagascar Plover** *Charadrius thoracicus* is restricted to grassy coastal areas of south-west Madagascar, and is treated as Rare. Its total population is low, possibly under 1,000, and the reasons for this rarity are unclear. It may be that it is out-competed by the common Kittlitz's Plover *C. pecuarius*.

The **Madagascar Red Owl** *Tyto soumagnei* has been collected on a number of occasions since it was first recorded in 1874, but today is known with certainty only in the rain-forest area of east-central Madagascar, where it was last seen in 1973. This was the only sighting during the past 50 years and the species is now undoubtedly extremely scarce, but is given Indeterminate status.

Four of the five species of ground-roller, a family endemic to Madagascar, are considered Rare. The **Short-legged Ground-roller** *Brachypteracias leptosomus*, **Scaly Ground-roller** *B. squamiger* and **Rufous-headed Ground-roller** *Atelornis crossleyi* are all confined to deep rain-forest in the centre and northeast of Madagascar, and are threatened by forest destruction. The **Long-tailed Ground-roller** *Uratelornis chimaera* has a restricted range, similar to that of the Subdesert Mesite, in south-west Madagascar. Although numerically safe at present, the restricted range is a source of concern especially as the species enjoys no habitat protection and is also trapped by local villagers.

Among the endangered small endemic birds of the island, the **Yellow-bellied Sunbird-asity** *Neodrepanis hypoxantha* (Plate XVIII) is one of the least known and is also difficult to distinguish from its only congener, the Wattled Sunbird-asity *N. coruscans*, which occurs in simi-

lar forest habitat. It is known from 13 specimens all collected before 1930 and was actually not recognised as a true species until 1933. Since then it has been found only twice; once in 1976 at Périnet-Analamazaotra Special Reserve, and once a decade later at Ranamafana, near Fianarantsoa. It is listed by ICBP as Indeterminate.

Three Madagascar bulbuls are considered threatened and classified as Rare. **Appert's Greenbul** *Phyllastrephus apperti* is known with certainty from only two remote regions in south-west Madagascar. The habitat it frequents is dry forest which is being destroyed by cutting and burning. The **Dusky Greenbul** *P. tenebrosus* is a little-known species from two localities in eastern central Madagascar, where the forest is rapidly disappearing. The **Grey-crowned Greenbul** *P. cinereiceps* from eastern Madagascar is almost totally unknown, having been found only twice in the past 50 years until the discovery of a population at Ranomafana in 1986.

Van Dam's Vanga *Xenopirostris damii* is known from a single site which partly falls within the Ankarafantsika Nature Reserve in north-west Madagascar. Recent observations indicate that it is present in fairly good numbers, but because of its highly restricted range it is classified as Rare.

Long-tailed Ground-roller

Pollen's Vanga *Xenopirostris polleni* (Plate XVIII), also Rare, is known from a wide variety of localities in eastern Madagascar, but is everywhere scarce and threatened by forest destruction.

Benson's Rockthrush *Monticola bensoni* was not described until 1971, although two old museum specimens collected at an unknown locality in Madagascar already existed. In 1962 a possible new species (later identified as Benson's Rockthrush) was recognised in several localities in the Mangoky River region and in the Isalo Massif. It was found again in 1969 and 1970, and in 1971 was located again 150 km south of the Isalo Massif. In 1977 two were observed on telegraph wires in the Zombitsy Forest Reserve. All these sightings were in dry, rocky areas between the Mangoky and Onilahy Rivers in southwest Madagascar. Although six birds were found within 2 km in one locality the total population is believed to be very small, but not under any threat. It is listed as Insufficiently Known.

The very distinctive **Madagascar Yellowbrow** *Crossleyia xanthophrys*, which is confined to the rain-forest in the east-central part of the island, was collected in large numbers for museums between 1880 and 1920, but from then until 1986 only two were found: one in the Tsaratanana Massif in 1966 and the other to the east of Antananarivo in 1968. In 1986 it was found at Ranomafana. It is described as difficult to observe because of its skulking behaviour in undergrowth and may therefore have been overlooked. Although the forests have been greatly reduced in areas where it was recorded, it should still gain some protection from the Tsaratanana Nature Reserve and the Périnet–Analazamaotra Special Reserve if it still exists in these localities. Its status is Indeterminate.

Occasionally, when only a single specimen of a species exists in the world's museums, there is debate that it might be merely an aberrant bird of a closely similar species. This was the case with the only skin of the **Red-tailed Newtonia** *Newtonia fanovanae*, which very closely resembles a female Red-tailed Vanga *Calicalicus madagascariensis* except for details of the bill and eye-ring. It is, however, now regarded as a true species. It was collected in 1931 in the Fanovana Forest in east-central Madagascar and no trace of the species has ever been found since then. As 50 years have now passed it could be treated as extinct under the criteria of CITES, but ICBP lists it as Indeterminate, as it is more likely to have been overlooked because of its difficult habitat and elusiveness.

Africa's Islands

The threatened bird species of the islands close to the African continent are here regarded as within the Afrotropical Region. There are 11 from the Mascarene Islands, 6 from the Comoros and Mayotte, 8 from the Seychelles and Aldabra Islands, 7 from São Tomé and Príncipe, 4 from the Canary Islands, 3 from Madeira, 2 from the Cape Verde Islands, 5 from the Tristan da Cunha group including Gough, and one each from Fernando Po, Ascension, St. Helena and Amsterdam Island. Of all the threatened species of birds of the Afrotropical Region 44% are on islands and the majority of extinctions have also occurred there. For the sake of convenience, species are treated by island groups rather than in systematic order.

Mascarene Black Petrel

The islands of Mauritius, Rodrigues and Réunion in the **Mascarene** group lie in the western Indian Ocean to the east of Madagascar. They became famous for their now extinct Dodo and Solitaires and today have little resemblance to their once well-vegetated appearance. Their surviving birds are suffering severely from the loss of native forests and also from predation or competition by introduced species of mammals and birds.

One of their endangered seabirds is the **Mascarene Black Petrel** *Pterodroma aterrima*. This small gadfly-petrel is known only from Réunion and Rodrigues and has been recorded so rarely that it is considered by the ICBP to be at least Endangered on the former and extinct on the latter. It has been seen at sea only twice and is known from Rodrigues only from fossil remains. The records from Réunion are mostly from nineteenth century specimens and a few taken since. Nesting is presumed to occur in mountain forests near Entre-Deux and Bois Rouge. Numbers are unknown but must be extremely small. Cats, dogs and rats probably prey on nestlings, which may also be taken by local people as food.

One of the rarest and most closely studied of the world's small birds of prey is the **Mauritius Kestrel** *Falco punctatus* (Plate XIX), listed as Endangered. A lot

of time and money has been spent on skilled efforts to save it from the threat of extinction. It is a forest-dwelling bird endemic to Mauritius and now confined to the Black River gorge and Magenta escarpment. Its population was reduced in the early 1970s to single figures for uncertain reasons. There has been a slight recovery, but its future remains in doubt. In the 1850s it was described as "plentiful wherever indigenous woods exist", but when the WWF/ICBP project to study and conserve the birds of Mauritius began in the early 1970s, it had become so rare that extinction seemed inevitable. Only one pair and two isolated adults could be found, but in 1973 a more thorough search revealed a total of eight or nine birds. Two of these were shot by hunters and two were caught for captive breeding. In 1974 the captive female died and was replaced by another from the wild. In the following breeding season all the known wild birds paired, one rearing three young and another none, while the captive pair raised one chick which died. Perhaps owing to a severe cyclone none of the birds bred in 1975. Three pairs were present in 1976, two of which nested on cliffs and raised three and two young respectively, the third nesting unsuccessfully in a tree. The captive pair also failed, so that by the end of 1976 there were eleven wild birds and two captive. In 1977 three wild pairs nested on cliffs and raised seven young, the captive pair again failing. Three of the wild young were brought into captivity, making twelve in the wild and five captive at the end of 1977. In 1978 a captive pair died and an adult pair taken from the wild as a replacement fledged one young bird. One wild pair raised three young. By the beginning of 1980 all the captive birds had died and the wild population was estimated at 15, only one pair of which bred and produced two young. In 1981 two clutches of eggs produced in the wild were taken for the captive breeding project. In 1982 one wild pair produced two young which disappeared, another an infertile clutch and then a second clutch from which three young were reared in captivity, bringing the captive population to six. In 1983 three wild pairs between them produced only three nestlings, two of which were taken into captivity; the third pair was given supplementary food and produced three clutches, from which two young were reared in captivity. By the end of 1983, ten Mauritius Kestrels were captive and six pairs in the wild, of which half were capable and half probably capable of breeding. Ten years of very difficult but devoted work had at least maintained this species in being and the effort is continuing.

The factors which caused the decline in the population appear to be irreversible. The main problem has been the chronic loss of forest habitat. The relict forest is subject to steady degeneration caused by vigorous introduced plants and the ravages of introduced deer, pigs, monkeys and rats. Major cyclones, hunters and wood-cutters are additional factors. Kestrels are shot by hunters in the mistaken belief that they take domestic poultry, hence the local name "Mangeur de Poules". Habitat quality and food abundance are regarded as the controlling elements in the survival of this species. The government has introduced protective legislation and has enlarged the Macabée/Bel Ombre Nature Reserve to 3,594 hectares. ICBP and Jersey Wildlife Preservation Trust (JWPT) are now cooperating with the government in an effort to improve the state of wildlife in Mauritius under a scheme called the Mauritius Wildlife Research and Conservation Programme, and a campaign of public education recently begun is partially aimed at reducing hunting pressure.

Pink Pigeon

Another seriously threatened species listed as Endangered is the beautiful **Pink Pigeon** *Nesoenas mayeri*, endemic to Mauritius and now restricted to the south-west of the island. Like the Mauritius Kestrel it has suffered severely from the combination of loss of habitat, uncontrolled hunting and cyclonic damage. Its population has been critically low since 1960, falling to only 18 birds in 1984. Breeding is confined to a very small grove of *Cryptomeria* trees. However, a very successful captive-breeding project has now produced about 100 zoo-birds from which it is hoped to re-establish the wild population. Those taking part in the captive-breeding project are the Mauritius Government, the Jersey Wildlife Preservation Trust, the New York and Albuquerque Zoos and the Vogelpark Walsrode in West Germany.

Yet another Mauritius species is on the brink of extinction and classified as Endangered, the **Mauritius Parakeet** *Psittacula eques* (Plate XIX), which now has a wild population of between four and a possible maximum of eleven birds. It is extinct on Réunion, where it occurred until 1800, but was regarded as common in the forested areas of Mauritius until about 1830 and still fairly numerous until

1900. By 1982 the very few surviving birds had apparently ceased to breed. Excessive hunting and the conversion of forests to cultivation, combined with predation by monkeys and competition for nest-sites by introduced Ring-necked Parakeets *Psittacula krameri* and Indian Mynahs *Acridotheres tristis*, were responsible for the decline. The species has been of major concern since the WWF/ICBP conservation effort on Mauritius began in 1970 and its remaining habitat is fully protected by the new Macabée/Bel Ombre Nature Reserve.

Two species of forest-dwelling cuckoo-shrikes, from the islands of Mauritius and Réunion respectively, are now listed as Vulnerable. The **Mauritius Cuckoo-shrike** *Coracina typica* (Plate XIX) is suffering severely from habitat loss and, more seriously, from very heavy nest-predation by introduced Crab-eating Macaque Monkeys and Black Rats. Introduced Red-whiskered Bulbuls *Pycnonotus jocosus* and Indian Mynahs are believed to be preventing the expansion of this species into disturbed native forests. Its present population is thought to have been reduced to about 180–190 pairs. The **Réunion Cuckoo-shrike** *C. newtoni* is restricted for unknown reasons to one very small and inadequately protected area in the north-

Rodrigues Warbler

west of Réunion, where its habitat is being degraded by introduced deer and where it is at risk from bird-lime poachers and tourist activity. Its population is estimated at between 100 and 150 pairs. Both species should benefit from current initiatives designed by ICBP to improve conservation on these islands.

The **Mauritius Black Bulbul** *Hypsipetes olivaceus* is an endemic species confined to one area in eastern Mauritius, and also considered Vulnerable. It is a frugivorous forest-dwelling bird, which was reduced to some 200 pairs by the mid-1970s and has probably declined further since then. Nest-predation and competition from introduced bird species and monkeys are the main threats. It is also vulnerable to the effects of cyclones during the fruiting season. During the last century it was regarded as one of the commonest of the endemic species, but like so many others its population declined steeply with the rapid exploitation of the island's forests. It has long been protected by law and should benefit from the new Mauritius Wildlife Research and Conservation Programme.

Several of the small birds of the Mascarenes are also at risk. One is the **Rodrigues Warbler** *Acrocephalus rodericanus*, of which only 20–25 pairs remain. It is threatened by habitat destruction by man and by cyclones and will be further endangered if, as seems possible, rats and monkeys are brought to the island. It is listed by ICBP as Endangered.

The **Mauritius Olive White-eye** *Zosterops chloronothus* was, until recently, very threatened by habitat clearance. There are probably only about 275 pairs, confined to the forested upland area of south-west Mauritius, where its future is by no means secure because of the threat of further habitat destruction (see p. 134). The planting of nectar-bearing vegetation in the area has been recommended on behalf of this and other species under the current Mauritius Wildlife Research and Conservation Programme. The species is listed by ICBP as Vulnerable.

Considerable effort has been made to save the endangered and colourful little **Mauritius Fody** *Foudia rubra* (Plate XIX). At the beginning of this century it was described as "fast disappearing" and it is now confined to what remains of the forested area in the south-west of the island. It has suffered catastrophically from the destruction of its original habitat and from extremely heavy nest predation by introduced animals. An ill-conceived project financed by the World Bank for the clearance of the dwarf forest at Les Mares on Plaine Champagne in 1971–1974 destroyed more than half of the population of 400 pairs which existed there. The very low rate of breeding success since then is attributed chiefly to nest predation by introduced Crab-eating Macaques and mongooses. The species has long been protected by law and in 1974 its remaining habitat received almost complete protection with the creation of the Macabée/Bel Ombre Nature Reserve. It is classified by the ICBP as Endangered and work to safeguard the small surviving population is proceeding under the Mauritius Wildlife Research and Conservation Programme with the help of ICBP.

The **Rodrigues Fody** *F. flavicans* is also listed as Endangered. It was described in 1864 as "exceedingly numerous" throughout the island. A steady decline was noted in the 1960s and by 1980 only about 100 pairs survived. It is a species which occupies high, mixed evergreen forest, though it is also seen in low scrub. Almost all of the mature forest on the island has now disappeared and the Rodrigues Fody has suffered severely

from competition by the more successful introduced Madagascar Fody *F. madagascariensis*. Reports that Black Rats have recently reached Rodrigues make the situation even more critical. The species is legally protected and a captive-breeding programme has been started. Consideration is being given to releasing captive-bred birds on a small coralline islet off Mauritius, or on neighbouring Réunion.

The granitic **Seychelles** archipelago has no fewer than seven threatened species, most now the subject of urgent ICBP conservation projects.

The **Seychelles Swiftlet** *Collocalia elaphra* (Plate XX) has a total population of under 1,000. Its distribution is limited by the availability of nest-caves, and the scarcity of these is compounded by disturbance and deliberate vandalism. It has been recommended that metal grilles be erected in the cave entrances to block human access, and so prevent further decline of this species, which is listed as Rare.

One of the best-known of the threatened species is the **Seychelles Magpie-robin** *Copsychus sechellarum* (Plate XX), which is at present confined to Frégate Island. This handsome black and white bird was described in the last century as "widespread and extremely numerous" on the islands of Mahé, Praslin, Marianne, La Digue and Aride, as well as on some of the small satellite islands. A plague of feral cats gradually exterminated them on one island after another. Some were transferred to other islands in the hope of a recovery, but these were also destroyed by cats, even as far away as on the small coral island of Alphonse in the Amirantes, where introduced Magpie-robins appeared to hold their own from about 1896 to the 1950s. When the species was first noted on Frégate in 1871 the then owner prohi-

Seychelles Magpie-robin

bited collectors from taking any specimens on the grounds of rarity and by 1940 this may have been the only surviving population apart from the birds on Alphonse. The Frégate population fluctuated from about a dozen to a possible maximum of 40 birds between 1964 and 1985, when, after falling, the total had risen again to about 25. An attempt was made to introduce some of the Frégate birds to Aride Island in 1978, but within a few years only a single male survived there.

The struggle to save the Seychelles Magpie-robin has been an epic of skill and perseverance. Following a report that cats had reached Frégate in 1960 a government campaign resulted in between 80 and 90 being killed. Thereafter a bounty system operated by successive owners of the island has kept cats under constant control. An outbreak of feline enteritis in 1965–1966 in the Seychelles aided the recovery of the birds. A strict ban on agricultural chemicals was enforced in 1973. In 1981 a sudden new increase in the cat population occurred and was immediately the subject of an eradication campaign mounted by ICBP with the technical help of the New Zealand Wildlife Service. About 51 cats were killed and the population of

Magpie-robins ceased its decline. The island is now believed to be really cat-free, but the Magpie-robin remains an Endangered species.

A remarkable success was scored by ICBP in saving the **Seychelles Warbler** *Acrocephalus sechellensis* (Plate XX), which exists only on Cousin Island. In 1967 barely 25 of these small birds survived and there seemed little likelihood that they could be prevented from becoming extinct. In a final effort to prevent this, ICBP purchased the island with funds subscribed in Great Britain and turned it into a fully protected reserve with a resident trained staff. By excluding all disturbance and restoring the natural habitat of scrub and forest, the population of warblers rapidly increased and now numbers about 250. It is classified by ICBP as Rare.

Other threatened species inhabiting the 25 hectares of the island including various seabirds, have also begun to thrive and Cousin, which is a particularly beautiful palm-fringed island, has become internationally famous as a conservation show-piece.

The **Seychelles White-eye** *Zosterops modestus* (Plate XX) is definitely an Endangered species. The very rapid and unexplained decrease in its population and its confinement to three very small areas of mixed secondary forest on the single island of Mahé suggest that it may very soon be extinct. It gains some protection from the fact that part of its range is within the Morne Seychellois National Park and there appears to be no evidence that it is suffering from lack of suitable habitat. The related Chestnut-flanked White-eye *Z. mayottensis semi-flava* of Marianne Island was, however, a casualty of wholesale habitat destruction and became extinct in the last century. The Seychelles White-eye is being studied in the hope of reversing its decline.

The **Seychelles Fody** *Foudia sechellarum* (Plate XX), classified as Rare, is confined to 3 small islands—Cousin, Cousine and Fregat—in the Seychelles. It is abundant on Cousin and fairly widespread on the other two, but its tiny distribution means that its survival depends on the continued absence of rats from these islands, its ability to withstand nest predation from the introduced Indian Mynah *Acridotheres tristis*, and successful competition with its cogener, the Madagascar Fody *F. madagascariensis*, also introduced.

The Seychelles Government has co-operated actively with ICBP in promoting conservation throughout the archipelago. A number of rare birds require constant vigilance. A notable example is the **Seychelles Black Paradise Flycatcher** *Terpsiphone corvina* (Plate XX) of La Digue and Praslin islands, which is listed as Rare; a special reserve has been created for it on La Digue which is wardened by the government with assistance from the Royal Society for Nature Conservation.

Another species in need of protection is the **Seychelles Scops Owl** *Otus insularis* (Plate XX), which was believed to be extinct on Mahé in 1959 but is now thought to number about 80 pairs. It is listed as Rare.

Aldabra atoll, 800 km south-west of the Seychelles, only just escaped becoming a staging post for military aircraft and is now administered by the Seychelles Government. Aldabra itself is a coral atoll raised on volcanic rock from a great depth of ocean. It has two endemic species of birds and 12 endemic subspecies. The **Aldabra Warbler** *Nesillas aldabranus* is very near extinction and is classified as Endangered. It was not discovered until 1967 and it occupies only a tiny part of the main atoll; indeed, like the Seychelles Warbler, the Aldabra Warbler appears to be confined to about 25 hectares, and these must be among the smallest total ranges of any bird species in the world. Although extensively searched for, little is known about the Aldabra bird beyond the fact that its population is not known to exceed two individuals. Black Rats and feral cats prey on all the small birds of Aldabra, while feral goats and a large population of giant tortoises threaten the vegetation. Various conservation measures are in hand, but landing on the atoll is often

PLATE XVII Madagascan Marsh. 1 Madagascar Little Grebe (p. 126), 2 Sakalava Rail (p. 128), 3 Madagascar Heron (p. 126), 4 Madagascar Teal (p. 127), 5 Madagascar Fish Eagle (p. 127).

PLATE XVIII Madagascan Rain Forest. 1 Pollen's Vanga (p. 130), 2 Brown Mesite (p. 128), 3 Yellow-bellied Sunbird-asity (p. 129).

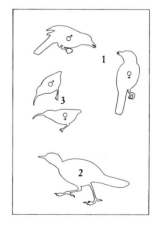

Norman Arlott 87

Norman Arlott

Norman Arlott 87

hazardous and much of the ground honeycombed with razor-sharp crevasses in the coral, which make exploration difficult. The atoll has been designated a Special Reserve and is on the World Heritage Site list.

The **Comoros** lie between the northern tip of Madagascar and the northern coast of Mozambique. The **Madagascar Heron** *Ardea humbloti* (see page 126) has been recorded from the islands and may possibly breed there; in addition to this species some of the endemics on Grand Comoro are at risk. They are all associated with the forest and/or heath around Mount Karthala, and are threatened by destruction of the habitat. At present the forest is relatively unaffected, with some cutting of lower patches for local use, but a road is under construction to take cars to the crater rim and this will inevitably cause disturbance. The heath is also vulnerable from eruption of the active volcano; in 1958 areas near the summit were burnt, presumably as a result of volcanic activity.

The species concerned, all classified as Rare, are the **Grand Comoro Scops Owl** *Otus pauliani* from the forest/heath intergradation zone, the **Grand Comoro**

Flycatcher *Humblotia flavirostris* from the forest, the **Mount Karthala White-eye** *Zosterops mouroniensis* restricted to the small area of summit heathland, and the **Grand Comoro Drongo** *Dicrurus fuscipennis*, found in clearings in the 500–900 m altitudinal zone.

The **Mayotte Drongo** *Dicrurus waldeni* is restricted to forest on the French possession of Mayotte, in the otherwise independent Comoro Islands. The overall condition of the forests here is poor and the species is listed as Rare.

The islands of **São Tomé** and **Príncipe**, on the Equator in the Gulf of Guinea, have an interesting if now much threatened avifauna. In past decades many of their endemic species must have suffered severely from loss of habitat and particularly from the destruction of forested areas. An ICBP project to investigate the status of birds on the islands has recently been carried out. As the following entries show, there is an urgent need for research and a comprehensive conservation programme.

One of the rarest species on the islands is the **Dwarf Olive Ibis** *Bostrychia bocagei* (Plate XVI). It is a dwarf form of the Olive Ibis *B. olivacea* of West and

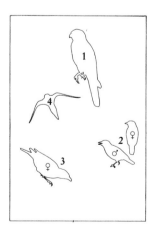

PLATE XIX   Mauritius.
1 Mauritius Kestrel (p. 131),
2 Mauritius Fody (p. 133),
3 Mauritius Cuckoo-shrike (p. 132), 4 Mauritius Parakeet (p. 132).

PLATE XX   Seychelles.
1 Seychelles Black Paradise Flycatcher (p. 136), 2 Seychelles White-eye (p. 135), 3 Seychelles Fody (p. 136), 4 Seychelles Scops Owl (p. 136), 5 Seychelles Magpie-robin (p. 134), 6 Seychelles Warbler (p. 135), 7 Seychelles Swiftlet (p. 134).

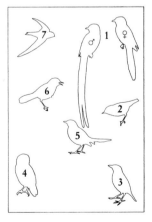

Central Africa and occurs only on São Tomé. It has not been recorded for more than 50 years. It may have been exterminated by mammalian predators, or loss of its forest habitat. By the criteria of CITES it should now be regarded as extinct; however, in the hope of rediscovering it, ICBP lists it as Indeterminate.

The **Maroon Wood-pigeon** *Columba thomensis* (Plate XVI), being the largest of the pigeons of the West African region, has suffered heavily at the hands of illegal hunters. It is confined to São Tomé, where until the 1960s it was fairly numerous. It is now restricted to the mountain in the centre of the island. In 1955 it was given legal protection but this has proved ineffective. ICBP lists it as Vulnerable.

The **São Tomé Scops Owl** *Otus hartlaubi* (Plate XVI) is a fairly widespread but low density species confined to forest growth. It is difficult to understand why the species is absent from other habitats but hunting, cats and competition from the ubiquitous Barn Owl *Tyto alba* may all be excluding factors. Heavy use of pesticides in the 1960s and 1970s may also have been significant. The species is listed as Rare.

A very little-known bird, the **São Tomé Fiscal Shrike** *Lanius newtoni* (Plate XVI), may not survive. According to a museum collector in 1928 it was then uncommon and it has not been recorded since. The reasons for its disappearance might have been loss of habitat, introduced avian diseases or mammalian predation. ICBP give its status as Indeterminate.

Yet another species which has not been seen with total certainty for 50 years and which could therefore now be extinct is the **São Tomé Short-tail** *Amaurocichla bocagii* (Plate XVI). This is a curious little forest-bird of puzzling affinities and apparently both tree-creeping and ground-feeding habits. It was reported in 1928 to be particularly elusive. As much of the habitat where it occurred is still intact, there is hope that it may still survive, and indeed a bird best answering its description was observed along a river in April 1987. It is listed as Indeterminate.

The **São Tomé White-eye** *Zosterops ficedulinus* is found on both São Tomé and Príncipe. Its populations on both islands have given cause for concern. Habitat destruction on Príncipe has been very extensive, but on São Tomé the species was reported to inhabit both forests and cultivated regions, which is a hopeful sign that it is adaptable to change and this seems to be borne out by observations made in August 1987. Its status was given by ICBP as Indeterminate but this has now be altered and the species is now judged as Out of Danger.

Finally, there is the **Grosbeak Bunting** *Neospiza concolor* (Plate XVI), a species which was apparently always uncommon, and only ever reported from two different areas of the island. It has not been seen this century and may possibly be extinct. Logging and mammalian predation would be the likeliest causes for its disappearance. There is, however, still some hope that it survives and it is therefore classified as Indeterminate.

The nearby island of **Fernando Po** (Bioko), off Equatorial Guinea, harbours the rarely recorded **Fernando Po Speirops** *Speirops brunneus*, the only endemic species of the island. It occurs in fairly open lichen forest on the slopes of Pico de Santa Isabel, and as the area which it inhabits is tiny it is classified as Rare.

On the **Cape Verde Islands**, to the west of Senegal, there is a species of lark which has had a very fluctuating history.

This is the **Raso Lark** *Alauda razae*. At the beginning of this century, when 60 specimens were collected, it was described as common and widespread on the tiny, arid island of Razo. Visits between 1960 and 1981 showed that the population was declining rapidly, perhaps because of protracted drought, and the last report in 1981 was that only 15–20 birds could be found. Given the large number of skins already in museums, a further collection taken in 1970 was thoroughly irresponsible. Fieldwork in 1985, however, resulted in an estimate of more than 200; presumably this rise in numbers was at least partly the result of recent rains. No measures have yet been taken to protect this little-known species, which ICBP lists as Endangered.

Another gravely threatened island species is the **Freira** *Pterodroma madeira*. Only a very few pairs of these gadfly-petrels are known to nest on the island of **Madeira**, where they make their burrows in inland cliffs in the mountainous region around Pico do Cedro. They are constantly threatened by collectors of birds and eggs but chiefly by rats. The exact breeding site is kept secret and rat poison is set out in the vicinity, but breeding continues to fail and extinction is now very close at hand. The species is listed as Endangered.

The **Gon-gon** *Pterodroma feae* breeds on Bugio off Madeira and on some of the Cape Verde islands, and has a total population of only a few hundred. It is assumed formerly to have nested in burrows in the floor of mountain woods, but all the woodland has now gone and it has adapted to nesting in rubble, scree, turf and cracks in rocky outcrops. The introduction of cats, rats and other mammals limits the species to inaccessible areas. Even so the species has been, and indeed still is, exploited for food. The species is classified as Rare by ICBP.

The **Madeira Laurel Pigeon** *Columba trocaz*, listed as Rare, is confined to the dense laurel forests in the northern part of Madeira. At the time of first settlement in the mid-fifteenth century it was exceptionally plentiful; in fact the pigeons were so common and tame they could be snared off branches with ease. This persecution and destruction of their forest has reduced their numbers to something over 500 today. Regrettably hunting is still permitted as it is claimed that the pigeon damages crops.

The related **Dark-tailed Laurel Pigeon** *Columba bollii* and **White-tailed Laurel Pigeon** *C. junoniae* from the

Madeira Laurel Pigeon

Fuerteventura Stonechat

laurel forests on Tenerife, La Palma, Gomera and Hierro in the **Canary Islands** are also in trouble and listed as Rare. However, much of the remaining forest is now protected and hunting has been prohibited since 1973.

The **Fuerteventura Stonechat** *Saxicola dacotiae* is confined to Fuerteventura in the Canary Islands. It occurs throughout the island, but only locally where there is suitable habitat of rocky slopes and reasonably developed scrub. Predation by introduced mammals (cats, rats and hedgehogs) and the expansion of tourism resulting in disturbance and habitat loss are considered the principal threats. The total population is in the order of 850 birds and the species is classified as Rare.

The **Blue Chaffinch** *Fringilla teydea* is confined to pine forests on Gran Canaria and Tenerife in the Canary Islands. Although not currently known to be at risk, the species is listed as Rare because of the differing impressions of its abundance to different observers. About a century ago the market in specimens was so great that shooting on a large scale by local people was considered likely to exterminate it. The species was also trapped and commonly kept as a cage-bird until at least 1956. Now the Blue

Chaffinch is fully protected by law and showing signs of recovery. Replanting of pines on Tenerife in the mid-1950s led to several tens of thousands of hectares being reafforested, and this must have been instrumental in the species's maintenance of numbers.

On the remote South Atlantic island of **St. Helena** is a small population of very distinctive plovers with long, slender legs. These are **St. Helena Plovers** *Charadrius sanctaehelenae*. Little is known about them except that their population does not exceed 200–300. They are believed to be suffering competition for food by the very numerous introduced Indian Mynahs *Acridotheres tristis*. ICBP lists the species as Rare.

The entire breeding population of **Ascension Frigatebird** *Fregata aquila*, estimated at around 5,000 birds, can be found on the tiny Boatswainbird Islet off **Ascension Island**. In the eighteenth century the species is reported to have bred in huge numbers on Ascension Island itself, but rapidly died out there following human settlement and the advent of cats in 1815. Because of the vulnerability of the species, pleasure boat trips to the islet have been prohibited. Cat eradication programmes have been suggested for Ascension Island in the hope that it will be recolonised, not only by the Frigatebird but by other seabird species too. The Ascension Frigatebird is classified as Rare.

The **Tristan da Cunha** group of islands harbours a number of endemics, which are especially threatened by the possibility of mammalian introductions and all have Rare status. The **Inaccessible Rail** *Atlantisia rogersi*, for instance, is currently numerous but, being flightless, would fall easy prey to cats and rats. The **Tristan Bunting** *Nesospiza acunhae* is at present widespread on Inaccessible, Nightingale, Middle and Stoltenhoff Islands and numbers several thousand birds. However it once occurred on Tristan da Cunha and became extinct in under 56 years, probably from habitat alteration—the almost complete extermination of tussock-grass, illustrating clearly the vulnerability of these island species. A second bunting from this area is the **Grosbeak Bunting** *N. wilkinsi*, restricted to woodland on Nightingale and Inaccessible Islands. The total population of this species numbers in the low hundreds giving it a very precarious existence.

Amsterdam Albatross

Gough Island lies to the south-east of the Tristan da Cunha group and also harbours a flightless rail, the **Gough Moorhen** *Gallinula comeri*, estimated to have a population of 2,000–3,000 pairs. The endemic passerine, the **Gough Bunting** *Rowettia goughensis*, may only number 200 pairs. Once again these birds are threatened by potential introductions of cats and rats, the likelihood of this having increased since the establishment of a permanent manned weather station. Both species are classified as Rare.

Amsterdam Island is an isolated wind-swept lava cone north of the Antarctic Convergence and nearer to South Africa than to Western Australia. Here in the late 1970s French ornithologists discovered the breeding grounds of a new species, since named the **Amsterdam Albatross** *Diomedea amsterdamensis*. The colony is small, only about 30–50 birds including immatures, and is producing only one to eight chicks a year. Judging by the accumulated bones on the plateau, the population was once larger than it is today. The island has been seriously despoiled and there are rats, cats and feral cattle on it. The species is listed by ICBP as Endangered.

ADDITIONAL CANDIDATE BIRDS OF AFRICA'S ISLANDS

LARIDAE Gulls, terns
Kerguelen Tern *Sterna virgata* breeds on the islands of Prince Edward, Crozet and Kerguelen in the southern Indian Ocean. The largest colonies, 2,000 pairs, occur on Kerguelen and are vulnerable to predation from feral cats.

NECTARINIIDAE Sunbirds
Giant Sunbird *Dreptes thomensis* appears to be a low density species on the São Tomé.

ZOSTEROPIDAE White-eyes
Príncipe Speirops *Speirops leucophaeus* is a low density species on Príncipe.

ORIOLIDAE Orioles
Príncipe Drongo *Dicrurus modestus* is an extremely uncommon bird from Príncipe.

145

Chapter 6
The Oriental Region

The Oriental Region lies approximately between 68° and 135°E and between 10°S and 32°N. Its northern boundary, dividing it from the Palaearctic, runs from the Hindu Kush along the high barrier of the Himalayas through northern Burma to Yunnan and Sichuan in China, then along the valley of the Chang Jiang River and the frontier of Manchuria to the East China Sea. In the west it runs southward to the west of the valley of the Indus River in Pakistan, around the west coast of India and Sri Lanka and south-east across the Bay of Bengal to include Burma, Malaysia, Sumatra and Borneo, where the boundary swings north-east through the Indonesian islands. According to Alfred Russel Wallace the demarcation between Oriental and Australasian bird species was a line drawn between the islands of Bali and Lombok and northwards between Borneo and Sulawesi, where the species of the two regions mingled in about equal proportions. Later opinion, however, has abandoned the so-called 'Wallace Line' in favour of one further east, along the Molucca Passage between Sulawesi and the northern Molucca Islands, then northwards around the Philippines, but (except for the Ryukyu archipelago) excluding Japan, which clearly belongs to the Palaearctic Region. It is a fascinating experience to follow in Wallace's footsteps from Java along the 1,700 km of the Indonesian island chain to West Irian in New Guinea and to observe the transition from Indo-Malayan species of birds to those with obvious Australo-Papuan affinities, such as the Mallee-fowl and Cockatoo.

The vegetation of the Oriental Region is broadly classified as tropical forest. In Pakistan, north-west India and parts of China there are large areas of steppe and desert. The great coniferous forests on the slopes of the Himalayas give way to mixed subtropical forests in the foothills and then to the rich lowland terai, now largely cultivated. From the foothills through Bhutan, Assam and the Bangladesh Hill Tracts is (or was) tropical rain-forest, stretching east and south throughout most of the remainder of South-East Asia and the Indonesian islands. The Indian subcontinent is more varied. To the south of the Nepalese terai is the great alluvial Gangetic Plain, one of the most densely populated regions in the world. Further south is peninsular India and the Deccan Plateau. Alongs its western coast is the long range of the Western Ghats, with a narrow strip of tropical rain-forest on its seaward side and a smaller and more interrupted forested range, the Eastern Ghats, down the eastern shore. The enormous Sundarbans delta of the Ganges and

Brahmaputra, stretching from Calcutta eastwards across Bangladesh, is the largest area of mangrove forest in the world. Some of the world's greatest rivers are in the Oriental Region, such as the Indus in Pakistan, the Ganges and Brahmaputra in India, the Irrawaddy and Salween in Burma, the Mekong in Indo-China and the Chang Jiang in China. All life in India and South-East Asia is governed by the vagaries of the monsoon, which sweeps back and forth between the Indian Ocean and the weather-barrier of the Himalayas. Sometimes it capriciously misses some areas, condemning them to devastating drought, while depositing on others between one-and-a-half and ten metres of torrential rain every year. Migratory birds time their arrival to coincide with the monsoon and the explosive abundance of insects and fresh vegetation which it brings.

The rain-forests of southern Asia, like those in the Amazon basin, are rich in bird species and in variety of vegetation. In Malaysia alone there are 2,000 different species of trees. The now widespread felling of these forests is having a terrible effect on all wildlife, including the majority of the 1,500 species of birds of the Oriental Region. China has removed vast areas of forest in order to increase its agricultural output, and thousands of square kilometres of rice-paddies have replaced forests throughout much of South-East Asia. Following the felling, the litter is usually burnt, causing further losses. In Indonesia, for example, 35,000 sq km of primary forest and a large national park were recently destroyed by a fire which got out of hand. Wherever forests have been clear-felled, soil-erosion follows and ground temperatures rise steeply. Millions of tonnes of precious top-soil are washed into the valleys by the monsoon rains, choking water-courses and causing serious flooding. What is left behind is often semi-desert in which only coarse grasses and creeping vines can grow. A crop or two can be raised by subsistence farmers in the ash left by the forest fire, but soon after that no nutrients remain in the soil.

Nevertheless, in spite of these ecological tragedies, conservation is now making progress in the Oriental Region. India and Indonesia are particularly active, with major conservation programmes involving heavy expenditure. India already has 52 national parks and 223 wildlife reserves of various kinds. Pakistan, India, Nepal and Bhutan have created a number of Himalayan reserves to protect high-altitude wildlife and several captive-breeding projects are in hand in an attempt to restore some of the rarest species of pheasants and ducks. There are wildlife reserves in Malaysia, Thailand, many Indonesian islands, Kampuchea, Vietnam, Korea, Laos, Hong Kong, China and the Philippines, and some of these countries are now signatories of CITES. Only Burma, which is still preoccupied with northern and southern tribal conflicts, has not yet joined the international conservation movement, although it is already co-operating with IUCN in restoring and managing its economically important elephant population. In all the other countries ICBP and WWF are working in close harmony with the governments and with numerous local natural history societies.

As will be seen in the following pages, conservation may be too late to save some of the endemic bird species of the region. There is an urgent need for exploration and research to ascertain the present status and distribution of many species about which nothing whatever has been heard for upwards of fifty years, particularly in China and the war-ravaged regions of South-East Asia. Fortunately, access to these countries is again possible, if often still difficult.

Abbott's Booby *Sula abbotti* is classified as Endangered. It breeds on the isolated Australian territory of Christmas Island in the Indian Ocean, where its population is estimated at a maximum of 2,000 breeding pairs. The species lays one egg every 2 years and does not breed until it is 5 to 6 years old, so recruitment to the already tiny population is slow. In addition to its low reproductive potential, the areas of rain-forests it selects for nesting coincide with rich phosphate deposits, and since 1965 there has been large scale extraction. As a result of mining activities much of the booby's habitat has been bulldozed into a moonscape. In an effort to save the species the National Park, created in 1980, has been extended to encompass about 30% of the nesting sites. However, one can only speculate as to whether a reduced population will be a viable one in the long term.

The **Christmas Frigatebird** *Fregata andrewsi* also breeds on Christmas Island, and although it was suspected of breeding on the Anambas Islands in Indonesia there is little evidence in support of this latter location. The current population is estimated at less than 1,600 pairs and none of the three colonies in which it is known to breed is protected. It is therefore greatly at risk from habitat destruction, disturbance and poaching. It is listed by ICBP as Vulnerable.

The **White-bellied Heron** *Ardea imperialis* (Plate XXI) is possibly very close to extinction. It is now recognized as extremely rare throughout its range in Nepal, Assam, Bangladesh and Burma and is too large to have been easily overlooked. Very few living ornithologists have seen it. It is a Candidate Red Data Book species.

The **Milky Stork** *Mycteria cinerea* is threatened throughout its range by habitat destruction and, in some countries, also by trapping for food. Its range is from western peninsular Malaysia to Sumatra and Java, where it has some protection in reserves. Its population was recently estimated at only 1,000 birds. The bulk of its breeding population is in Sumatra, the birds then dispersing to Java. After the Vietnam War it became very rare there. It is officially protected in Malaysia, although the forest tribes are permitted to kill it for food; a recent expedition found no immature birds there. Trappers also take it for food in Java. The military devastation and napalm bombing in Vietnam, and Kampuchea undoubtedly caused losses. The species is listed by ICBP as Vulnerable.

Storm's Stork *Ciconia stormi* is scarce but probably widespread in south-east Sumatra and Kalimantan in Indonesia. There are recent records from Malaysia and a breeding record from Thailand but

Christmas Frigatebird

no significant populations are likely to exist on the peninsular. It is restricted to forested wetlands and once the land is cleared is replaced by the Woolly-necked Stork *C. episcopus*. It is classified as Indeterminate.

The **White-shouldered Ibis** *Pseudibis davisoni* is another likely casualty of the Vietnam War. Although once widespread in Burma, Thailand, Kampuchia, Laos and southern Vietnam, its population has been seriously reduced. Precise details are lacking, but the prolonged hostilities in most of its range have undoubtedly affected it. Most of the human population, deprived of cereal harvests for several years, have had to eat whatever could be found and this conspicuous bird was an easy target. It is possible that some survive in the less populated areas of the Mekong River and in Kalimantan, where it was seen recently. There are also unconfirmed reports of it still breeding in Thailand, the only country where it is legally protected from hunting or capture. Its status is given by ICBP as Indeterminate.

The **Giant Ibis** *Pseudibis gigantae* also formerly occurred in the Mekong River basin in South-East Asia. This shy ibis has always been scarce, but agricultural development and the hostilities in much of its range must have made it more so. It is almost certainly extinct in Thailand and its status is not known in Laos or Kampuchea. The only recent records are from southern Vietnam. It is listed as Rare, but the most recent evidence suggests it deserves Endangered status.

One of the world's rarest ducks is the **White-winged Wood Duck** *Cairina scutulata*. It was formerly fairly common in north-eastern India, the Bangladesh Hill Tracts, Burma, western Thailand, western peninsular Malaysia, Sumatra and Java. Both its range and population have been greatly reduced, due to the extensive destruction of its habitat, increased hunting, the pollution of water sources and the isolation of its very small surviving populations. It present numbers are critically small. There are perhaps 15 pairs in protected forest in Assam, a small group in the Chittagong Hill Tracts of Bangladesh and an unknown number in Burma. It is also reported to have small numbers in nine or ten localities in Sumatra, including Siberut Island. The most promising recent report is of at least four birds seen in 1985 in the Padang-Sugihan Reserve. Its total population is probably not more than 200 pairs. Captive breeding has been successfully established by the Wildfowl Trust in England and eggs are being sent for hatching in Thailand. A reintroduction programme could succeed if a sufficient number of fully protected reserves with suitable habitat could be found. At present only those in Assam are functioning. The species is legally protected in India and Indonesia. It is listed by ICBP as Vulnerable.

The most important rare bird in the Philippines is undoubtedly the **Philippine Eagle** *Pithecophaga jefferyi*. This large and powerful bird is under severe pressure from shooting, trapping and the progressive felling of its dipterocarp forest habitat. It once bred on the islands of Samar, Luzon, Leyte, Mindanao, a small island in the Surigas Strait and

Maleo

possibly Negros. It is now known only in the forests of Mindanao, (its main stronghold), Luzon, Samar and Leyte, although this latter population is likely to die out soon. In 1910 there were 1,200 of them in Mindanao alone. Its population is still declining in spite of considerable efforts to educate the forest people not to shoot or harass it. A careful census in 1973 suggested a possible total of 309 birds and an annual loss by shooting or trapping of 5–10%. The loss of habitat is certainly much greater; in 1910 65% of Mindanao was forested, but by 1973 only 30% of the island was still a suitable forest habitat and about 650 sq km are still being felled every year; the losses from shooting and trapping also continue. This magnificent eagle is fully protected by law and its capture for zoos is strictly controlled. Eighteen of them are held in captivity by the Philippines Parks and Wildlife Service for breeding and return to the wild, but the species has never yet been successfully bred in captivity anywhere. Considerable sums from the United States and Europe have been spent on this project. It now seems that much of the money may have been wasted. First the breeding installation was attacked and robbed by guerillas. President Marcos then suddenly sold half of the essential forests to land speculators and halved the government grant

to the project. The enclosures became little more than repositories for locally confiscated eagles. It remains to be seen how the recent change of government in the Philippines will affect the project. The total population of the species in the wild has dropped to about 300. It is listed by ICBP as Endangered.

About 13 colonies of **Maleo** *Macrocephalon maleo* (a member of the megapode family), totalling perhaps 5,000 birds, nest regularly on the sand beaches or in forest clearings of Sulawesi, burying their eggs one metre deep, leaving them to be incubated by the sun or by subterranean hot-springs. Egg harvesting by the local natives is still a serious problem though now being reduced by paid guards. Existing new reserves are being given improved protection and it is planned to established a system of hatcheries in which the eggs can be allowed to develop without interference. The species is listed by ICBP as Vulnerable.

The most spectacular birds of the Oriental Region are its many species of pheasants, most of which are now rare, although familiar in collections in many countries. They are shot and trapped for food by hill tribesmen and harassed by commercial collectors, but the destruction of the forests they occupy is the main threat to their survival.

A typical example is the **Cheer**

Pheasant *Catreus wallichi*. It is endangered throughout most of its range, which is the Himalayan foothills from Hazara in northern Pakistan through Kashmir and northern India to Nepal and perhaps Bhutan. It may already be extinct in Pakistan and Azad Kashmir, but appears to be holding its own in Nepal. It is protected by some reserved forests in northern India, but poaching still occurs in these areas. The results of attempted reintroductions in the states of Himachal Pradesh and Uttar Pradesh are not yet documented. Eggs have also been supplied by the World Pheasant Association (UK) to Pakistan, where captive-breeding and release are being tried. Some birds have been released in the Margalla Hills National Park near Islamabad and in the Malkandi Forest of the Kaghan Valley in Hazara. The Cheer is protected by law in Pakistan and is listed by ICBP as Endangered.

Swinhoe's Pheasant *Lophura swinhoii* is unique to Taiwan. It inhabits the hardwood forests and also some secondary growth on the slopes of the central, northern and eastern mountains of the island, where it is under considerable pressure from the commercial pheasant-trappers, though this is now declining. Its population of a few thousand birds is diminishing as its preferred habitat disappears, but like the Mikado Pheasant *Syrmaticus mikado* (see below) which shares the same island and is also threatened, it might be adaptable to change. There is, however, much disturbance from the expansion of agriculture, forestry, mining, tourism and hydro-electric development, all of which affect the species. It is protected by Taiwan law and its export is prohibited. Further protection is provided by a ban on hunting and by a large reserve which was created primarily for the Mikado Pheasant. A number of captive-bred Swinhoe's from the Pheasant Trust in England have been successfully released in the Che Chi experimental forest belonging to the National Taiwan University. The species is treated by ICBP as Vulnerable.

A much more threatened species is **Elliot's Pheasant** *Syrmaticus ellioti* of the forested mountains of eastern China. It formerly ranged from Jiangxi, southern Anhui, Zhejiang and Fujian to northern Guangdong, but its distribution is now much reduced. It has also suffered from great losses of habitat and uncontrolled hunting. No recent information about its numbers or distribution is available, though it is reported to be plentiful where suitable habitat exists. No part of its range is protected. There are, however, 1,500 Elliot's Pheasants in captivity in various countries and wild-caught birds are common in zoos. It is hoped to organise a captive-breeding project if suitable protected habitat can be found within the range of the species. ICBP lists it as Endangered.

The **Mikado Pheasant** *Syrmaticus mikado*, which is found only in Taiwan, is still fairly widespread in the central mountains. In spite of the pressures it shares with Elliot's Pheasant it is apparently maintaining a stable population of a few thousand birds. It appears to be unusually adaptable to man-made changes to its habitat. The Taiwan Government created a 3,680 hectare high-altitude reserve to protect it and the equally vulnerable Swinhoe's Pheasant in 1970. Three additional reserves have been proposed. The Mikado is legally protected in Taiwan where its export was banned in 1974. It is listed by ICBP as Vulnerable.

Hume's Pheasant *Syrmaticus humiae* is a Rare species of the same genus as Elliot's and Mikado Pheasant. It is found in northern Burma and adjacent hill country in southern China and in north-east India. No population estimates have been made, but enquiries in Burma indicate that the species may be more abundant than hitherto believed. Although trapping may have had deleterious effects in some areas, in others it is still found in considerable numbers.

The striking **Cabot's Tragopan** *Tragopan caboti* is also threatened. It is confined to the mountain forests and above the tree-line in the four provinces of Fujian, Guangdong, Jianxi and Hunan in south-eastern China, where it is declining and now very scarce. The extensive destruction of the forests and constant human persecution have been responsible for its now precarious state. The species is nominally protected by Chinese law, but there is little enforcement in the remote regions inhabited by this bird. The Pheasant Trust in England is planning a programme of captive breeding and release if a suitably protected and appropriate area of habitat can be found within the range of the species. It is listed by ICBP as Endangered.

The **White Eared Pheasant** *Crossoptilon crossoptilon* is distributed in small numbers over a very wide range, from northern Assam and eastern Tibet through northern Burma to western China. There are very few recent reports on its status and it is regarded as Vulnerable. Significantly it is rarely offered for sale to foreign collectors. There are no hunting restrictions in most of its range and it is protected only in Tibet, on religious grounds. The new reserve in the Mishmi Hills in northern Assam and several in Bhutan may provide some protection for the species. Attempts at captive breeding are being made by the Jersey Wildlife Preservation Trust, but as more than 200 of these birds held in European and North American collections are descended from this stock the

problem of in-breeding will be difficult to overcome without new stock from the wild.

Sclater's Monal *Lophophorus sclateri* replaces the Himalayan Monal *L. impejanus* of the western Himalayas from Assam and south-east Tibet eastwards through northern Burma to western Yunnan in southern China. It was regarded as rare in 1910 and is undoubtedly much more so today. Trappers in Assam are no longer able to find it, but a report in 1968 stated that it was still quite common at elevations of 2,400 to 2,750 metres in some parts of northern Burma. This area is now inaccessible to ornithologists because of tribal hostilities and no further information has been obtained. South-eastern Tibet, northern Burma and south-west China have, in fact, remained a *terra incognita* for the past 50 years and are in urgent need of exploration by ornithologists. Meanwhile, Sclater's Monal is classified by ICBP as Rare. If it still survives in Assam, the new Mishmi Hills Reserve may provide some protection.

The **Crested Argus** *Rheinardia ocellata* occurs in dense undergrowth in the forests of Vietnam, Laos and peninsular Malaysia. Throughout these countries there has been very extensive logging and, in the first two, also prolonged hostilities and shortages of food which has affected the survival of all pheasants. This species has some protection in the Taman Negara National Park in Malaysia, where it is still fairly numerous. It is listed by ICBP as Rare.

The island of Borneo (which is now Indonesian Kalimantan except for the north-west which belongs to Malaysia as Sabah and Sarawak, plus the small independent state of Brunei) is the home of the **Bulwer's Pheasant** *Lophura bulweri*. It is still fairly widespread, although only locally distributed in the submontane primary forests of Kalimantan, Sabah and Sarawak. Until 1974 its range appeared to be unaltered, but its numbers are now diminishing because of the extensive felling of forests. One third of the big Kutai National Park in Kalimantan has already been deforested and oil exploration is in progress there. By 1980 nearly all of Sabah's magnificent forests except the Mount Kinabalu and Palau Gaya National Parks had been felled. By 1995 all those in Kalimantan will have been converted to agriculture or secondary growth, though the outlook is less bleak in Sarawak and Brunei. However, thanks to the efforts of the Indonesian branch of WWF, a protected highland forest reserve called the Bukit Raya is being planned for central Kalimantan; this would include Mount Gunung Bodang which has a population of these pheasants. The species has no legal protection but still has some safety in the reserves mentioned above. ICBP lists it as Vulnerable.

Edwards's Pheasant *Lophura edwardsi* is found only in Vietnam where it is rare and very localised. It is now apparently restricted to the area of Quang Tri, Hue and Hoi An, just south of the former demarcation line between former North and South Vietnam. There is no recent evidence of any alteration in range. Information about this elusive species is difficult to obtain. A report in 1975 stated that it was still thriving in secondary growth following the defoliation of forests by the US Army during the Vietnam War. Many were killed for food by military personnel on both sides. A studbook of all those in captivity is kept by the World Pheasant Association and it is hoped to release captive-bred birds in Vietnam. The species is listed by ICPB as Vulnerable.

A near neighbour of Edwards's Pheasant is the **Imperial Pheasant** *Lophura imperialis*, listed as Vulnerable, which is also restricted to the area of the Vietnam demarcation line and the neighbouring forests of Laos. It has been recorded in Dong Hoi Province (formerly North Vietnam) and Quang Tri (formerly South Vietnam), also in the adjacent part of Laos. Access to these areas has for many years been restricted by the military situation and by the very rugged, densely vegetated terrain. The Imperial's present population is not known, but believed to be small. Food shortage during the war greatly increased the hunting pressure. Both the Imperial and Edwards's Pheasants obviously suffered losses from the defoliant spraying in the area of the demilitarised zone. It is ironic that the zone now serves as an unintentional protected area for both species where any trespasser can be shot on sight by trigger-happy sentries! The small captive stocks held in collections are likely to die out unless fresh blood can be obtained from the wild.

Edwards's Pheasant

There are three subspecies of the **Green Peafowl** *Pavo muticus*. The nominate race is restricted to Java and peninsular Malaysia as far north as the Isthmus of Kra; in Java it is now known only in the Udjung Kulon and Baluran reserves and in Malaysia its presence is in doubt. The subspecies *P. m. imperator* formerly had a wide range, occuring throughout Indo-China, southern Yunnan in China, Thailand north of the Isthmus of Kra and southern Burma. Intensive searches in Thailand between 1972 and 1974 failed to find it except in the Petchabun Range and along the Burmese border. Its distribution in Indo-China is probably similarly reduced. There is no recent information from Yunnan or Burma, but it is certainly persecuted there. The third race, *P. m. spicifer*, has disappeared from the Chittagong and Lushai hills of Bangladesh, Manipur and Assam where it used to occur, but it probably still survives in

Green Peafowl

small numbers in western Burma. Loss of habitat to cultivation, combined with hunting, have caused serious declines in numbers in all three races. The species is legally protected in Indonesia, Malaysia and Thailand. The populations in the Udjung Kulon and Baluran reserves are well protected and stable; a reported population in the national park on Terutao Island (Indonesia) should also be secure. The Green Peafowl is plentiful in collections. It is listed by ICBP as Vulnerable.

The **Palawan Peacock-pheasant** *Polyplectron emphanum* is a Vulnerable status pheasant restricted to the island of Palawan in the Philippines. Although totally protected by law, it has been widely trapped for food and for export to aviculturists. The coastal primary forests which the pheasant inhabits appear to be doomed, and so if this pheasant is to survive it will have to adapt to scrub and cut-over forest.

Blyth's Tragopan *Tragopan blythi* (Plate XXII) inhabits the thick, damp forests of Tibet, Assam, Bhutan and Burma. Although in a few parts of its range it is apparently still locally fairly common, it is hunted excessively and is listed by ICBP as Rare.

Last of this lamentably long list of threatened Oriental pheasants is the superbly colourful **Western Tragopan** *Tragopan melanocephalus* of the western Himalayas. This magnificent bird, amongst the most arboreal of pheasants, has been nearly exterminated by excessive hunting, collecting, forest destruction and disturbance by humans and their herds of goats. It now survives in only a few localities. The species's range is divided into small isolated populations, probably numbering no more than 100 each. The total population is unlikely to exceed 5,000 birds, and could be as low as 1,600. Its former range was from

Swat in the Pakistan Himalayas east-wards to the Bhagirathi River in Tehri Garhwal, India. It was recorded in Himachal Pradesh State until 1969 and was recently seen in Azad Kashmir and the adjacent area of northern Kashmir. There have also been records from Hazara, Indus Kohistan and the rugged Hunza region of Gilgit. None of these sightings suggested numerous popula-tions. In 1977 and 1978 a serious attempt to estimate the size of the population was made in Pakistan and Azad Kashmir. This provided proof that the species is now very rare. Its last stronghold appears to be the Neelum and Jhelum valleys in Azad Kashmir. About 12 males were heard calling in the Salkhala Reserve and six were flushed within 31 sq km; nine were also flushed in the Kuttan Reserve and a few in the Machiara National Park. All these places are in the Neelum Valley. The Gilgit population is thought to be very small. In Himachal Pradesh 22 birds had been sighted in 1969. Small numbers are believed to survive in Hazara Kohistan and the Duber Valley in Swat. The typical habi-tat was found to be rhododendron, bam-boo and other dense vegetation in con-iferous or oak forests at between 2,400 and 3,600 metres elevation, the birds moving lower to 2,000 metres in winter. Parts of this habitat are within protected reserves. The Pakistan National Wildlife Council has set up facilities for raising nestlings from eggs taken in the wild for later release and a similar project exists in Himachal Pradesh in India. Both are supported by WWF. No captive stocks are held in other countries. The Western Tragopan is protected by law in India and Pakistan and is listed by ICBP as Endangered.

Very few birds have lost 98.3% of their former geographical distribution and still survived, yet this is what has happened to one of the world's largest flighted birds, the **Great Indian Bustard** *Ardeotris nigriceps*. Its range once span-ned most of Pakistan and India and in some regions it was sufficiently numer-ous for a single Indian hunter to have claimed to have shot 961 of these great birds between 1808 and 1829 in the Ahmadnagar district alone. Today it is found regularly only in lowland and semi-arid plains in Rajasthan and in a few small areas in the states of Gujarat, Madhya Pradesh and Maharashtra. Its total population is probably fewer than 1,000, although difficult to estimate because small numbers often wander widely in winter, even occasionally into eastern Pakistan. The large areas of un-disturbed grassland essential to the spe-cies are now exceedingly rare in India and there is constant disturbance by domestic cattle and agriculture. Poaching in protected areas is common-place by nomads and town-dwellers, often using bullock-carts to stalk the unsuspecting birds. The Great Indian Bustard has legal protection in every state where it still occurs, but enforce-ment is very difficult. Reserves such as the Jaisalmer Desert National Park have been created for it and the guard-force is to be increased. It is classified by ICBP as Endangered.

The floricans belong to the bustard family and are miniatures of their much larger relatives. There are two species, both endemic to the Indian subconti-nent. They are difficult to observe in their long-grass habitat except when the males are doing their jumping courtship display. For this reason they have been somewhat neglected by ornithologists and it was only recently that it was realised how rare they had become. The **Lesser Florican** *Sypheotides indica* is the most widely distributed of the two and until 1980 was believed to be still fairly plentiful in the grasslands of the Deccan in peninsular India, where in the old days it used to be shot by the hundred as a very tasty gamebird. In 1981 a careful survey was conducted which showed that the species had suffered a dramatic decline and that its grassland habitat had all but disappeared, having been converted to growing various crops. The main breeding areas are now in parts of Maharashtra, Madhya Pradesh and Haryana States and in the Kathiawar peninsula of Gujarat. In the winter a few birds wander as far as the Nepalese terai and the Mekran coast in Baluchistan. Although now very scarce, they are still occasionally shot or netted. It has been recommended that the Lesser Florican should be moved from Schedule 4 of the Indian Wildlife (Protection) Act of 1972 to Schedule 1. It is a Red Data Book Candidate species.

The larger **Bengal Florican** *Houbaropsis bengalensis* (Plate XXI) has become even more scarce and may now be on the verge of extinction. It used to occupy a fairly wide range from the Nepalese terai through Bhutan and Assam to Bengal and Uttar Pradesh. A few birds were found in the 1920s in Indo-China, but

their breeding grounds remain unknown and very possibly no longer exist. Most of the species's long-grass habitat has now been claimed for agriculture and the species is believed to occur only in a very few parts of the Nepalese terai and in reserves in Assam such as Kaziranga, Dudhwa and Manas. There may be some in Thailand and Burma. The total population is believed not to exceed 100 in Nepal and perhaps a total of 300–400 elsewhere. It is a Red Data Book Candidate species.

The **Javan Wattled Lapwing** *Vanellus macropterus* used to be found in Java, Sumatra and Timor, but its present distribution is unknown. All the cultivated lowland areas in these islands where it might be expected to occur are subjected to constant trapping and hunting and the species may now be extinct. It has not been seen since 1940, although frequently looked for. For the last 100 years it was regarded as rare. Its status is given by ICBP as Indeterminate.

Jerdon's Courser *Cursorius bitorquatus* is a rare and very elusive fast-running bird of the dense scrub jungle, found only in the Godavari River region of Andra Pradesh in India. It was known

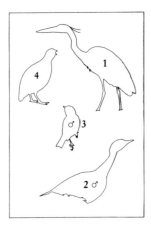

PLATE XXI Indian Grassland. 1 White-bellied Heron (p. 148), 2 Bengal Florican (p. 156), 3 White-browed Bushchat (p. 163), 4 Swamp Partridge (p. 164).

PLATE XXII Burmese Forest. 1 Beautiful Nuthatch (p. 172), 2 Blyth's Tragopan (p. 154), 3 Green Cochoa (p. 169), 4 Rufous-necked Hornbills (p. 168).

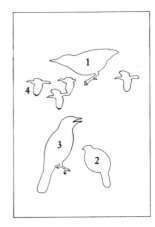

Norman Arlott 87

Norman Arlott 87

Norman Arlott, 87

to the early ornithologists, but by 1900 had seemingly disappeared and was listed in the last Red Data Book as Extinct. Eighty-five years later, after a long search, it was rediscovered by members of the Bombay Natural History Society. Part of the secret of the bird's elusiveness is that it has proved to be nocturnal. It is now on ICBP's list of Candidate Red Data Book species.

The **Negros Fruit Dove** *Ptilinopus arcanus* is known only from a specimen collected on Mount Canlaon, on Negros Island in the Philippines. Nothing is known of its present status and it is a Candidate Red Data Book species.

The majestic, arboreal and fruit-eating **Christmas Imperial Pigeon** *Ducula whartoni* is found only on the remote and once heavily forested Christmas Island, in the Indian Ocean. It is ruthlessly hunted and has suffered severely as a result of phosphate mining on the island, because the access roads which were constructed enabled hunters to invade its last sanctuary. It is planned to strip 30% of the island of all vegetation by 1994 to get at the phosphate. Most of the 3,000 human inhabitants will also be removed. In 1887 this fine pigeon was common. By 1974 only 100 survived, but it recovered slightly in 1977. It was given legal protection in the 1930s, but enforcement was impossible. It is still protected, but poaching is rampant in spite of the appointment of a Conservation Officer in 1975. The reserves which are now being created on the island to protect the habitat of the Endangered Abbott's Booby *Sula abbotti* will perhaps help the pigeons and also the Vulnerable Christmas Frigatebird *Fregata andrewsi* (see p. 148). The Imperial Pigeon is listed by ICBP as Vulnerable.

The continued existence of the **Forest Owlet** *Athene blewitti* has been tentatively supported by a recently published photograph, supposedly of the species, taken in 1968. It is known to have occurred in the past from the Tapti River, 200 km north of Bombay, eastward to Sambalpur, in Orissa, and was recently reported near Nagpur in Madhya Pradesh. It could not be found during a search of its presumed range in 1975 and 1976. Only six specimens have ever been collected, the last of these near Bombay in 1914. There is an obvious need to establish the status of this interesting species. It can easily be con-

PLATE XXIII Malaysian Forest. 1 Giant Pitta (p. 168), 2 Black Wood Partridge (p. 164), 3 Marbled Wren-babbler (p. 170).

PLATE XXIV Biak Island. 1 Biak White-eye (p. 194), 2 Biak Black Flycatcher (p. 194), 3 Biak Scops Owl (p. 193), 4 Biak Monarch (p. 194), 5 Biak Paradise Flycatcher (p. 193).

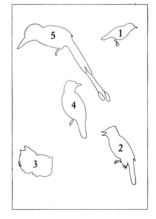

fused with the partly sympatric Spotted Little Owl. *A. brama*. ICBP give its status as Indeterminate.

The big **Helmeted Hornbill** *Rhinoplax vigil* is still fairly widespread in some parts of South-East Asia, but is heavily persecuted and its closed-canopy forest habitat is rapidly being destroyed. It is hunted by the forest tribes for food, for its feathers and for the bony casque on its bill as a material for carving. Its flesh is believed to have medicinal value (I ate one during the Burma Campaign when meat was very scarce and found it preferable to Python). Formerly it was common in the tropical forests of southern Burma, Malaysia, Thailand, Borneo and Sumatra. It has some protection in the various national parks and reserves in these countries, such as the Mount Kinabalu and Palau Gaya in Sabah and the Taman Negara in peninsular Malaysia, but in Kalimantan virtually all forests up to an altitude of 1,500 metres have been felled and most of those within the range of the species are due to be felled within the next 15 years. The Helmeted Hornbill is legally protected in Malaysia and Indonesia. Its status given by ICBP as Indeterminate.

The Second World War devastated the island of Okinawa, in the Ryukyu Islands to the south of Japan. It is surprising that the **Okinawa Woodpecker** *Sapheopipo noguchii* survived, but it still has a population of between 20 and 100 pairs inhabiting about 1,500 hectares of remaining hill forest. In 1973 it was declared a Natural Monument and a Special Bird for Protection. A small seven-hectare reserve containing two or three pairs of woodpeckers was created on Yonaha Mountain and small areas of forest are nominally protected on Ibu and Nashime Mountains. Much of the forest is used by the US Marines for training purposes which at least discour-

ages tree-felling by local residents but causes great disturbance. There has been some replanting with exotic tree species useless to the woodpeckers which require dense undergrowth and a debris-strewn forest floor with large old trees in which to nest. It is listed by ICBP as Endangered.

On the same island Japanese ornithologists recently discovered a new species, now named the **Okinawa Rail** *Rallus okinawae*. It occurs in the northern one-third of the island and is apparently adaptable to habitat disturbance. It is being closely studied and has been given protection. It is currently a Candidate species.

Gurney's Pitta *Pitta gurneyi* is at present the only one of the many attractive little short-tailed pittas of the Indo-Malayan region which is listed as threatened, though several others are now giving cause for concern. It was relatively common 50–100 years ago, but became increasingly rare as the lowland evergreen forests it inhabited in southern Burma and Thailand disappeared. Almost nothing now remains within its range. Six years of searching by local ornithologists were finally rewarded in 1986 when a nesting pair was found in Trang Province of Thailand. Strenuous efforts are now being made to save the last few patches of forest and to reduce the pressure of bird-catchers in the region. Its last ICBP status was Indeter-

Gurney's Pitta

minate, but recent developments show the species to be Endangered indeed perhaps the most threatened of all Oriental birds.

In 1968 a new species of martin was discovered wintering at Lake Boraphet in central Thailand. It was named the **White-eyed River Martin** *Pseudochelidon sirintarae*. The location of its breeding area is still unknown (south-west China, along one of the major rivers there has recently been suggested), as is the size of its population, so it was classified as Indeterminate. It was immediately put under legal protection in Thailand. There are plans to turn Lake Boraphet into a protected reserve, because at present bird-catchers net thousands of birds every year in the reed-beds. It is interesting that the only other member of this sub-family of the Hirundinidae, the Pseudochelidoninae, is the Zaire River Martin *P. eurystomina* from the Zaire River, 10,000 km away in west-central Africa.

The **White-browed Bushchat** *Saxicola macrorhyncha* (Plate XXI) used to occur in open, desert-like habitat in southern Afghanistan, Pakistan and northern India. Very little is known about it. It may no longer exist in Pakistan and there are very few recent records from India, where it was usually seen in habitat favoured by the Great Indian Bustard. I could not find it in Afghanistan in 1977, and it is currently a Candidate species.

The numerous species of babblers in Asia are often difficult to identify because of the dense vegetation most of them skulk in. This may explain why so little is known about some of them. One species is known only from a single specimen; the **Rusty-throated Wren-babbler** *Spelaeornis badeigularis* from the Mishmi Hills in north-east Assam.

The **Doubtful Leiothrix** *Leiothrix*

White-eyed River Martin

astleyi is known only from a pair of live birds shipped from an unknown locality in south-east China but its taxonomy is in doubt. Both are classified as Candidate Red Data Book species.

As recently as 1925 the very striking **Bali Starling** *Leucopsar rothschildi*, listed as Endangered, could still be seen in many parts of the island of Bali, in Indonesia. By 1967, after a careful search, the total population was put at 500–1,000 birds. Today the number is only about 180 and its distribution is reduced to a small north-eastern coastal part of this beautiful but over-populated island. Although now officially protected by Indonesian law, it is still extensively trapped for the cage-bird trade and is suffering increasingly from competition for nest-sites by the Black-winged Starling *Sturnus melanopterus*, which is spreading throughout the island. This invasive species has benefited from the human modification of the forests and is already three times more numerous than the Bali Starling. Part of its range is within the protected Bali-Barat National Park, where the government is planning to remove the 4,500 people living inside its boundaries. There are at least 700 in captivity in various countries and some birds have been released experimentally on the nearby island of Lokrum; however, two of the pairs soon moved back to Bali, suggesting that the habitat on Lokrum was insufficient.

ADDITIONAL CANDIDATE BIRDS OF THE ORIENTAL REGION

PELECANIDAE Pelicans
Spot-billed Pelican *Pelecanus philippensis* has suffered a serious decline in India and Burma, though its population in Sri Lanka may be stable.

ARDEIDAE Herons, bitterns
White-eared Night-heron *Gorsachius magnificus* is very little known and rare in densely forested mountains in south-east China. It breeds only in Hainan. Its preference for bamboo thickets makes it vulnerable to habitat destruction.

CICONIIDAE Storks
Greater Adjutant *Leptoptilos dubius* is a nomadic species but largely restricted to Burma in the breeding season, where the massive seasonal influxes reported last century no longer occur.

ACCIPITRIDAE Old World vultures, hawks, eagles
Nicobar Serpent-eagle *Spilornis klossi* is known from the Nicobar Islands where it is suffering from deforestation.
Kinabalu Serpent Eagle *Spilornis kinabaluensis* is only known from Sabah and Sarawak, Malaysia.
Dark Serpent Eagle *Spilornis elgini* is a little-known endemic resident of the Andaman Islands.
Small Sparrowhawk *Accipiter nanus* is believed to be scarce in mountain forest in Sulawesi, Indonesia.
Javan Hawk-eagle *Spizaetus bartelsi* is endemic to the forests of Java, Indonesia, there it is confined to a few forest reserves, probably as a consequence of the extreme trapping and hunting pressure it suffers in other areas.
Philippine Hawk-eagle *Spizaetus philippensis* is a scarce forest eagle from the Philippines.

MEGAPODIIDAE Megapodes
Nicobar Scrubfowl *Megapodius nicobariensis* is quite common on the Nicobar Islands but threatened by egg-collecting.
Sula Scrubfowl *Megapodius bernsteinii* is known from a few specimens from Banggai and Sula Islands in Indonesia.
Moluccan Scrubfowl *Megapodius wallacei* is known from some of the larger islands of the Moluccas, Indonesia, where it is probably vulnerable to egg-harvesting.

PHASIANIDAE Pheasants, quails, partridges
Swamp Partridge *Francolinus gularis* (Pl. XXI) occurs in north-east India, Nepal and Assam, has a similar habitat to the Bengal Florican (see page 156) and is possibly as scarce outside reserves such as the Sukla Phanta and Kaziranga.
Black Wood Partridge *Melanoperdix nigra* (Pl. XXIII) is confined to peninsular Malaysia, Sumatra and Borneo, where it is threatened by habitat destruction.
Manipur Bush Quail *Perdicula manipurensis* inhabits wet grassland, and sometimes swamps, in the hills of Assam and Manipur, India. It is believed to be getting scarcer.
White-cheeked Partridge *Arborophila atrogularis* from India and Burma inhabits lowland forest, a disappearing habitat.
Rickett's Partridge *Arborophila gingica* is confined to the wooded hills of south-east China, where little is known of it.
Orange-necked Partridge *Arborophila davidi* is known from one specimen collected near the city of Ho Chi Minh, Vietnam, in 1927.

Chestnut-headed Partridge
Arborophila cambodiana is known
from the mountains of south-east
Thailand, where one specimen was
described in 1930, and adjacent
Kampuchea.

White-eared Partridge *Arborophila
ardensis* is confined to the hills of the
island of Hainan, China.

Chestnut-necklaced Partridge
Arborophila charltonii is found in the
lowlands of peninsular Thailand and
Malaysia, Borneo and Sumatra.

Vietnam Pheasant *Lophura
hatinhensis* is a recently described
pheasant from the old demilitarised
zone of central Vietnam.

Crested Fireback *Lophura ignita* is
found in Burma, Thailand, Malaysia,
Sumatra and Borneo. It is confined to
level lowland forest, particularly along
river terraces, a habitat that is easily
logged.

Siamese Fireback *Lophura diardi* is
restricted to a narrow altitudinal zone
above lowland cultivation in Thailand,
Laos, Kampuchea and Vietnam.

Germain's Peacock-pheasant
Polyplectron germaini is a resident of
southern Vietnam and was, at least
formerly, common but its current
status is unknown.

Malaysian Peacock-pheasant
Polyplectron malacense is known from
South-East Asia and is threatened by
logging.

Bornean Peacock-pheasant
Polyplectron schleiermacheri has not
been recorded recently and is known
from only a few old records from
Kalimantan, Indonesia.

TURNICIDAE Buttonquails
Sumba Buttonquail *Turnix everetti* is
known from three specimens collected
on Sumba, Indonesia, in 1949. Its
status is unknown.

Worcester's Buttonquail *Turnix
worcesteri* from the Philippines remains
virtually unknown.

RALLIDAE Rails
Snoring Rail *Aramidopsis plateni* is an
elusive rail from Sulawesi, Indonesia.
All but one specimen were collected
over 40 years ago.

Bald-faced Rail *Gymnocrex rosenbergii*
is believed to be a rare rail of primary
forest on Sulawesi, Indonesia.

Invisible Rail *Habroptila wallacii* is a
rare rail confined to the dense thickets
of Halmahera, Indonesia.

HELIORNITHIDAE Finfoots
Masked Finfoot *Heliopais personata* is
a secretive bird and a rare resident of
Bangladesh, Assam and Manipur in
India and Burma.

SCOLOPACIDAE Snipes,
woodcocks, sandpipers
Sulawesi Woodcock *Scolopax celebensis*
is a little-known species of mountain
forest in Sulawesi, Indonesia.

Obi Woodcock *Scolopax rochussenii* is
confined to Obi Island in the
Moluccas, Indonesia.

Wood Snipe *Gallinago nemoricola* is
believed to breed only in wooded
habitats in the Himalayas, and outside
the breeding season is dispersed
sparingly through the hill ranges of
India and Pakistan.

COLUMBIDAE Pigeons, doves
Nilgiri Wood Pigeon *Columba
elphinstonii* is confined to the hill
forests in south-west India. It was not
seen during recent visits to the Western
Ghats and Nilgiri Hills.

Sri Lanka Wood Pigeon *Columba
torringtoni* is confined to the montane
forests in Sri Lanka, where it is
declining as its habitat is destroyed, or
replaced by eucalyptus or coniferous
plantations.

Pale-capped Wood Pigeon *Columba punicea* is known from few records from South-East Asia. Recent records are from Thailand only.

Grey Wood Pigeon *Columba argentina* is a small island species from Indonesia and Malaysia. Some of its islands are still forested and the species is assumed to survive.

Mindoro Bleeding-heart *Gallicolumba platenae* is endemic to Mindoro in the Philippines where its status is unknown.

Negros Bleeding-heart *Gallicolumba keayi* is endemic to Negros in the Philippines where its status is unknown.

Sulu Bleeding-heart *Gallicolumba menagei* is endemic to the Sulu archipelago in the Philippines. Its status is unknown but it is assumed to be scarce.

Wetar Ground Dove *Gallicolumba hoedtii* is a very rarely recorded species from Wetar and Timor, Indonesia.

Sumba Green Pigeon *Treron teysmanni* is found in the lowlands of Sumba, Indonesia, where its status is unknown.

Flores Green Pigeon *Treron floris* is widespread in the Lesser Sundas, Indonesia. It is uncommon on Flores and its status on the other islands is unknown.

Timor Green Pigeon *Treron psittacea* is restricted to a few remaining pockets of deciduous forest on Timor, Indonesia.

Large Green Pigeon *Treron capellei* is a scarce but widespread species of South-East Asia. It is largely restricted to lowland forest.

Red-naped Fruit Dove *Ptilinopus dohertyi* is believed to be threatened on Sumba, Indonesia, where it is endemic.

Flame-breasted Fruit Dove *Ptilinopus marchei* is scarce and local in stunted vegetation on mountain peaks on Luzon and Polillo Islands in the Philippines.

Mindoro Imperial Pigeon *Ducula mindorensis* is endemic to montane forest in Mindoro, Philippines, but there have been no records in the past few decades.

Spotted Imperial Pigeon *Ducula carola* from the Philippines is locally common at certain times of the year, but is generally poorly known.

PSITTACIDAE Lories, parrots, macaws

Red-and-blue Lory *Eos histrio* is known only from Taland and Sangihe Islands, and is threatened by the bird trade.

Purple-naped Lory *Lorius domicella* is found in mountain forest in Seram and Ambon, Indonesia, where it is considered uncommon.

Blue-fronted Lorikeet *Charmosyna toxopei* is known only from Buru, Indonesia, where its status is unknown.

Yellow-crested Cockatoo *Cacatua sulphurea* from Indonesia is in great demand as a cage-bird.

Salmon-crested Cockatoo *Cacatua moluccensis* has declined in recent years on Seram, Indonesia, and still faces considerable pressure from trapping.

White Cockatoo *Cacatua alba* is found on Halmahera and Obi, Indonesia, and is another species being heavily traded.

Red-vented Cockatoo *Cacatua haematuropygia* is largely restricted to remote coastal areas in Palawan, Philippines, where thousands are trapped each year for the markets.

Tanimbar Corella *Cacatua goffini* is common on Tanimbar, Indonesia, but threatened by the bird trade.

Green-crowned Racket-tailed Parrot *Prioniturus luconensis* from the Philippines is trapped for bird markets.

Blue-headed Racket-tailed Parrot *Prioniturus discurus* from the Philippines is also trapped for the bird markets.

Red-crowned Racket-tailed Parrot *Prioniturus montanus* is patchily distributed in the Philippines.

Wallace's Hanging Parrot *Loriculus flosculus* is endemic to Flores, Indonesia. It is described from a single specimen and has only been recorded once.

Sangihe Hanging Parrot *Loriculus catamene* is endemic to Sangihe, Indonesia, where the original vegetation has been almost completely replaced by cultivation.

Rothschild's Parakeet *Psittacula intermedia* was long described from seven specimens of uncertain origin, but recently one or two birds have appeared each year in bird markets in India.

Nicobar Parakeet *Psittacula caniceps* is restricted to forest on the Nicobar Islands, India.

CUCULIDAE Cuckoos

Green-cheeked Bronze Cuckoo *Chryococcyx rufomerus* is a very little-known bird of the Lesser Sundas, Indonesia.

Red-faced Malkoha *Phaenicophaeus pyrrhocephalus* is largely restricted to wet evergreen forest in Sri Lanka, and has declined markedly in recent years.

Sunda Ground Cukoo *Carpococcyx radiceus* has been recorded in Borneo and Sumatra, but could not be found in Sumatra during recent extensive searches.

Green-billed Coucal *Centropus chlororhynchus* is endemic to Sri Lanka and severely threatened by loss of habitat.

Steere's Coucal *Centropus steerii* is confined to deep forest on Mindoro, Philippines. There is little habitat left.

Javan Coucal *Centropus nigrorufus* is known from one site on the coast of

Java. Much of its habitat has been long usurped for fish ponds and paddy.

TYTONIDAE Barn owls

Taliabu Owl *Tyto nigrobrunnea* is known from a single specimen from Taliabu, Indonesia.

Minahassa Owl *Tyto inexspectata* is a little-known bird from Sulawesi, Indonesia.

Lesser Masked Owl *Tyto sororcula* is presumed to occur in lowland forest on Buru and Tanimbar, Indonesia.

STRIGIDAE Owls

White-fronted Scops Owl *Otus sagittatus* is found in Burma, Thailand, Malaysia and possibly Sumatra, mainly in lowland forest. There are few records of this species, but as the call is unknown there may be more than records suggest.

Sumatran Scops Owl *Otus stresemanni* is known from one specimen from Sumatra, Indonesia.

Javan Scops Owl *Otus angelinae* is known from only two localities in Java, Indonesia.

Flores Scops Owl *Otus alfredi* is known from three specimens from Flores, Indonesia, taken late last century.

Mindoro Scops Owl *Otus mindorensis* is known only from the type-specimen collected in 1896 on Mindoro in the Philippines.

Philippine Eagle Owl *Bubo philippensis* is little known but probably restricted to forest in the Philippines.

David's Owl *Strix davidi* is a recently revised taxonomic split. It has a tiny population in China.

PODARGIDAE Frogmouths

Dulit Frogmouth *Batrachostomus harterti* is a submontane species from Borneo known from few specimens.

CAPRIMULGIDAE Nightjars

Satanic Nightjar *Eurostopodus*

diabolicus is endemic to Sulawesi, Indonesia, and known only from the type-specimen.

Salvadori's Nightjar *Caprimulgus pulchellus* is a little-known montane species of Sumatra and Java, Indonesia.

APODIDAE Swifts

Giant Swiftlet *Hydrochous gigas* is found in peninsular Malaysia, Sumatra and Java. It is little known and seems scarce. It may have very specific breeding-site requirements.

Dark-rumped Swift *Apus acuticauda* is known from Nepal and Assam, where it has a very limited range with a small population.

ALCEDINIDAE Kingfishers

Blyth's Kingfisher *Alcedo hercules* is a widespread species in South-East Asia but known from few records.

Jungle Kingfisher *Ceyx melanurus* is apparently scarce in lowland forest in the Philippines.

Winchell's Kingfisher *Halcyon winchelli* is a poorly-known species from the Philippines.

Lazuli Kingfisher *Halcyon lazuli* is uncommon in the Lesser Sundas, Indonesia, where it inhabits mangroves and lowland swampy woodland.

Cinnamon-banded Kingfisher *Halcyon australasia* is a woodland species from the Lesser Sundas, Indonesia, where it is local.

Blue-capped Wood Kingfisher *Halcyon hombroni* from Mindanao, Philippines, has not been recorded since 1939.

BUCEROTIDAE Hornbills

Brown Hornbill *Ptilolaemus tickelli* is believed to occur in Assam, India, and in Burma, Laos and Vietnam. Although locally common, its distribution is imperfectly known.

Rufous-necked Hornbill *Aceros nipalensis* (Pl. XXII) occurs from Nepal and Bhutan to northern Indo-China. It is threatened by hunting and depletion of big-tree habitat.

Plain-pouched Hornbill *Aceros subruficollis* is an enigmatic species from South-East Asia. Its status remains essentially unknown.

Narcondam Hornbill *Aceros narcondami* is confined to the forest on Narcondam Island in the Andaman Islands. It has a small population but the island is not yet under threat.

Sumba Hornbill *Rhyticeros everetti* is a little-known bird endemic to Sumba Island in Indonesia. Little forest habitat is thought to remain. It is considered to be the most threatened of the hornbills.

Sulu Hornbill *Anthracoceros montani* is from the Sulu archipelago, Philippines, where the limited forest is probably disappearing.

CAPITONIDAE Barbets

Black-banded Barbet *Megalaima javensis* is locally distributed in the isolated pockets of forest that remain in the lowlands and hills of Java, Indonesia.

PICIDAE Woodpeckers

Red-collared Woodpecker *Picus rabieri* is believed to be scarce in forest in eastern Laos and Vietnam.

EURYLAIMIDAE Broadbills

Wattled Broadbill *Eurylaimus steeri* is from the Philippines. Although believed common earlier this century there appear to be few recent records.

PITTIDAE Pittas

Schneider's Pitta *Pitta schneideri* occurs in Sumatra including Kerinci Ceblat National Park. It was not found during recent extensive searches in northern Sumatra.

Whiskered Pitta *Pitta kochi* is confined to the north of Luzon, Philippines, where its population is small.

Giant Pitta *Pitta caerulea* (Pl. XXIII) is known from peninsular Malaysia,

Sumatra, south Thailand and Borneo, where it is considered scarce through loss of habitat.

Bar-bellied Pitta *Pitta ellioti* is found in southern Indo-China, where it is very little known. It is dependent on lowlands and may be threatened by habitat destruction.

Blue-headed Pitta *Pitta baudi* is confined to Borneo, where it is little known, but dependent on lowlands and therefore seriously threatened by habitat destruction.

Fairy Pitta *Pitta nympha* is widespread in South-East Asia and suffering from loss of its forest habitat especially in China.

CAMPEPHAGIDAE Cuckoo-shrikes
Blackish Cuckoo-shrike *Coracina coerulescens* is a lowland forest bird from Luzon and Cebu, Philippines, recently extinct on the latter.

White-winged Cuckoo-shrike *Coracina ostenta* occurs on the middle islands of the Philippines where its habitat is disappearing fast.

PYCNONOTIDAE Bulbuls
Wattled Bulbul *Pycnonotus nieuwenhuisi* is known only from two specimens, one from Kalimantan and one from Sumatra, Indonesia.

Mottled-breasted Bulbul *Hypsipetes siquijorensis* is a scarce and little-known species from the Philippines.

(MUSCICAPIDAE) TURDINAE
Thrushes
Rusty-bellied Shortwing *Brachypteryx hyperythra* is a little-known species from India and China.

Black Shama *Copsychus cebuensis* is endemic to Cebu in the Philippines. Although there is no original forest left on the island, and the bird was thought to be extinct, it appears to have adapted to secondary growth.

Luzon Redstart *Rhyacornis bicolor* is restricted to clear mountain streams on Luzon in the Philippines where it is apparently intolerant of disturbance.

Blue-fronted Robin *Cinclidium frontale* is known from a few records from South-East Asia.

Green Cochoa *Cochoa viridis* (Pl. XXII) has a large range in India, Burma, Thailand, Laos, Vietnam and China, where it inhabits dense forest undergrowth. It is a rarely recorded species which may be partly due to its secretive nature but also because it is genuinely declining as a result of destruction of its forest habitat.

Sumatran Cochoa *Cochoa beccari* is endemic to the mountains of Sumatra, Indonesia. It is known from a handful of specimens and only one recent recorded sighting.

Javan Cochoa *Cochoa azurea* is currently known from only a few locations in west Java, Indonesia.

Sri Lanka Whistling-thrush *Myiophoneus blighi* is endemic to Sri Lanka in dense mountain forests near running streams. It is threatened by loss of forest habitat.

Geomalia *Geomalia heinrichi* is a shy bird endemic to Sulawesi, Indonesia, where it was not discovered until 1930.

Slaty-backed Thrush *Zoothera schistacea* is found in the Tanimbar Islands, Indonesia. It probably lives in lowland forest but its status is unknown.

Red-backed Thrush *Zoothera erythronota* is a little-known bird from Sulawesi and Peleng, Indonesia.

Orange-banded Thrush *Zoothera peronii* is becoming increasingly local and uncommon in the Lesser Sundas, Indonesia.

Everett's Thrush *Zoothera everetti* is a scarce endemic of the mountains of Borneo.

Spot-winged Thrush *Zoothera spiloptera* is endemic to Sri Lanka.

Fawn-breasted Thrush *Zoothera machiki* is known from three specimens from the Tanimbar Islands, Indonesia. It is believed to inhabit lowland forest but its status is not known.

Grey-sided Thrush *Turdus feae* has a restricted breeding range in China and winters in India, Burma and Thailand. It is a forest inhabitant and its overall distribution is poorly understood.

(MUSCICAPIDAE) TIMALIINAE
Babblers

Marsh Babbler *Pellorneum palustre* is confined to reed beds and wet grasslands in north-east India.

Black-browed Babbler *Trichastoma perspicillatum* is known from the unique type-specimen collected in Kalimantan, Indonesia, in the middle of the last century.

Bagobo Babbler *Leonardina woodi* is a secretive and little-studied species from Mindanao in the Philippines.

Short-tailed Scimitar-babbler *Jabouilleia danjoui* is a scarce endemic species from Vietnam. Its status is unknown.

Bornean Wren-babbler *Ptilocichla leucogrammica* is an uncommon endemic resident of lowland forest in Borneo.

Striated Wren-babbler *Ptilocichla mindanensis* is a declining species from the Philippines.

Rabor's Wren-babbler *Napothera rabori* is endemic to Luzon in the Philippines, and known only from the type-localities of the three recognised subspecies.

Marbled Wren-babbler *Napothera marmorata* (Pl. XXIII) is found in central Malaysia and known from one specimen in western Sumatra. Despite extensive searches it has not been found since in the latter locality.

Deignan's Babbler *Stachyris rodolphei* is an endemic resident of bamboo forest

in north-west Thailand.

Striped Babbler *Stachyris striata* is restricted to mountain slopes on northern Luzon in the Philippines.

White-breasted Babbler *Stachyris grammiceps* is confined to the subtropical wet forest of south-west Java. It is extremely localised in tiny remnant patches of forest.

Sooty Babbler *Stachyris herberti* is an endemic resident at low elevations in central Laos. Its status is unknown.

Miniature Tit-babbler *Micromacronus leytensis* is a rarely recorded species from the Philippines.

Jerdon's Moupinia *Moupinia altirostrus* is found in three disjunct populations in Pakistan, India and Burma, though the last population may be extinct.

Ashy-headed Laughingthrush *Garrulax cinereifrons* is endemic to Sri Lanka in the wet forests of foothills and mountains. It is threatened by loss of habitat and disturbance.

Black-hooded Laughingthrush *Garrulax milleti* is an endemic species of forests of Vietnam. Its status is unknown.

Grey Laughingthrush *Garrulax maesi* occurs in four distinct populations in China. Its status is unknown.

White-cheeked Laughingthrush *Garrulax vassali* is found in forest and scrub in Vietnam and Laos. Its status is unknown.

Yellow-throated Laughingthrush *Garrulax galbanus* is known from India, Bangladesh and China. The populations are fragmented.

White-speckled Laughingthrush *Garrulax bieti* is found in central-west China. Its status is unknown.

Nilgiri Laughingthrush *Garrulax cachinnans* is restricted to the Nilgiri Hills in south-west India.

Collared Laughingthrush *Garrulax versini* is known only from one plateau in Vietnam. Its status is unknown.

Red-winged Laughingthrush *Garrulax formosus* frequents mountain forest in China and Vietnam.

Gold-fronted Fulvetta *Alcippe variegaticeps* is found in forest undergrowth in central and south-east China. Its status is unknown.

Grey-crowned Crocias *Crocias langbianis* is a scarce endemic of Vietnam.

(MUSCICAPIDAE) PANURINAE Parrotbills

Greater Rufous-headed Parrotbill *Paradoxornis ruficeps* is found in reedbeds, bamboo and dense grassland in Bhutan, India, Burma, Laos, Vietnam and China.

Black-breasted Parrotbill *Paradoxornis flavirostris* from India, Burma and China has few recent records. Its habitat is not known.

(MUSCICAPIDAE) SYLVIINAE Old World warblers

Large-billed Bush Warbler *Bradypterus major* is found in the western Himalayas, Turkestan and China. It is little known and its rarity gives cause for concern.

Sri Lanka Bush Warbler *Bradypterus palliseri* is a scarce endemic of Sri Lanka, confined to the dense undergrowth of mountain jungle. It was formerly widespread but has declined in recent years.

Long-tailed Prinia *Prinia burnesi* occurs in two disjunct populations in Pakistan and India. It is dependent upon expanses of wet grassland that adjoin the larger rivers.

Bristled Grass Warbler *Chaetornis striatus* is a local and declining species from India and Nepal.

(MUSCICAPIDAE) MUSCICAPINAE Old World flycatchers

Streaky-breasted Jungle-flycatcher *Rhinomyias addita* is endemic to forest on Buru, Indonesia.

Brown-chested Jungle-flycatcher *Rhinomyias brunneata* is found in south-east China, and winters in Malaysia and India, and may reach Sumatra, Indonesia.

Henna-tailed Jungle-flycatcher *Rhinomyias colonus* has a curious distribution in Indonesia, and is believed to be scarce.

White-throated Jungle-flycatcher *Rhinomyias albigularis* is confined to Guimaras and Negros in the Philippines. The fragments of standing forest on the islands, which are its major habitat, are being cleared.

White-browed Jungle-flycatcher *Rhinomyias insignis* inhabits montane forests in Luzon, Philippines. Its habitat is being rapidly cleared for agriculture.

Lompobattang Flycatcher *Ficedula bonthaina* is known only from the Lompobattang massif on Sulawesi, Indonesia. It was evidently common in dense forest undergrowth but its current status is unknown.

Sumba Flycatcher *Ficedula harterti* is endemic to Sumba, Indonesia, where its status and habitat are unknown.

Cryptic Flycatcher *Ficedula crypta* is known from one locality on Luzon and by a few specimens from Mindanao in the Philippines.

Damar Blue Flycatcher *Ficedula henrichi* is endemic to Damar, Indonesia, and known only from nine specimens collected in 1899.

Black-banded Flycatcher *Ficedula timorensis* is endemic to Timor, Indonesia, where it is restricted to remnant patches of deciduous forest.

Matinan Flycatcher *Cyornis sandfordi* is known only from the Matinan mountains in Sulawesi, Indonesia.

Rueck's Blue Flycatcher *Cyornis ruecki* is unknown in the field. There are two specimens that were collected

from peninsular Malaysia and two from north-eastern Sumatra. Its taxonomic standing from Malaysia is questionable.
Blue-Breasted Flycatcher *Cyornis herioti* is endemic to Luzon, Philippines, where it is scarce in threatened hill forest.

(MUSCICAPIDAE)
MONARCHINAE Monarchs
Caerulean Paradise Flycatcher *Eutrichomyias rowleyi* is known only from the island of Sangihe, north of Sulawesi. It was described from a single skin in 1873, and rediscovered in 1978. Recent surveys failed to observe it. It may already be extinct as all its forest habitat has been destroyed.
Short-crested Monarch *Hypothymis helenae* occurs in the Philippines where it is scarce on the larger islands.
Celestial Monarch *Hypothymis coelestis* occurs in the Philippines and has been observed by few ornithologists in the past decade.
White-tipped Monarch *Monarcha everetti* is known only from Tanahjampea, Indonesia.
Black-chinned Monarch *Monarcha boanensis* is known only from the type-specimen from a small island off Seram, Indonesia.
Flores Monarch *Monarcha sacerdotum* was discovered in 1971 on Flores, Indonesia.
White-tailed Monarch *Monarcha leucurus* is endemic to the Kai Islands, Indonesia, where its status and habitat are unknown.

(MUSCICAPIDAE)
RHIPIDURINAE Fantails
Tawny-backed Fantail *Rhipidura superflua*, of unknown status, is endemic to mountain forest on Buru, Indonesia.

(MUSCICAPIDAE)
PACHYCEPHALINAE Whistlers
Sangihe Shrike-thrush *Colluricincla*

sanghirensis is restricted to forest on Sangihe, Indonesia.

PARIDAE Titmice, chickadees
White-winged Tit *Parus nuchalis* is confined to north-west India, where its status and distribution give cause for concern.
Yellow Tit *Parus holsti* is a scarce endemic resident of Taiwan, occurring in primary broadleaf forest.

SITTIDAE Nuthatches
White-browed Nuthatch *Sitta victoriae* is known only from Mt. Victoria in the Chin Hills, Burma.
Black-masked Nuthatch *Sitta yunnanensis* is a resident of mountain forests in central China.
Yellow-billed Nuthatch *Sitta solangiae* is a little-known species from Vietnam.
Giant Nuthatch *Sitta magna* is resident in Burma, China and Thailand.
Beautiful Nuthatch *Sitta formosa* (Pl. XXII) occurs from the eastern Himalayas across South-East Asia to northern Laos. It is scarce in Nepal and Bhutan. Its distribution and status give cause for concern.

RHABDORNITHIDAE Philippine treecreepers
Long-billed Rhabdornis *Rhabdornis grandis* is found in Luzon, Philippines. It is currently known only from two specimens but may prove to be widespread in remnant mountain forests.

DICAEIDAE Flowerpeckers
Brown-backed Flowerpecker *Dicaeum everetti* from Malaysia and Indonesia is either scarce or overlooked.
Legge's Flowerpecker *Dicaeum vincens* is restricted to the wettest forest of Sri Lanka.

NECTARINIIDAE Sunbirds
Apricot-breasted Sunbird *Nectarinia buettikoferi* is endemic to Sumba, Indonesia, where its status is unknown.

Elegant Sunbird *Aethopyga dryvenbodei* is confined to remnant patches of forest on the Sangihe Islands, Indonesia.

ZOSTEROPIDAE White-eyes
Javan White-eye *Zosterops flava* is now scarce in the north-east of Java. There are a few recorded from east Kalimantan.
Ambon Yellow White-eye *Zosterops kuehni* occurs on Ambon and possibly Seram, Indonesia.
Rufous-throated White-eye *Madanga ruficollis* is found on Buru, Indonesia. It was described in 1923 and has not been recorded since.
Crested White-eye *Lophozosterops dohertyi* is known from Sumbawa and Flores, Indonesia. Its status is unknown on the former and it is described as uncommon on the latter.
Pygmy White-eye *Oculocincta squamifrons* is very local in mountains in Sabah, Malaysia. Its distribution elsewhere in Borneo is unknown.
Spot-breasted White-eye *Heleia muelleri* is scarce in remnant pockets of deciduous woodland on Timor, Indonesia.

MELIPHAGIDAE Honeyeaters
Crimson-hooded Honeyeater *Myzomela kuehni* is endemic to Wetar, Indonesia, where it has not been recorded for over 50 years.
Dusky Friarbird *Philemon fuscicapillus* occurs on Halmahera and its satelite islands in Indonesia.
Black-faced Friarbird *Philemon moluccensis* is found only in the Lesser Sundas, Indonesia.

ESTRILDIDAE Waxbills
Green Munia *Estrilda formosa* is confined to central India, where its rarity gives cause for concern.
Green-faced Parrotfinch *Erythrura viridifacies* occurs on Luzon in the Philippines. The nest has not been described and its status is unknown.
Red-eared Parrotfinch *Erythrura coloria* is known from Mindanao in the Philippines. Its status is unknown.
Timor Sparrow *Padda fuscata* is local in the lowlands and coastal scrub of Timor, Indonesia.

PLOCEIDAE Weavers
Finn's Baya Weaver *Ploceus megarhynchus* is confined to the southern slopes of the Himalayas and north-west India. It is now extremely local, with disjunct populations.

STURNIDAE Starlings
Sri Lanka White-headed Myna *Sturnus senex* is scarce and confined to high virgin forest in Sri Lanka, where it is threatened by loss of habitat.

ORIOLIDAE Orioles
Isabela Oriole *Oriolus isabellae* has a small range in Luzon, Philippines, where it is threatened by forest destruction.
Silver Oriole *Oriolus mellianus* breeds in forest in China and is not well known.

CORVIDAE Crows
Sri Lanka Magpie *Urocissa ornata* is endemic to virgin forests in the mountains and foothills of Sri Lanka, where it is threatened by loss or disturbance of habitat.
Hooded Treepie *Crypsirina cucullata* was common in the central plains of Burma but has not been recorded recently.
Racket-tailed Treepie *Temnurus temnurus* is found in Vietnam and Hainan, China. Its status is unknown.
Banggai Crow *Corvus unicolor* is endemic to Banggai, Indonesia, and known only from two specimens.
Flores Crow *Corvus florensis* is endemic to Flores, Indonesia, and known from very few specimens.

Chapter 7
The Australasian Region

The Australasian Region includes the Australian continent, New Guinea, Tasmania and New Zealand. Related islands such as the Solomons and New Caledonia are included, as is the Indonesian island chain as far west as the Molucca Sea where it adjoins the Oriental Region. The more remote Pacific islands are dealt with in the final main section of this book.

The origins of the avifauna of the Australasian Region can be traced back to the Mesozoic or Tertiary periods and the break-up of the super-continent of Gondwanaland, as can be seen in the affinities of some species with those of Africa and South America, such as the flightless cassowaries and emus. New Zealand also probably carried from Gondwanaland the ancestors of some species such as the now extinct giant moas. Some infiltration of Asiatic species probably took place along the Indonesian island chain and colonisation between New Guinea and the Australian mainland is still continuing. The speciation of birds has been assisted by the climatic and physiographical boundaries, such as the great central Australian desert, which during the late Tertiary and the Pleistocene isolated parts of once continuous populations, forming "island" groups where differentiation and new species could evolve. The absence of large mammalian predators also had a major effect on the evolution of Australian wildlife, permitting, for example, the development of an extraordinary diversity of defenceless marsupial animals. There is no evidence of penetration of Australasian bird species into the Palaearctic, but great numbers of Palaearctic waders from eastern Asia migrate regularly into the region. Australia now has more than 700 species of birds, 60% of which are endemic and about 125 of which do not breed on the continent. About 50 are vagrants or irregular visitors. Because of the vast areas of hostile and unexplored environment, much still remains to be learned about the avifauna of the region. By comparison with Europe or the Americas the study of bird migration in the Australasian Region is as yet only imperfectly developed, although rapid progress has been made in recent years. It is believed that many species are irregularly nomadic rather than regularly migratory, because of the vagaries of the climatic conditions and the frequency of devastating and protracted drought in some areas.

To visit Australia, the land of million-acre farms, yet where 70% of the land is uncultivated, is to learn a whole range of new terms to describe habitat types. These can be almost as confusing as the 54 unfamiliar species of parrots or the

67 species of Australian honeyeaters (Meliphagidae). There is, for example, the very distinctive hard-leafed sclerophyll forest of tall eucalypts with an open canopy among graceful tree-ferns, found in the west and south-west. There is brigalow, a mixture of dense low scrub and acacia trees, much favoured by nectar-eating and insectivorous birds. In the southern coastal regions is mallee scrub of dense, low-growing eucalypts with a tangled undergrowth, the habitat of, among others, the remarkable Mallee-fowl *Leipoa ocellata*. Further inland are vast areas of mulga scrub—an arid region uninhabited by humans but important to many birds, whose populations change radically if any rain falls. And gibber desert, one of the world's least hospitable regions of prehistorically rounded stones, with extremely high temperatures by day, falling to sub-zero at night. In the arid empty centre of the continent, where total drought may extend for years, only a few clumps of sharp-spined spinifex, porcupine grass or salt-bush grow and the very rare Night Parrot *Geopsittacus occidentalis* still contrives to exist. In the rich northern savanna grasslands, the few coastal monsoon-forests and the lush surviving rain-forests of Queensland, both vegetation and wildlife abound in immense variety. Unfortunately, as elsewhere in the world, more than half of the country's tree cover had been destroyed by 1985, resulting in a serious increase in erosion and a depletion of ground-water sources. New deserts have been created by faulty irrigation leading to soil salination, by immense bush-fires and by persistent over grazing by sheep and cattle. But across the vastness of the great Australian continent there are great riches in wildlife.

The relatively small island of Tasmania, with its mossy high-altitude temperate rain-forest, is also rich in wildlife. The south-west part of the island is protected under the World Heritage Trust. While the majority of its birds originated in southern Australia, some, such as the ultra-rare Orange-bellied Parrot *Neophema chrysogaster*, are endemic and of particular interest.

New Zealand has suffered greatly from over-exploitation of its wild environment and the replacement of forests by sheep, as well as from the ravages of countless predatory animals introduced by the early settlers. Many species of native birds have been lost, but there are still some unique birds of very primitive origin, such as the fightless Kiwis (Apterygidae) and the almost flightless wattlebirds (Callaeidae). Some 30 bird species have been thoughtlessly introduced from other countries, to the detriment of native birds. Several of the now largely deforested offshore islands have been the scenes of some outstanding conservation successes, which are described later. New Guinea, only one-tenth the size of Australia, has almost as many bird species thanks to the richness of its magnificent forests. These include the incomparably beautiful birds of paradise, which although heavily exploited by the forest tribes who use their feathers for head-dresses, still gain some protection from the remoteness of the cloud-covered tropical mountain forests they inhabit. Conservation is making good progress in Papua New Guinea and a number of important reserves and research centres have recently been created there.

Scientific ornithology and conservation are controlled by a number of highly qualified bodies such as the Wildlife Division of the Commonwealth Scientific and Industrial Research Organization (CSIRO) and the Royal Australian Ornithologists' Union. These are supported by the Australian branch of the WWF and the Australian Conservation Foundation, as well as by many state societies, museums and universities. Ornithology is also well represented in New Zealand, where the Wildlife Service and the Royal Forest and Bird Protection Society do admirable work. Every state in both countries has a number of national parks and wildlife reserves which provide a high degree of public education. However, being by tradition independently minded, not all Australian states take kindly to federal authority in matters of conservation and there is some variation between the needs of public recreation and the protection of endangered species and habitats. Nevertheless, conservation is increasingly given precedence.

The flightless and tail-less **Little Spotted Kiwi** *Apteryx owenii* is probably extinct on North, South and D'Urville Islands of New Zealand, where it used to occur. The present population of 500–600 birds on Kapiti Island originated from those introduced in 1913. The future of the species depends on preventing the introduction of predators, against which it is defenceless. It is currently a Candidate species.

The **Magenta Petrel** *Pterodroma magentae*, is presumed to be restricted as a breeding bird to the Chatham Islands, New Zealand. After being known from only one specimen it was rediscovered in 1978. Its future is threatened by introduced predators and the destruction of its habitat by introduced herbivores. It is listed by ICBP as Endangered.

Beck's Petrel *P. becki* was discovered at sea, where two specimens were

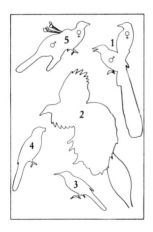

PLATE XXV Huon Peninsula (Papua New Guinea). 1 Huon Bird of Paradise (p. 195), 2 Emperor of Germany Bird of Paradise (p. 195), 3 Foerster's Melidectes (p. 195), 4 Huon Melipotes (p. 195), 5 Wahne's Parotia (p. 195).

PLATE XXVI Australian Interior. 1 Plains Wanderer (p. 192), 2 Night Parrot (p. 186), 3 Chestnut-breasted Whiteface (p. 194), 4 Eyrean Grass-wren (p. 188), 5 Grey Grass-wren (p. 194).

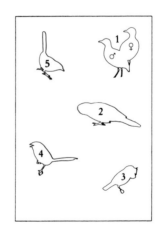

Norman Arlott 87

Norman Arlott 87

Norman Arlott 87

Norman Arlott 87

collected near the Solomon Islands in 1928. Information has been lacking since then. Its status is listed as Indeterminate.

The **Chatham Island Petrel** *Pterodroma axillaris* (Plate XXVII) is known to breed only on Rangatira Island in the Chathams, off New Zealand. The island has been managed as a reserve since 1954 and there has been a recovery of the vegetation. Nevertheless, the total population has remained very small, estimated at less than 500 birds, and ICBP classify the species as Endangered.

Another Endangered New Zealand petrel is the **Black Petrel** *Procellaria parkinsoni* which breeds on Little and Great Barrier Islands and has a population of fewer than 1,000 pairs. Predation by cats appears to have been the biggest threat, but eradication programmes on Little Barrier Island have recently been successfully implemented.

The **Westland Black Petrel** *Procellaria westlandica* breeds on one small mountain range on South Island, New Zealand. It is subject to predation by introduced mammals and is also vulnerable to timber milling in the area. However, industrial development is not always deleterious, because there has been a recent increase in numbers to 1,000–5,000 breeding pairs attributed to increased offal from large commercial fisheries within the petrel's feeding range. The species is listed as Vulnerable.

Heinroth's Shearwater *Puffinus heinrothi* is known from a handful of specimens from the northern coast of New Britain. The breeding site has not been found, but two individuals recently recovered on Bouganville suggests that it could breed there. Meanwhile, ICBP list the species as Indeterminate.

The **New Zealand Brown Teal** *Anas aucklandica* was once common throughout New Zealand but is now severely depleted or absent from most of its former range and is listed as Vulnerable. Its decline is due to drainage, forest clearance, possibly unidentified disease and predation by cats.

There are 13 species of megapodes, or mound-building birds. Most of them are confined to the Australasian Region, although others occur as far west as the Nicobar Islands to the north of Sumatra and some as far north as the Marianas and the Philippines and eastwards to Tonga. All have the unique habit of incubating their eggs by burying them deep in the

PLATE XXVII Chatham Islands. 1 Chatham Island Oystercatcher (p. 183), 2 New Zealand Shore Plover (p. 184), 3 Chatham Island Petrel (p. 181).

PLATE XXVIII Choiseul. 1 Sandford's Sea Eagle (p. 192), 2 Solomon Island Crowned Pigeon (p. 184), 3 Imitator Sparrowhawk (p. 192), 4 Fearful Owl (p. 193).

Takahe

ground, or under large heaps of fermenting vegetation, or in warm volcanic ash. The unattended young have to dig themselves out and are capable of flying to cover almost immediately. The temperature of the incubating eggs is regulated by the parents adding or subtracting material in the huge covering mound. The eggs are large and numerous and the nest-sites conspicuous, so all the species suffer heavy predation by natives who harvest the eggs regularly and also from foxes, dingos, pigs, monitor lizards and other animals which easily dig up the eggs or kill the chicks. Some of the Australian species such as the **Malleefowl** *Leipoa ocellata*, a Candidate species, have disappeared completely from some areas where they were once common.

The **Waigeo Brush-turkey** *Aepypodius bruijnii*, which is confined to primary hill forest on Waigeu Island, off western Irian Jaya, is considered sufficiently restricted in range to be a Candidate species. I found two nest-mounds of this species on an un-named islet in this region in 1973.

In the Solomon Islands a single specimen of the large and flightless **San Cristóbal Mountain Rail** *Gallinula sylvestris* was collected in 1929 on the island of that name. It was reported to be not uncommon in the central forested mountains and a second bird was seen in 1953. There have been no reliable reports about the species since then. Its status is given by ICBP as Indeterminate. A United States company has acquired timber rights for the whole island and will probably clear 80,000 ha; there is little planning for reserves and the operation will have a heavy impact on the whole wildlife community.

On Lord Howe Island, off eastern Australia, the **Lord Howe Island Woodhen** *Tricholimnas sylvestris* is struggling to survive. It is a flightless rail and completely fearless of man. In consequence, it has been mercilessly persecuted. In the eighteenth century it was numerous, but in 1975 only ten breeding pairs remained and by 1980 only three. Between 1978 and 1981 it was closely studied by the National Parks and Wildlife Service of New South Wales, who found it was suffering from predation by rats, cats and pigs and also by the magpie-like Currawongs *Strepera graculina* and introduced Masked or Chestnut-faced Owls *Tyto novaehollandiae* from Australia and Tasmania. Projects to eliminate this combination of pests were put in hand and some of the woodhens were taken for captive breeding. Their population was increased to about 200 birds, of which 85 had been captive-bred. After 1984, however, there was a sudden unexplained drop to only 18–20 birds. These were in the moss-forest of Mount Gower and Mount Lidgbird. The species is listed by ICBP as Endangered.

The **Takahe** *Notornis mantelli* is an Endangered species restricted to the Murchison Mountains on South Island, New Zealand. Subfossil remains indicate that the species was once much more widespread, even occuring on North Island. Competition from introduced deer for food and predation by stoats are suspected of being the major factors in its decline to a population of about 180 birds. Improved deer control has resulted in an improvement of vegetation and a captive breeding and release programme is showing a promise of success.

The island of New Caledonia, half way between eastern Australia and Fiji, is the only place in the world where the strange **Kagu** *Rhynochetos jubatus* (Plate XXIX) is found. It is the sole representative of its family and is flightless, though able to glide briefly. At first glance it is an inconspicuous though fairly large slate-grey pigeon-like bird, but when it raises its copious crest and spreads its strongly russet-barred black and white wings it is transformed. Its pre-dawn "song" is a succession of richly melodious notes. Inevitably it has been constantly trapped and much sought after by collectors, but the main losses have been caused by introduced cats, dogs, pigs and rats and by the increasing loss of its forest habitat to open-cast nickel-mining. It is now very localised in those few valleys in the central mountains inaccessible to man. The recent violent conflict over the political future of the islands has resulted in a cessation of logging, hunting and mining. Many Europeans have fled and it is impossible to forecast the future for this splendid bird. It is nominally protected by French law. Plans to create a national park in the Rivière Bleue failed, but a small park was developed near Noumea which provided semi-wild facilities for six pairs of Kagus, which have produced 20 juveniles. If the species is to survive, a comprehensive conservation plan is essential. It is listed by ICBP, which is undertaking this plan, as Endangered.

Chatham Island and its neighbouring smaller islands 800 km east of New Zealand are the home of several threatened species of birds which have received much attention from the New Zealand Wildlife Service. In spite of the increasing threats to the natural ecology of the islands, some notable successes have been achieved. One of the endangered species is the **Chatham Island Oystercatcher** *Haematopus chathamensis* (Plate XXVII), which in the past used to occur not only on Chatham but also on Mangere and Rangatira Island. Today the total population is only about 50 birds, concentrated mainly on Chatham, with a few breeding occasionally on Rangatira Island, Pitt and Mangere. The species is now fully protected by law and both Chatham Island and Mangere are Reserves for the Preservation of Flora and Fauna. A slight increase in numbers is reported as a result of the reduction (ultimately the complete removal) of the introduced sheep and carnivores from the islands. It is listed by ICBP as Endangered.

Another New Zealand bird which is nearing extinction is the **Black Stilt** *Himantopus novaezealandiae*. This interesting species is restricted to breeding in a valley on the upper Waitaki River, in South Island, and this region is threatened by hydroelectric development and irrigation. Its present population is about 50 birds. Unfortunately it now hybridises with the Pied Stilt *H. h. leucocephalus*, and this is likely to increase as the Black Stilts find it more difficult to find their correct mates. In

Black Stilt

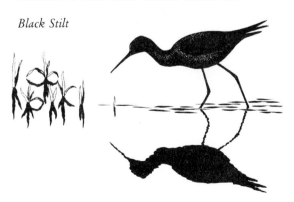

1974 only four juvenile Black Stilts were known to have reached maturity. The species is protected by New Zealand law and is being carefully studied by the Wildlife Service who have successfully reared some young birds in the Mount Bruce Reserve. A special reserve on the Waitaki River is planned, but much of the habitat favoured by the birds has already been lost. They are listed by ICBP as Endangered.

The **New Zealand Shore Plover** *Thinornis novaeseelandiae* (Plate XXVII) is now known only on the small Rangatira Island in the Chatham group, where its population is very limited. It formerly occurred on the coastal areas of North and South Islands of New Zealand and on several of the Chatham islands. By the end of the last century it had disappeared from New Zealand and from Chatham, Pitt and Mangere, having been exterminated by feral cats. For the last 75 years it has been restricted to Rangatira Island, where between 1890 and 1910 it was seriously depleted by commercial collectors. By 1937 the population was estimated at only 70 pairs, rising by 1985 to about 120, of which only about 80 were breeding, perhaps because of a vigorous regeneration of vegetation following the removal of sheep and cattle. Attempts to reintroduce the species on Mangere failed because of the strong homing instinct of the plovers, which soon returned to Rangatira Island. The species is fully protected by law and the island was turned into a reserve in 1954. It is the sole representative of its genus and it is regrettable that its docile and confiding nature makes it particularly vulnerable to predation. It is listed by ICBP as Endangered.

The **New Zealand Snipe** *Coenocorypha aucklandica* occurs in five races, each confined to a different oceanic island off south-east New Zealand. Four are relatively common but at risk because of their restricted range; the fifth was exterminated by rats when they over-ran the South Cape Islands in 1964. The species is currently classified as Rare.

A large number of endemic species of pigeons and doves in the Australasian Region are at risk, particularly those restricted to islands. A typical example is the **Solomon Island Crowned Pigeon** *Microgoura meeki* (Plate XXVIII). Although considered by some to be extinct, it may still survive in primary rain-forest on the island of Choiseul, which has been less exploited than some of the Solomons. It is classified as Extinct by ICBP.

A bird which has suffered greatly from the logging and nickel-mining in New Caledonia is the very attractive **Cloven-feathered Dove** *Drepanoptila holosericea* (Plate XXIX). It was once common in all the forested areas of the island and also on the offshore Ile des Pins, but barely 1,000 now survive and these are decreasing. In spite of legal protection, the doves are still hunted everywhere, even in the remotest remnant forests. It is listed as a Vulnerable species.

The **Giant Imperial Pigeon** *Ducula goliath* (Plate XXIX), because of its large size, is even more intensely hunted throughout New Caledonia and has been exterminated on the Ile des Pins. It is now seen only in the mountain forests, where mining and logging make it increasingly easy for hunters to gain access. Hunting is legally permitted only between 15th March and 15th April, but is continuous and is the main cause of its decline. It is also listed by ICBP as Vulnerable.

The **Golden-shouldered Parrot** *Psephotus chrysopterygius* is found in two subspecies, the nominate in isolated parts of central and southern Cape York, Queensland, Australia, and *dissimilis* in semi-arid north-east Northern Territory. It is nowhere common and it is threatened by illegal trapping, fire and pastoralism. ICBP classify it as Rare.

The very beautiful **Paradise Parrot** *Psephotus pulcherrimus* is probably already extinct. The last confirmed sighting was in 1927, but recent unconfirmed reports suggest that a few may still survive somewhere along the Queensland coast of Australia. Until the close of the nineteenth century it was not uncommon in Queensland and New South Wales, but a succession of severe droughts and the expansion of cattle grazing may have contributed to a decline from which it never recovered. Its capture for sale and the very high prices paid by bird fanciers also contributed. The species requires open savanna woodlands and grassy scrubland with plenty of the termite mounds which it habitually used as nest-sites. It is legally protected. ICBP list it as Endangered.

The **Princess Parrot** or **Pilpul** *Polytelis alexandrae* is a rare and nomadic species known only in the dry central-eastern Australian deserts. Neither its population size nor the causes for its apparently small numbers are yet known and it is currently a Candidate species.

The big **Vulturine** or **Pesquet's Parrot** *Psittrichas fulgidus* is endemic to New Guinea and is the only parrot to feed entirely on fruit, taking no nuts or seeds. It is hunted by the forest tribes for its wing and tail feathers, which are used as head-dresses. Its distribution in the dense montane forests is limited and its population both small and declining. Any logging in its range will endanger it. ICBP list it as a Candidate species.

The **Orange-bellied Parrot** *Neophema chrysogaster* is a Rare parrot which breeds in Western Tasmania and migrates to the southern coast of the Australian mainland in winter. In Tasmania it breeds on heath and sedgelands and in mainland Australia it feeds on saltmarshes and dunes. The decline in the population over the last century is poorly understood, but has been correlated with the development of large areas of the wintering habitat for saltworks and sewage farms.

The **Splendid** or **Scarlet-chested Parakeet** *Neophema splendida* is another Rare species which occurs locally in the interior of Australia. This gaudy little bird seems to have packed the brightest possible colours into the smallest possible space and consequently is highly prized as a cage-bird. However, captive stocks are self-sustaining because the birds are relatively easy to breed in captivity. Trapping wild birds is therefore not a problem and it seems as if this species is just naturally rare.

The **Orange-fronted Parakeet** *Cyanoramphus malherbi*, classed as Endangered, is known with certainty only

Vulturine Parrot

185

from South Island, New Zealand. It was found in 1980–1981 in Lake Summer area, North Canterbury, otherwise there are fewer than ten reliable records this century. Its decline is probably due to introduced mammals. Recent research indicates that this species is a colour morph of the Yellow-crowned Parakeet *C. auriceps*.

A very large ground-dwelling parrot, the **Kakapo** *Strigops habroptilus* of New Zealand, lived in safety until the arrival of the first Maoris about 950 AD. Although it can glide briefly on its small wings, it is virtually flightless and easily caught. When the first Europeans arrived and introduced cats, dogs and rats to South, North and Stewart Islands, where the Kakapos lived, the species was at once critically endangered. It is the only member of its sub-family and the world's only flightless parrot. It is also unique in being the only parrot to establish lek mating grounds, to which males attract females by a loud, booming call-note. In spite of strenuous efforts by the New Zealand Wildlife Service it is now on the brink of extinction. Its required habitat is apparently either climax forest of *Podocarpus* and *Nothofagus*, or forest margins in sub-alpine scrub and tussock on avalanche scree. More than three-quarters of such habitat in New Zealand has now disappeared under various developments. In 1978 it appeared that only 12 Kakapos survived, all of them males. In 1979 a colony of about 100 was discovered on Stewart Island. By 1985 only about 50 of these could be found, though others may still exist. Feral cats had killed the remainder, but these have now been removed. On Little Barrier Island there were 21 (12 males and 9 females), most of them having been transferred from Stewart Island in 1982. In Fjordland in south-west New Zealand, one male is known to exist; but

early in 1985 a number of males were heard booming in the north-west corner of South Island, a former stronghold of the species where there used to be heavy predation by rats, stoats and Brush-tailed Possums *Trichosurus vulpecula*. Intensive studies, using telemetry, infra-red video-recorders, helicopters and laboratory incubators for hatching eggs, are now in progress in the hope of saving the species. Captive-breeding by the New Zealand Wildlife Service has so far not succeeded. The species is listed by ICBP as critically Endangered.

One of Australia's most mysterious and least-known birds is the **Night Parrot** *Geopsittacus occidentalis* (Plate XXVI). During the nineteenth century it was reported in the arid interior of every Australian state, but the only specimen taken this century was shot at Nichol Spring, in Western Australia, in 1912. There have, however, been a number of sightings since then in western and southern Australia in regions where it is most likely to have survived. In June 1979 four birds were found on Cooper's

Kakapo

Creek in far north-eastern South Australia. There are still thousands of square miles of unexplored spinifex grasslands in the centre of the continent where the species may well still exist. The fact that it is both nocturnal and very secretive make it exceptionally difficult to locate. The reasons for its scarcity are unknown, but cattle-grazing and predation by feral cats and rats may have contributed. The species is legally protected throughout Australia and there are several large national parks in areas where it may exist. Its status is given by ICBP as Indeterminate.

A close relative, the **Ground Parrot** *Pezoporus wallicus*, is also threatened. It resembles the Night Parrot but has a longer tail. The Western Ground Parrot *P. w. flaviventris* is found only in parts of the coast of Western Australia. The size of its population is unknown, but it is locally protected. It is listed by ICBP as Endangered. The Eastern Ground Parrot *P. w. wallicus* of eastern Australia is listed as Vulnerable. It is seriously threatened by the rapid development of both mineral mining and human settlements in the coastal regions it inhabits. It is regarded as extinct in South Australia and almost extinct in Queensland, apart from a single breeding area at Cooloola. Its range in Victoria and New South Wales is much restricted and discontinuous. The total population is unknown, but is certainly declining. It is legally protected and still occurs in a number of reserves and national parks in Queensland, Victoria and New South Wales. The southern Tasmanian race *P. w. leachii* (not recognised by some) may now also be at risk.

The **Noisy Scrub-bird** *Atrichornis clamosus* was listed in 1889 as extinct, but was rediscovered in 1961. It had originally occurred to the south of Perth and along the coast as far as Mount Barker. In 1961 it was found in densely vegetated gulleys on a headland at Two Peoples Bay, 40 km east of Albany and later also on nearby Mount Manypeaks. Both are now protected reserves. It earned international renown owing to the personal interest of HRH the Duke of Edinburgh in its protection during his visit to Western Australia in the early 1970s. As a result of his concern, a proposed new town was relocated in order not to disturb the Scrub-birds. This admirable conservation effort brought well-deserved credit to the government of Western Australia. The species now has a population of about 185. It is listed by ICBP as Endangered. The related **Rufous Scrub-bird** *A. rufescens* of eastern Australia is now also scarce with small, isolated populations in the highlands of the Great Dividing Range. It is is classified as Rare.

There used to be three distinct and quite common subspecies of the **New Zealand Bush Wren** *Xenicus longipes*. In each case they have been the victims of predatory animals introduced by European settlers into their forest and scrub habitat. The North Island Bush Wren *X. l. stokesi* was known to inhabit the central and southern part of the island. The last two unconfirmed records of it were from the Gisborne area in 1949 and 1955, and it is now probably extinct. The South Island race *X. l. longipes*, which used to be common throughout the forests, might still exist in very small numbers according to unconfirmed reports from the Fjordland area. Stead's Bush Wren *X. l. variabillis* was known from Stewart Island and several small neighbouring islands. It was last reported on Stewart in 1951 and was finally exterminated on Big South Cape Island in 1965 by Black Rats which had been accidentally introduced. A last-resort relocation of the birds to nearby Kaimohu

Island was attempted but birds were last seen there in 1972. The New Zealand Wildlife Service did its utmost to save the Stead's Bush Wren and gave the South Island race full protection, but it remains critically endangered, if indeed it still survives—indeed the species has recently been added to the extinct list. The related Stephen Island Wren *X. lyalli*, found only on that island, was swiftly exterminated in 1894 by a single domestic cat.

In 1874 the first **Eyrean Grass-wren** *Amytornis goyderi* (Plate XXVI) was discovered in the east of South Australia. It was not recorded again until 1931 and a third specimen was found in 1961. In 1976 a considerable population was discovered in the sandhills of the Simpson Desert in the extreme north-east of the state, near Eyre Creek and also near Birdsville, just over the Queensland border. The following year the spinifex grass and other vegetation had died throughout both areas and only a small population of the Grass Wrens survived in the dunes. Part of the habitat is protected by the Simpson Desert National Park. The species is protected by Australian law and is listed by ICBP as Indeterminate.

The **Eastern Bristlebird** *Dasyornis brachypterus* occurs in scattered groups in dense heath, scrub and reed-beds along the coastal region from eastern Victoria to south-east Queensland. It has some protection in national parks and reserves, but is threatened by habitat destruction and unsuitable fire regimes. The **Western Bristlebird** *D. longirostris* formerly had a range in coastal Western Australia from Perth to Esperance. It is now rare and restricted to southern coastal areas such as the Two Peoples Bay Reserve and the Fitzgerald River National Park. Its total population is very small and is threatened by fire. Both species are Candidate Red Data Book species.

The most widely acclaimed effort by the New Zealand Wildlife Service to save an endangered bird species from extinction concerns the **Chatham Island Black Robin** *Petroica traversi*. This engaging little bird was once fairly common on Chatham, Pitt, Mangere and Little Mangere, in the Chatham Islands. It disappeared from the first two of these islands by 1871 and from Mangere later in the nineteenth century when cats were introduced. It then survived only in the 16 hectares of scrub forest on Little Mangere until this entire small population was transferred to Mangere between 1974 and 1977. Its habitat on Little Mangere had been severely damaged by a large population of "muttonbirds" (petrels and shearwaters) which were regularly harvested and had spoiled the scrub forest by their nest-burrows. Severe winds, rain and drought had also contributed to the destruction of the habitat. A survey in 1961 suggested a total population of only 20–30 pairs of robins. By 1976 it was only seven. By the

Eastern Bristlebird

time the translocation to Mangere was complete in 1979, it was down to only five birds, of which only one pair was capable of breeding. The future of the species then depended on one already aged female, known as "Old Blue". Mangere meanwhile had been converted to a protected nature reserve with a newly-planted forest of 120,000 native trees, where all predatory animals had been removed. Moving the surviving robins from Little Mangere involved scaling the 200 m cliffs, catching the birds and transporting them in rubber boats to Mangere. It was decided to attempt to make the robins lay more than their normal single clutch of three eggs by cross-fostering, the first clutch being transferred to the nest of a Chatham Island Warbler *Gerygone albofrontata*. The experiment succeeded, the warblers hatching the eggs, leaving the robins to lay another clutch in their own nest. However, the warblers abandoned the chicks after only ten days. The Wildlife Service therefore decided the following year to try to place the robin eggs under Chatham Island Tits *Petroica macrocephala chathamensis* on nearby Rangatura Island. The tits proved to be ideal parents, rearing the nestlings successfully, and raising the total population of Black Robins to 12.

The 1982–1983 breeding season was a very bad one and only two chicks were raised, the post-breeding population actually dropping to 11, of which two died during the winter. The 1984 season began with the advantage that the cross-fostering technique with the Chatham Island Tits had been perfected and that from the young produced there were now four pairs of Black Robins capable of breeding. Moreover, the robins on Rangatira Island (with 100 hectares of suitable habitat) had a greater opportunity for expansion than those on Mangere, which had only 4.2 hectares. With a total combined stock of only nine birds, the year would be critical and it was decided to try to make the robins lay three clutches each, by transferring the first two to the foster parents. The results were quite astonishing: the robins laid a total of 22 eggs, of which 17 hatched. From these, 13 nestlings fledged and 11 survived, bringing the total population to 30 in 1984 and to 38 in 1985. Without the cross-fostering programme no more than four or five young could have been expected. For the first time ever, four 3-egg clutches had been laid and, even more remarkably, one female had laid three 3-egg clutches. "Old Blue" was the most successful breeder since 1979 and, as mother of eight and grandmother of 11, had produced 19 live robins. She was transferred to Rangatira Island for a well-earned rest and in 1985 died at the ripe old age of at least 14 years, having played the leading role in saving her species from imminent extinction. It was a fitting accolade to this remarkable little bird that her death was officially announced in the New Zealand Parliament! The species is listed by ICBP as Endangered.

The **Forty-spotted Pardalote** *Pardalotus quadragintus* is a scarce flowerpecker with ICBP Candidate status. It is confined to mature eucalyptus forests in south-east Tasmania, where it is threatened by habitat destruction, unsuitable fire regimes and competition from other pardalote species for nest sites.

The **White-breasted White-eye** *Zosterops albogularis* of Norfolk Island, unlike most other members of the white-eye family, is solitary and not very vocal, and is therefore difficult to find. Judged by the large numbers collected, it must once have been common. It is now confined to the remnant rain-forest in the Mount Pitt Reserve, where it is threatened by feral cats, and possibly by competition from the related Grey-breasted Silvereye *Z. lateralis*, which reached the island in 1904. Its population in 1982 was fewer than 50 birds and it may now be extinct. It is listed as critically Endangered.

The **Stitchbird** *Notiomystis cincta*, listed as Vulnerable, formerly occurred throughout New Zealand and several offshore islands, but suffered severely as soon as predatory animals were introduced. Further losses were caused by collectors and avian diseases. By 1888 it was rare and shortly afterwards disappeared from North Island. It is now restricted to Little Barrier Island, with a population of about 200 pairs, which suffer predation from feral cats. The cats also prey on the numerous Cook's Petrels *Pterodroma cookii* and Black Petrels *Procellaria parkinsoni* which occupy the island (see p. 181). A project to eliminate the resident cats was introduced by the New Zealand Wildlife Service, but this has not yet been effective. The Stitchbird was recently introduced to Hen, where it now breeds, Cuvier and Kapiti Islands. Little Barrier was made a Reserve for the Protection of Flora and Fauna in 1890. The species is legally protected.

The **Kokako** *Callaeas cinerea* (not to be confused with the Kakapos; see p. 186) belongs to the family of primitive remnant New Zealand wattlebirds and have distinctive fleshy wattles at the base of the bill. The Huia, one of the three species in this family (each in its own genus) is already extinct: it was especiallly unique as it is the only species known, to have shown sexual dimorphism in its bill shape and so presumably in its feeding habits. In addition, the **South Island Kokako** *C. c. cinerea* is nearly or probably already extinct. Only a few scattered and unconfirmed reports of its presence during the past 35 years suggest

that it may still survive. Until the arrival of the Europeans settlers it was widely distributed throughout South Island and Stewart Island. The New Zealand Wildlife Service has thoroughly searched for it and recently it has been rediscovered on Stewart Island. Much of the forest habitat preferred by it has been destroyed on both islands and there is predation on all birds by cats and rats as well as much destruction of vegetation by introduced herbivores. The North Island subspecies *C. c. wilsoni* is still fairly widely distributed in North Island and on the adjacent Great Barrier Island, but is decreasing owing to the felling of the forests and predation by introduced mammals. Its now discontinuous distribution in the remaining stands of mature forest and its weak powers of flight inhibit it from colonising new areas. The total population is thought to be about 1,000 birds, scattered in small groups. It is fully protected and cooperation between the Wildlife and Forest Services has resulted in several reserves being created for the Kokakos. Competition for food by introduced Brush-tailed Possums *Trichosurus vulpecula* as well as deer and goats is a problem, as is predation by feral cats, rats and weasels. The species is listed by ICBP as Endangered.

There is better news of the third wattlebird, the once widespread **Saddleback** *Creadion carunculatus*. Until recently its population was declining owing to predation and it existed only on Hen Island, off North Island, and on three small islets south-west of Stewart Island. Since 1962 it has been reintroduced on several islands free from rats and cats and is making good progress. The North Island race *C. c. rufusater* now numbers about 500 birds and the South Island race *C. c. carunculatus* about 200–250 birds. The species is listed by ICBP as a Candidate species.

Bowerbirds, which are related to the

Adelbert Bowerbird

birds of paradise, specialise in constructing decorated "bowers" to attract females. Several species in New Guinea are beginning to be threatened by deforestation. In particular, the **Adelbert Bowerbird** *Sericulus bakeri*, which inhabits the higher summits of the Adelbert Range, also has a very restricted distribution and has become very rare. It is currently listed by the ICBP as a Candidate Red Data Book bird.

Eleven birds of paradise are listed as Candidate species, mainly because of the growing disturbance to their former habitats and to a lesser extent because they are hunted for their spectacular plumes by natives. **Wallace's Standardwing** *Semioptera wallacei* is a magnificent bird with emerald-green plumage and two long white feathers hanging from each shoulder. It represents the westernmost limit in the distribution of the birds of paradise, inhabiting hill forests on Halmahera and Batjan Islands in the Moluccas, where it was recently rediscovered after having been reported extinct for 30 years or more.

ADDITIONAL CANDIDATE BIRDS OF THE AUSTRALASIAN REGION

SPHENISCIDAE Penguins
Yellow-eyed Penguin *Megadyptes antipodes* is confined to New Zealand where it is threatened by farm development, human disturbance and predation at its nesting sites.

PROCELLARIDAE Petrels,
shearwaters
Cook's Petrel *Pterodroma cooki* breeds on a few New Zealand off-shore islands. Introduced predators are the main threats.
Pycroft's Petrel *Pterodroma pycrofti* breeds on islands off North Island,

New Zealand. Its population is below 1,000 pairs with low breeding success.

PHALACROCORACIDAE
Cormorants
New Zealand King Cormorant *Phalacrocorax carunculatus* is endemic to New Zealand. Its total population is estimated at less than 7,000.

ANATIDAE Ducks, geese, swans
Freckled Duck *Stictonetta naevosa* is declining in New South Wales and Western Australia, where it is threatened by habitat reduction and excessive hunting.

ACCIPITRIDAE Hawks, Old World vultures

Black Honey Buzzard *Henicopernis infuscata* is confined to primary rain-forest and forest edges in New Britain, off New Guinea.

Sandford's Sea Eagle *Haliaeetus sanfordi* (Pl. XXVIII) is confined to the Solomon Islands, where it is now theatened by deforestation and mineral mining.

Red Goshawk *Erythrotriorchis radiatus* is confined to forest and woodland and sparsely distributed across northern and eastern Australia, but is now rarely sighted.

New Britain Sparrowhawk *Accipiter brachyurus* is confined to rain-forest and forest edges in New Britain.

Imitator Sparrowhawk *Accipiter imitator* (Pl. XXVIII) is confined to primary and tall secondary rain-forest in northern Solomon Islands.

New Guinea Harpy Eagle *Harpyopsis novaeguineae* is confined to undisturbed forest in New Guinea, where it is little known. It is most frequent in mountains.

FALCONIDAE Falcons

Grey Falcon *Falco hypoleucos* is widespread in Australia but is rarely seen. A recent census produced only five records of breeding pairs.

TURNICIDAE Buttonquails

Black-breasted Buttonquail *Turnix melanogaster* is confined to dry rain-forest of eastern Queensland, Australia, where it is adapting to man-modified environment.

PEDIONOMIDAE Plains wanderer

Plains-wanderer *Pedionomus torquatus* (Pl. XXVI) occurs in sparse grassland habitat in south-east Australia with largest numbers around Denilquin, New South Wales. It is threatened by habitat destruction and introduced

predators. Recent work shows the species to be more numerous than once feared.

RALLIDAE Rails

Woodford's Rail *Nesoclopeus woodfordi* is confined to primary rain-forest on Bougainville, Santa Ysabel, and Guadalcanal, Solomon Islands, where it is threatened by deforestation.

CHARADRIIDAE Plovers

Hooded Plover *Charadrius rubricollis* is declining in Australia probably because of increased use of the beaches by humans.

SCOLOPACIDAE Snipes, woodcocks, sandpipers

Cox's Sandpiper *Calidris paramelanotos* is a new species described in 1982. It has been recorded only in Australia although it presumably breeds in the Northern Hemisphere. It could be a hybrid as no juveniles have been seen.

LARIDAE Gulls, terns

Pacific Gull *Larus pacificus* is endemic to Australia but it is nowhere common.

Black-fronted Tern *Sterna albostriata* is confined to South Island, New Zealand, where it is local and possibly declining. Its major breeding sites are threatened by hydro-electric development.

COLUMBIDAE Pigeons, doves

Yellow-legged Wood Pigeon *Columba pallidiceps* is a rarely recorded species of lowland forest in the Bismarck archipelago and the Solomon Islands.

Santa Cruz Ground Dove *Gallicolumba sanctaecrucis* is found in the Solomon Islands and Vanuatu, and not recorded recently.

Thick-billed Ground Dove *Gallicolumba salamonis* is confined to primary rain-forest on islands of the

San Cristóbal group, Solomon Islands.
Scheepmaker's Crowned Pigeon
Goura scheepmakeri occurs in lowland
forest in New Guinea. It is a prized,
large and easy target for hunters.
Victoria Crowned Pigeon *Goura
victoria* from New Guinea is also
prized by hunters and threatened in
areas accessible to man.
Island Imperial Pigeon *Ducula
pistrinaria* is widespread on small
islands in the Bismarck archipelago and
Solomon Islands. It is threatened by
hunting, especially as its communal
roosting habit makes it an easy target.

PSITTACIDAE Lories, parrots,
macaws
Biak Red Lory *Eos cyanogenia* is
confined to the coastal lowland
rain-forest and forest edges on islands
in Geelvink Bay, Irian Jaya.
Streaked Lorikeet *Charmosyna
multistriata* is known from a few
localities in the Snow Mountains of
Irian Jaya.
Hooded Parrot *Psephotus dissimilis*
occurs in the semi-arid north-east of
the Northern Territory, Australia. The
species has been heavily trapped in the
past and this may account for the
decline, but management of the
grasslands may be equally important.
Antipodes Islands Parakeet
Cyanoramphus unicolor is confined to
Antipodes Islands, New Zealand. It is
not greatly threatened so long as introduced predators are kept off the islands.

TYTONIDAE Barn owls
Golden Owl *Tyto aurantia* is confined
to primary rain-forest on New Britain.

STRIGIDAE Owls
Biak Scops Owl *Otus beccari* (Pl.
XXIV) from Biak Island, Geelvink
Bay, Irian Jaya is a forest habitat and
forest-edge species and is at risk from
the loss of its habitat.

Fearful Owl *Nesasio solomonensis* (Pl.
XXVIII) is confined to tall lowland and
hill rain-forest in Bougainville,
Choiseul and Santa Ysabel in the
Solomon Islands.

ALCEDINIDAE Kingfishers
New Britain Kingfisher *Halcyon
albonotata* is a scarce kingfisher from
lowland forest in New Britain, Papua
New Guinea.
Moustached Kingfisher *Halcyon
bougainvillei* is found on Bougainville,
Papua New Guinea, and Guadalcanal
in the Solomon Islands. It has not been
reliably reported since 1953.
Biak Paradise Kingfisher *Tanysiptera
riedelii* (Pl. XXIV) is confined to
primary rain-forest on Biak Island, off
west Irian Jaya.

PITTIDAE Pittas
Superb Pitta *Pitta superba* is confined
to primary rain-forest on Manus in the
Admiralty Islands.
Solomon Island Pitta *Pitta anerythra*
is known from Bougainville, Papua
New Guinea, and Santa Ysabel in the
Solomon Islands. It was formerly
described as common but has not been
recorded since 1936.

CAMPEPHAGIDAE Cuckoo-shrikes
Caledonian Greybird *Coracina analis*
(Pl. XXIX) is a mountain forest species
endemic to New Caledonia where it is
apparently scarce.

(MUSCICAPIDAE) TURDINAE
Thrushes
San Cristóbal Thrush *Zoothera
margaretae* is confined to montane
rain-forest on San Cristóbal island in
the Solomons.

(MUSCICAPIDAE) SYLVIINAE Old
world warblers
Kolombangara Warbler *Phylloscopus
amoenus* is endemic to Kolombangara,
Solomon Islands. Its status is unknown.

Fly River Grassbird *Megalurus albolimbatus* is known from the swampy grasslands of two localities in the Fly River region of southern Papua New Guinea, in Middle Fly and the Bensbach near the Irian Jaya border.
Whitney's Thicket Warbler *Cichlornis whitneyi* is confined to montane rain-forest thickets on Guadalcanal, Solomon Islands.

(MUSCICAPIDAE) MALURINAE Australian warblers
Purple-crowned Fairy-wren *Malurus coronatus* of Australia has declined in range and numbers due to pastoral development.
Thick-billed Grass-wren *Amytornis textilis* of Australia inhabits areas of thick scrub, and has declined where grazing has prevented young plants from maturing.
Grey Grass-wren *Amytornis barbatus* (Pl. XXVI) was first recorded in 1921 but it was not described until 1967. It is known from a number of locations in Australia and may prove to be more widespread than at first supposed.
Carpentarian Grass-wren *Amytornis dorotheae* is known from two locations in Northern Territory, Australia. It requires stands of spinifex that are slow to regenerate after burning.
Chestnut-breasted Whiteface *Aphelocephala pectoralis* (Pl. XXVI) is found in South Australia. It is nomadic and recorded rarely and incidentally.

(MUSCICAPIDAE) MONARCHINAE Monarchs
Rennell Shrikebill *Clytorhynchus hamlini* is confined to lowland rain-forest on Rennell Island, Solomon Islands. The island is well forested but a bauxite mining scheme could adversely affect the species.
Biak Monarch *Monarcha brehmii* (Pl. XXIV) is confined to lowland and hill

rain-forest on Biak Island, Geelvink Bay, Irian Jaya.
Biak Black Flycatcher *Myiagra atra* (Pl. XXIV) is confined to primary and tall secondary forest of interior hills of Biak and Numfor Islands, Geelvink Bay, Irian Jaya.

(MUSCICAPIDAE) RHIPIDURINAE Fantails
St. Matthias Rufous Fantail *Rhipidura matthiae* is confined to lowland and coastal rain-forest on St. Matthias Island in the Bismarck archipelago.

(MUSCICAPIDAE) PACHYCEPHALINAE Whistlers
Vogelkop Whistler *Pachycephala meyeri* is confined to hill rain-forest in the mountains of Vogelkop, Irian Jaya.

ZOSTEROPIDAE White-eyes
Biak White-eye *Zosterops mysorensis* (Pl. XXIV) is a forest species known only from Biak Island, Geelvink Bay, Irian Jaya.
Sudest White-eye *Zosterops meeki* is confined to lowland forest and forest edge on Sudest Island, Papua New Guinea.
Gezo White-eye *Zosterops luteirostris* is endemic to Gezo, Solomon Islands, where its habitat is being rapidly removed.
Nendo White-eye *Zosterops sanctaecrucis* is endemic to Nendo, Solomon Islands. Its status is unknown.
Sanford's White-eye *Woofordia lacertosa* is endemic to Nendo, Solomon Islands. Its status is unknown.

MELIPHAGIDAE Honeyeaters
Sudest Meliphaga *Meliphaga vicina* is confined to lowland rain-forest and forest edges on Tagula (Sudest) Island, Louisiade archipelago, in the Coral Sea.
Brass's Friarbird *Philemon brassi* is known from a single lagoon on the

Idenburg River, Irian Jaya.

Foerster's Melidectes *Melidectes foersteri* (Pl. XXV) is confined to montane rain-forest in the mountains of the Huon Peninsula, Papua New Guinea.

Huon Melipotes *Melipotes ater* (Pl. XXV) is also confined to the montane rain-forest on the Huon Peninsula, Papua New Guinea.

Red-faced Honeyeater *Gymnomyza aubryana* (Pl. XXIX) is endemic to New Caledonia, where it is local and little known.

Regent Honeyeater *Xanthomyza phrygia* has a declining range in eastern Australia.

Black-eared Miner *Monorina melanotis* is confined to mallee scrub in a small region at the junction of Victoria, New South Wales and South Australia. It is threatened by interbreeding with the Yellow-throated Miner *M. flavigula* and by clearance of the mallee.

ESTRILDIDAE Waxbills

Gouldian Finch *Erythrura gouldiae* from Australia is declining in parts of its range.

STURNIDAE Starlings

Rusty-winged Starling *Aplonis zelandica* is a lowland starling found on odd islands in the Solomon Islands. There are no recent records from Vanuatu.

CRACTICIDAE Bell magpies

Sudest Butcherbird *Cracticus louisiadensis* is endemic to Sudest Is., Papua New Guinea. It lives in lowland forest and forest edge and it is not well known.

PARADISAEIDAE Birds of paradise

Macgregor's Bird of Paradise

Macregoria pulchra is found in subalpine forests in New Guinea. Its range has contracted due to hunting pressure.

Long-tailed Paradigalla *Paradigalla carunculata* is confined to the montane rain-forest in the Vogelkop region and western Snow Mountains of Irian Jaya.

Black Sicklebill *Epimachus fastuosus* is patchily distributed in the mountains of western and central New Guinea. It is the largest plumed member of its family and is hunted both for its tail feathers and for food.

Brown Sicklebill *Epimachus meyeri* is very local in the central ranges of New Guinea where it is hunted.

Ribbon-tailed Astrapia *Astrapia mayeri* is confined to cloud-forest in the western part of the Central Highlands of Papua New Guinea.

Huon Bird of Paradise *Astrapia rothschildi* (Pl. XXV) is confined to montane rain-forest in the mountains of the Huon Peninsula, Papua New Guinea.

Wahnes's Parotia *Parotia wahnesi* (Pl. XXV) is confined to rain-forest in the mountains of the Huon Peninsula and the Adalbert Ranges, Papua New Guinea.

Goldie's Bird of Paradise *Paradisaea decora* is confined to hill rain-forest in the Fergusson and Normanby Islands of the D'Entrecasteaux archipelago.

Emperor of Germany Bird of Paradise *Paradisaea guilielmi* (Pl. XXV) is confined to hill rain-forest in the mountains of the Huon Peninsula, Papua New Guinea.

Blue Bird of Paradise *Paradisaea rudolphi* is confined to the edges of primary montane rain-forest in the mountains of central south-east Papua New Guinea.

Chapter 8
Pacific Islands

This final chapter deals with the threatened birds which are confined to remote islands scattered over the wide expanse of the Pacific Ocean. Other species which are also island birds, but which occur on islands clearly related to the nearest continent, have already been described under the headings of the six zoogeographical regions.

In his foreword to the report on the recent ICBP International Symposium on Island Birds, Dr Christoph Imboden said that time, isolation and the small areas of oceanic islands had led to the evolution of unique wildlife communities with high numbers of endemic plant and animal species. These include some of the most bizarre and fascinating birds to be found anywhere, for islands are the primary source of biological novelty. Most of the birds which have lost the powers of flight are, or sadly were, found only on islands. But they are all high-risk species and extremely vulnerable to any change in their restricted ecosystems. About three-quarters of the species of birds known to have become extinct in the last four centuries were island forms. This alarming trend is still continuing: at least two-thirds of today's threatened species occur only on islands and will probably disappear at the rate of one every year unless greater resources can be found for their conservation.

On a small island, habitat destruction can very easily be total. There is no

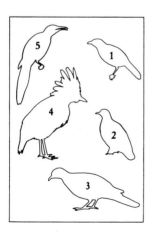

PLATE XXIX New Caledonia. 1 Caledonian Greybird (p. 193), 2 Cloven-feathered Dove (p. 184), 3 Giant Imperial Pigeon (p. 184), 4 Kagu (p. 183), 5 Red-faced Honeyeater (p. 195).

PLATE XXX Mariana Islands. 1 Marianas Fruit Dove (p. 204), 2 Marianas Crow (p. 205), 3 Micronesian Scrubfowl (p. 202), 4 Guam Flycatcher (p. 210).

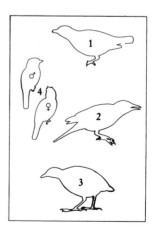

Norman Arlott 87

retreat for highly specialised creatures which have evolved without any defence against predators or aggressive competitors. Their struggle for survival in the face of human disturbance is a depressing spectacle which can be witnessed today in horrible reality on many islands, especially on those of the now highly "developed" Hawaiian and New Zealand archipelagos. In some instances species such as the Dodo and the Solitaires of the Mascarene islands were exterminated directly by man, but most of today's extinctions will be brought about either by predators introduced by man, or by the exploitation of island resources, by lumbering, by mining, by agriculture, or by touristic development.

However, the prospect is not entirely one of doom and gloom. Seemingly hopeless situations have led to some of the most imaginative and enterprising work in conservation management. Providing that destruction has not gone too far, the ecosystems of small islands often respond more readily to skilled management than do larger land-masses, so that restoration is sometimes possible. This book shows that projects initiated in despair have occasionally resulted in spectacular successes, proving that if the necessary skill, resources and dedication can be applied, endangered species can still be saved.

This book also indicates the extent of the problems faced by ICBP and also the many opportunities for saving species. The cooperation of governments is, of course, an essential element and it is pleasing that throughout the world this cooperation is now being more readily provided. Some of the great despoilers of extensive areas of wildlife habitat, such as the multi-national mining, petroleum and civil engineering companies, are beginning to regard restoration and conservation sympathetically and to provide funds for it. The main impediment to progress, however, is the lack of financial resources. Dedicated conservationists face this problem daily, striving against time and terrible odds to put off that final word: extinction. It is a sad reflection on humanity that

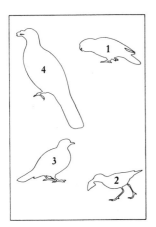

PLATE XXXI French Polynesia. 1 Tahiti Lorikeet (p. 204), 2 Tuamotu Sandpiper (p. 202), 3 Society Islands Ground Dove (p. 204), 4 Society Islands Imperial Pigeon (p. 203).

PLATE XXXII Hawaii. 1 Ou (p. 208), 2 Kauai Creeper (p. 210), 3 Nukupuu (p. 207), 4 Akialoa (p. 207), 5 Kauai Oo (p. 207).

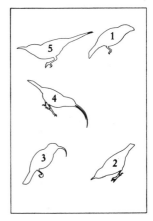

every year that passes sees more and more of the world's natural heritage of wildlife disappear for lack of the money so cheerfully paid for a few more miles of motorway, or for yet another space satellite. I hope this book will encourage readers to give tangible support to the International Council for Bird Preservation and to the World Wide Fund for Nature. Both these organisations draw on and contribute to scientific resources of the International Union for Conservation of Nature and Natural Resources and their partnership represents the main hope for the future of the world's wildlife.

The following description of threatened species of island birds refers to those known to be at risk. Without doubt there are many more and the list grows longer every year. Many remote oceanic islands have not been visited for decades by ornithologists and can be explored only by costly expeditions. To some there is now no access because of closely guarded military installations. A few others have been used as targets for testing atomic weapons and are now lifeless, although once the breeding grounds of countless seabirds. It should be borne in mind, therefore, that this chapter is inevitably incomplete.

On the small island of Ngau, in the Fiji group 1,500 miles east of Australia, a single (juvenile) specimen of a new species of petrel, the **Fiji Petrel** *Pterodroma macgillivrayi*, was collected in 1855. It was not seen again until an intrepid ICBP-backed explorer rediscovered it in 1984. A specimen was caught, photographed and released. Several others were subsequently caught or seen. A very small population evidently nests in the rocky summit of Ngau. Its status is Indeterminate.

The **Micronesian Scrubfowl** *Megapodius laperouse* (Plate XXX) is locally common in Belau and the Mariana Islands. The species remains threatened though by egg harvesting (see also p. 150) and the introduction of predators, and it is consequently listed as Rare.

Many oceanic island rails are gravely threatened. One is the **Guam Rail** *Rallus owstoni* which is endemic to Guam in the Mariana Islands. Like many isolated island rails it is flightless, but has the ability to adapt to both grasslands and

woodlands and moreover it is apparently continuing to survive in spite of the presence of numerous predators such as feral cats and pigs. However, a major decline in its population took place in 1971–1972 and fewer than 100 are believed to survive in the north, but it is still relatively numerous, a situation which in view of the pressure of predation has been described as little short of miraculous. It is protected by the Guam Government and may no longer be hunted. It is listed by ICBP as Vulnerable.

The Fiji Islands also have a rail with Endangered status, the **Barred-wing Rail** *Nesoclopeus poeciloptera*. It was believed to have been exterminated by introduced mongooses, cats and rats by 1920. They still threaten its survival. A single bird was rediscovered in 1973 on the island of Viti Levu. No measures have been taken to protect the species and its survival seems doubtful.

The original type-specimen of the **Tuamotu Sandpiper** *Prosobonia cancellatus* (Plate XXXI) was collected on

Christmas Island, in the Line Islands of the South Pacific. It is no longer found there but, in 1920, an American expedition collected 60 specimens from 16 of the 76 small atolls and 400 islets of the Tuamotu archipelago. This was evidently done in the then current belief in the axiom "shoot it before it disappears for ever". It is becoming extremely rare and is listed by ICBP as Vulnerable.

The **Tooth-billed Pigeon** *Didunculus strigirostris* of Western Samoa is also excessively hunted and now much at risk, being listed by ICBP as Vulnerable. It occurs only in virgin forest up to 1,400 metres on Upolu and Savai'i, where the felling of trees for timber, coconut plantations and pasture has resulted in a serious loss of habitat. Foreign lumber companies are destroying Western Samoa's forests at an alarming rate and the country also has a very rapid rate of population growth. The creation of a protected reserve on Nu'ulua Island has been recommended. This would also protect the scarce Friendly Ground Dove *Gallicolumba stairi* and a breeding beach of Green Turtles *Chelonia mydas*.

The **Society Islands Imperial Pigeon** *Ducula aurorae* (Plate XXXI) of Tahiti and the Makatea in the Tuamotu archipelago is another of the numerous species of island pigeons and doves which are now in danger. In 1972 there were only ten in Tahiti and about 500 on

Makatea. Following the cessation of phosphate mining on Makatea the vegetation has recovered and enabled the population to increase. It may now be secure there. The hunting of birds was prohibited throughout French Polynesia in 1967 but this is not properly enforced. A nature reserve has been established in the Papenoo Valley on Tahiti but it needs more efficient wardening to prevent hunting, burning and over-grazing. The species is listed by ICBP as Vulnerable.

In the Marquesas Islands a pigeon and a dove are endangered. The **Marquesas Imperial Pigeon** *Ducula galeata* has a population estimated in 1972 at between 200 and 400, confined to the wooded ridges and valleys of the western end of Nukuhiva. Although officially protected by French law, it is still hunted because of its large size and tasty flesh. Its habitat is threatened by the construction of an airport, the relocation of which has been recommended, as has the creation of a protected reserve. It is classified as Endangered.

The **Marquesas Ground Dove** *Gallicolumba rubescens* has an even smaller population, which in 1975 was estimated at not more than 225. It occurs only on the two widely separated small islets of Hatatu and Fatuhuku, which are 250 km apart, but it undoubtedly used to occur on others in this large archipelago, before the introduction of rats, cats, dogs and pigs. Considerable French military activity began on Eiao (barely 5 km from Hatatu) soon after Eiao was given protected status in 1971, which brought into question the reliability of the similar status given to Hatatu. If this island is used by the army, even for recreational purposes, there will be a grave risk that predatory animals and non-indigenous vegetation will be introduced. Both islands where the ground doves occur are officially protected and hunting was

Barred-wing Rail

banned in 1967. The future of the species will depend on keeping the islands intact and free from predators. The status of *G. rubescens* is given by ICBP as Indeterminate.

The **Society Islands Ground Dove** *Callicolumba erythroptera* (Plate XXXI) was thought to have been exterminated in the middle of the last century on several atolls in the Tuamotu archipelago, and also on Tahiti and Moorea in the Society Islands. In 1966 its population was said to be still quite large on three of the Tuamotu islands which had remained free of cats and rats, but accurate knowledge of its present status is lacking. No conservation measures have been taken apart from the (ineffective) prohibition of bird-hunting by the French Government in 1967. The species is listed by ICBP as Indeterminate.

The **Mariana Fruit Dove** *Ptilinopus roseicapilla* (Plate XXX) is restricted to four islands in the Mariana group in the Western Pacific. These are Guam, Rota, Tinian and Saipan. Until the islands were overrun in the Second World War the doves were numerous on all four. Since then they have suffered to some extent from hunting and deforestation, but perhaps 200 still survive on Guam and a few on Tinian. They may be suffering from competition from the Philippines Turtle Dove *Streptopelia bitorquata*,

which was introduced by hunters. The species is included in the Guam Endangered Species list and no longer hunted, but is not yet incorporated in the Endangered Species Act of 1975. It has been recommended for inclusion in the US Trust Territories list of endangered species. ICBP classifies it as Vulnerable.

The **Rapa Fruit Dove** *Ptilinopus huttoni* is restricted to the wooded hills of Rapa Island, near the eastern end of the Austral Islands chain, south of Tahiti. Its population is only 125 pairs. It is hunted for food, and is losing its habitat and is classified by the ICBP as Rare.

The range of the **Tahiti Lorikeet** *Vini peruviana* (Plate XXXI) has shrunk considerably to some of the islands in the Tuamotu archipelago, two in the Society Islands and an introduced population in the Cook Islands. It disappeared from the larger of the Society Islands shortly after the introduction of the Marsh Harrier *Circus aeruginosus* which probably preyed on it. Its decline in the Tuamotus may have been associated with the introduction of a mosquito which is a vector of avian malaria. Today the total population is thought to be under a thousand even though it frequents coconut groves, an abundant habitat. ICBP lists the species as Rare.

The **Ultramarine Lorikeet** *Vini ultramarina*, also considered Rare, is restricted to two of the Marquesas Islands and introduced on a third. In 1975 the population was estimated to be only 300 pairs, and these remaining birds are threatened by the continued degradation of the forests and the possible introduction of avian malaria.

The very little-known **Long-legged Warbler** *Trichocichla rufa* from Fiji was believed to have been extinct by 1894, but was seen again in 1967 and 1973 on Viti Levu and on the ridgetops of Vanua Levu in 1974. A new subspecies *T. r.*

Long-legged Warbler

cluniei was discovered in 1976 on the northern slopes of the Delanacau mountains in west-central Vanua Levu. Nothing is known about the population of either race, but the fact that the Long-legged Warblers have a local Fijian name suggests that they were once widespread. There is still sufficient scrub left on the islands to support them. They are listed by ICBP as Endangered.

An ornithological survey of the remote Cook Islands was carried out in 1973. It was found that the **Rarotonga Flycatcher** *Pomarea dimidiata*, which had been regarded as rather rare in 1899, had declined to only about 50–100 birds and that its habitat in the forested foothills was being rapidly destroyed by logging. It now has only 24–30 birds, which are threatened by three species of rats as well as by cats. Recommendations for a protected reserve to save it have been made. Meanwhile it is listed by ICBP as Vulnerable.

On Tahiti, in the Society Islands, a small population of the **Tahiti Monarch** *Pomarea nigra* still survives in the forested mountains behind Papeete, on Mount Mara. The reasons for its scarcity are not known and Mount Mara is now a wildlife reserve where the monarchs are protected by law. It is classified as Endangered. Of the other races, "*P. n. tabuensis*" from the Tonga Islands is now known to have been a Polynesian Triller *Lalage maculosa tabuensis*, while *P. n. pomarea* from Maupiti in the Society Islands is extinct.

The **Truk Monarch** *Metabolus rugensis* is endemic to Caroline Island in the Truk group, Western Pacific. Its habitat now includes plantations, indicating ability to accept changed conditions, but its single egg clutch gives low reproductive capacity and it is classified as Rare.

In the Truk group of the Caroline Islands in the Western Pacific the **Great**

Truk White-eye *Rukia ruki* has been seen and collected only on the forested summit of Mount Winibot on the small island of Tol in the Truk group, where its population is obviously very small. It was last seen in 1975 during an ornithological survey of the archipelago. The species is protected under the US Trust Territories Endangered Species Act. Mount Winibot has been recommended as a conservation area and it is deplorable that this has not yet been implemented in order to protect one of the world's rarest birds. Another species of the genus *Rukia* is also at risk: the **Great Pohnpei White-eye** *R. longirostra* from Pohnpei Island, which is classified as Rare.

The **Pink-eared Parrotfinch** *Erythrura kleinschmidti* is endemic to Viti Levu, Fiji. It is classified by ICBP as Rare and it seems that it has always been a scarce species. It is probably more widespread than once thought as there are now records from secondary scrub and *Cocos* plantations, but a secure population probably depends upon the protection of indigenous forest.

The **Santo Mountain Starling** *Aplonis santovestris* is thinly distributed in the interior highlands of Espíritu Santo, Vanuatu. Recent expeditions have failed to locate the species, although the habitat in which it is known to occur remains intact, and ICBP lists the species as Rare.

The **Marianas Crow** *Corvus kubaryi* (Plate XXX), an Endangered species, is declining on both the islands in the southern Marianas where it still occurs. It used to be well distributed throughout Guam in forests and coconut plantations but occurs now only between Mangilao and Tumon Bay. On Rota its total population is fewer than 200 birds. Part of its range is within the Pati Point Natural Area and the Anao Conservation Reserve. It is legally protected and on the Guam Endangered Species list.

Hawaiian Goose

The islands of **Hawaii** are famous for the great diversity of their endemic birds, their luxuriant vegetation and their spectacular mountain scenery. Unfortunately, they are equally famous for the number of their unique bird species which are now extinct and for the large number of exotic species of birds and other animals and also plants which have been introduced. Since the Second World War Hawaii itself has been so extensively "developed" that much of this island now resembles suburban Los Angeles or Miami. Nevertheless, the islands as a whole are still rich in fascinating wildlife and especially in the colourful birds which can be seen in the protected reserves and the forested and less extensively developed regions. The long list of those now regarded as threatened, in spite of the skilled efforts of conservationists, is, however, depressing.

The **Hawaiian Goose** or **Nene** *Branta sandvicensis* occurs on the sparsely vegetated lava slopes of two mountains on Hawaii. The species declined from an estimated 25,000 birds at the end of the last century to a low of perhaps 30 by 1952, and only the release of over 1,400 captive bred birds has maintained it in the wild. Even so it is doubtful whether the Hawaiian Goose can sustain the heavy predation pressure it is under from introduced rats, cats, dogs and mongooses. ICBP classifies the species as Vulnerable.

The **Hawaiian Hawk** *Buteo solitarius* is thinly but widely distributed on Hawaii and is listed as Rare by ICBP. Recent surveys suggest that it is increasing under protection and it may be that its status as a threatened species will be reassessed in the near future.

The **Puaiohi** or **Small Kauai Thrush** *Myadestes palmeri* is confined to a small part of the Alaha'i Swamp on the Hawaiian island of Kauai. It was apparently never very numerous and now has a very small population which is classed as Endangered. Its habitat is wet montane forest dominated by *Metrosideros* trees. No more than 15 were seen during a thorough search of the surviving rain-forest in 1960 and only seven were seen in 1981. The introduction of exotic plants, predatory animals and competing bird species carrying avian diseases have contributed to the rarity of the thrushes, as has habitat destruction by grazing and browsing animals. The range of the species is within the Alaha'i Swamp Wilderness Reserve and the thrushes are also protected by federal and state laws.

The **Nihoa Warbler** *Acrocephalus familiaris* is known only from the tiny Hawaiian island of Nihoa. It used to occur on Laysan too, but was extirpated some time between 1912 and 1923 following the destruction of the indigenous vegetation by introduced rabbits. The bird lives on brushy hillsides and, although it is quite common, it could easily be threatened by alteration of the habitat or introduction of predators such as cats or rats. ICBP gives the species a Rare status.

An even more critically Endangered species on the island of Kauai is the curiously-named **Kauai Oo** *Moho braccatus* (Plate XXXII). The name is the one originally given by the Hawaiians, whose language to Western ears consists mainly of glottals and vowel sounds. It is appropriate that many of the birds have retained their local vernacular names instead of being renamed by Westerners. The Oo is one of the numerous family of **honeyeaters**, but is mainly insectivorous, feeding like a woodpecker by climbing the trunks of trees. It was thought to be extinct, but was rediscovered in 1960 in the mountain rain-forest of the Alaha'i Swamp on Kauai. Its nest was found in 1971 and it was seen again in 1981, but its population, which was large in the nineteenth century, may now be only one or two pairs. It is protected by federal and states laws and its range is within the Wilderness Reserve area, but it risks predation by the tree-climbing Black Rats of the area and is classified as Endangered. It is the sole certain survivor of its genus, which included the now

extinct Hawaiian species *M. nobilis* and *M. apicalis*; the fourth species, **Bishop's Oo** *M. bishopi*, was reported to have been seen in 1981 on Mount Haleakala on Maui, prior to which it had last been seen in 1915 and was already classified as Extinct but has now been reclassified as a Candidate species.

The **Nukupuu** *Hemignathus lucidus* (Plate XXXII) is listed as Endangered. Between 1896 and 1967 the sub-species *H. l. affins* was regarded as extinct but has now been reclassified. It was rediscovered in 1968 in the remote high-altitude rain-forest on the slope of the Haleakala volcano on the Hawaiian island of Maui, and has been seen again in subsequent years. Its population is probably very small. It is protected by federal and state laws and its range is protected by the Haleakala National Park, access to the valley where it survives being restricted. The extension of US federal jurisdiction to other areas thought to be inhabited by the Nukupu'u and other honeycreepers is being considered. There is some invasion of even the remotest Hawaiian forests by harmful non-native plants and animals, including the Black Rat, which threatens the survival of all bird species. The Kauai Nukupu'u *H. l. hanapepe*, the only other surviving subspecies, is restricted to a small part of the Alaha'i Swamp on Kauai. It was similarly "lost" between 1890 and 1960 but has been recorded a few times in recent years. The nominate race *H. l. lucidus* of Oahu is already extinct.

Yet another critically Endangered and possibly extinct species is the **Akialoa** *Hemignathus obscurus* (Plate XXXII), which has a long, decurved bill. Its range, if it still exists, is within the Alaka'i Swamp Wilderness Reserve on Kauai Island, where it is protected by federal and state law. The three other races, *H. o. allisianus* on Oahu,

H. o. lanaiensis on Lanai and *H. o. obscurus* on Hawaii are all extinct.

The **Akiapolaau** *Hemignathus munori* is another honeycreeper, found in only two or three small areas of native forest on the island of Hawaii. It was formerly widespread in all the upland forests, but is now restricted to parts of the Kilauea Forest Reserve and adjacent regions and to the Olea Forest Reserve in Puna District. Single birds have recently been seen in the Kohala and Mount Hualalai regions. Its total population is in the low hundreds and declining. Little natural regeneration is taking place in the region it inhabits because of overgrazing by goats, sheep and pigs. The species also suffers from predation by tree-climbing rats and competition from introduced exotic birds. Little has been done to improve its habitat by the Hawaiian Department of Land and Natural Resources, but it is protected by federal and state laws. ICBP lists it as Endangered.

A honeycreeper which is suffering entirely because of human selfishness and neglect is the seed-eating **Palila** *Psittirostra bailleui*. The species is found only in the high-elevation forest on the western slope of Mauna Kea, Hawaii, and is dependent on the Mamane tree for its existence. A large part of the Mamane forest is managed by the Hawaii State Division of Fish and Game for hunting. In order to satisfy hunters it has been subjected to severe over-grazing, erosion and loss of natural regeneration. This has been much criticized by conservationists, but although the Palila is obviously declining, with a population of barely 2,000 in 1984, nothing is done apart from the protection it is supposed to receive under federal and state laws. ICBP lists it as Endangered.

Another Hawaiian honeycreeper, the **Poo Uli** *Melamprosops phaesoma*, was discovered in 1973 in the tangled forest on the north-east slope of Haleakala volcano on Maui. It has a very restricted range, within which it is apparently rare. Its status is given by ICBP as Rare.

The **Crested Honeycreeper** *Palmeria dolei* occupies the upper rain-forest of the Haleakala volcano on Maui and is threatened by the usual introduced cats, rats and avian diseases. It has not been seen on Maolokai, where it used to occur, since 1907 and its population on Maui is now very small. It is protected, like the other rare honeycreepers, by federal and state law and it has some protection in the fact that its range is within the Haleakala National Park, and it should also benefit from the new Waikamai Reserve on Maui. It is classified as Vulnerable.

The curious **Maui Parrotbill** *Pseudonestor xanthophrys*, which, although belonging to the honeycreeper family, has a stout, parrot-like bill, is now listed as Vulnerable. It is found only in the high Koa forests of Maui, on the north and east slopes of Haleakala volcano and in the upper Kipahulu Valley. Its population may still be fairly large, but is threatened by introduced pigs, rats, exotic birds and avian diseases. It is protected by federal and state law and the Kipahulu Valley is within the Haleakala National Park. The remaining native forest on the north-east of the volcano is one of the two most important habitats surviving in the Hawaiian Islands.

The last of the threatened Hawaiian honeycreepers is the **Ou** *Psittirostra psittacea* (Plate XXXII). It used to be found on the islands of Kauai, Oahu, Molokai, Lanai, Maui and Hawaii. Now it survives only in the centre of the Alaka'i Swamp on Kauai and on Hawaii in the Ula'a Tract and the Hilo Forest Reserve. In 1977 several thorough searches by the US Fish and Wildlife Service could find only 61 birds and the total population

certainly does not exceed the very low hundreds. The causes of its decline are exactly the same as for the other honeycreepers and, like them, it is fully protected by law. It is Endangered.

The **Alala'** or **Hawaiian Crow** *Corvus tropicus* is listed by ICBP as Endangered. A small relict population still survives on the island of Hawaii. It was very tame and fairly common until the 1930s, but is now reduced to about 130 birds, mostly on the slopes of Hualalai. The reasons for its precipitous decline are obscure, but increased grazing, hunting, habitat destruction, introduced predators and avian diseases probably contributed. The extent of both the wet and dry forest favoured by this species has greatly diminished and both have been invaded by feral pigs, goats and cattle and also by the arboreal Black Rat which preys on eggs and nestlings. The crows are protected by federal and state law and an attempted captive-breeding project is in hand.

ADDITIONAL CANDIDATE SPECIES OF THE PACIFIC ISLANDS

PROCELLARIIDAE Petrels, shearwaters
Murphy's Petrel *Pterodroma ultima* is a little-known species discovered during the 1920s at Tubuai Islands.
Newell's Shearwater *Puffinus newelli* has a much reduced breeding range in Hawaii. It has suffered from predation, destructon of some colonies by fire and mortality of fledglings attracted to street lights.

HYDROBATIDAE Storm-petrels
Sooty Storm-petrel *Oceanodroma tristrami* has colonies on the Hawaiian Islands with an estimated population of less than 10,000. It also occurs on some of the Japanese islands but its status there is unknown.

MEGAPODIIDAE Megapodes
Niuafo'ou Scrubfowl *Megapodius pritchardii* is confined to the remote island of Niuafo'ou (Tonga), where it incubates its eggs in hot volcanic ash. The major threats to the species are egg collecting and feral cats.

RALLIDAE Rails
Henderson Rail *Nesophylax ater* is confined to Henderson Island in the Pitcairn group. The island is undisturbed, but small and vulnerable, only recently escaping conversion to an American millionaire's home.

APODIDAE Swifts
Tahiti Swiftlet *Aerodramus lencophaeus* has declined on Tahiti

where it feeds over wet, rocky and forested valleys.

Atiu Swiftlet *Aerodramus sawtelli* was collected in 1973 from a cave in Atiu in the Cook Islands. Only 60 nests were recorded but local inhabitants reported that there were a few smaller colonies elsewhere on the island.

ALCEDINIDAE Kingfishers
Mangaia Kingfisher *Halcyon ruficollaris* is unique to Mangaria in the Cook Islands, where it is threatened by deforestation.
Tuamotu Kingfisher *Halcyon gambieri* is known from only one island in the Tuamotu archipelago.
Marquesas Kingfisher *Halcyon godeffroyi* is endemic to the Marquesas Islands. It is a shy forest dweller and has always been considered scarce.

(MUSCICAPIDAE) TURDINAE
Thrushes
Kamao *Myadestes myadestinus* is endemic to the Hawaiian Islands.
Olomao *Myadestes lanaiensis* is endemic to the Hawaiian Islands and requires monitoring.

(MUSCICAPIDAE) SYLVIINAE
Old world warblers
Nauru Warbler *Acrocephalis rehsei* is endemic to the Micronesian island of Nauru, where it is reported to be still present in the remaining bushy areas.

(MUSCICAPIDAE)
MONARCHINAE Monarchs
Marquesas Monarch *Pomarea mendozae* was common in the Marquesas Islands in the 1920s and has declined since due to deforestation.
Versicolour Flycatcher *Mayrornis versicolor* is confined to the small island of Ogea in the Lau Group, Fiji, where it has a very restricted distribution and .is very little known.
Guam Flycatcher *Myiagra freycineti*

(Pl. XXX) is endemic to Guam. It was once widespread in wooded areas but the population has crashed over the last decade.

ZOSTEROPIDAE White-eyes
Small Lifou White-eye *Zosterops minuta* is endemic to Lifou in the Loyalty Islands. Its status is unknown.
Large Lifou White-eye *Zosterops iriornata* is endemic to Lifou in the Loyalty Islands. It is a forest species very rarely found in native gardens.

DREPANIDIDAE Hawaiian honeycreepers
Kauai Creeper *Oreomystis bairdi* (Pl. XXXII) is endemic to Kauai in the Hawaiian Islands, where it is uncommon in high native forest.
Hawaii Creeper *Oreomystis mana* is endemic to Hawaii in the Hawaiian Islands.
Oahu Creeper *Paroreomyza maculata* is endemic to Oahu in the Hawaiian Islands where it is extremely scarce.
Maui Creeper *Paroreomyza montana* is only found on the slopes of one volcano on Maui in the Hawaiian Islands.
Akepa *Loxops coccinea* is found in the Hawaiian Islands where it is locally common on Hawaii and patchily distributed on Maui.
Nihoa Finch *Telespyza ultima* is only found on the tiny island of Nihoa in the Hawaiian Islands.
Laysan Finch *Telespyza cantans* is only found on Laysan in the Hawaiian Islands.

STURNIDAE Starlings
Rarotonga Starling *Aplonis cinerascens* is restricted to the forested interior of Rarotonga, Cook Islands. It was regarded as abundant early this century but conservative estimates made in 1984 put the population at 100.

Appendix I

A Systematic List of the World's Threatened Bird Species

Compiled by Nigel Collar and Paul Andrew, ICBP, December 1987, for the 1988 IUCN List of Threatened Animals

NAMES

The vernacular names used here are generally those commonly cited. Ornithologists vary as to which of the many authorities to follow, and thus standardisation between avifaunal regions and different groups of birds is a complex, controversial and lengthy task beyond the scope of this book. The scientific names and taxonomic order largely follow Morony, Bock and Farrand (1975) (see bibliography).

STATUS

Each bird is given a threat status according to the latest ICBP Red Data Book research. The categories used are as follows:

E, Endangered
> The species is known to be in danger of extinction, and is unlikely to survive if the causal factors continue operating.

V, Vulnerable
> The species is less threatened than those in the Endangered category, but is likely to move to the Endangered category.

I, Indeterminate
> The species is thought to be either Endangered, Vulnerable or at best Rare, but there is not enough evidence to place it definitely in one of these categories.

K, Insufficiently Known
> The species is suspected to be, but because of lack of information not definitely known to be, at risk.

R, Rare
> The species has a small but stable population which may be at risk (often as a function of a restricted range), and therefore requires careful monitoring.

S, Of Special Concern
> The species is at present safe but generates a great conservation interest.

K*, Candidate Red Data Book
> The species is being considered for the next editions of the Red Data Books. No particular status has been assigned to it because research has not yet been completed, but it could be any of the above.

REGION

Zoogeographic regions are numbered as follows:

1	Palaearctic Region	4a	Madagascar
2	Nearctic Region	4b	Africa's Related Islands
3	Neotropical Region	5	Oriental Region
	Afrotropical Region	6	Australasian Region
4	Mainland Africa	7	Pacific Ocean Islands

CITES

The Convention on International Trade in Endangered Species of Wild Fauna and Flora (CITES) seeks to regulate international trade in wild animals and plants by cooperation between exporting and importing countries. The Convention is implemented by means of licences issued in member countries, and no species listed in CITES can be traded without some sort of documentation.

It prohibits (except in extraordinary circumstances) international commercial trade in species that are threatened with extinction and which are or may be threatened by trade. These species are listed in CITES Appendix I.

It controls international trade in species whose survival is not yet threatened but may become so unless trade in these species is strictly controlled. These species are listed in CITES Appendix II.

It reinforces the protection of species already protected by national legislation. These species are listed on CITES Appendix III. Countries may seek international co-operation in enforcement of their laws, although this Appendix is not often used.

VERNACULAR NAME	SCIENTIFIC NAME	STATUS	CITES	ZOOGEOGRAPHIC REGION	RANGE	PAGE
RHEAS	**Order RHEIFORMES** **Family Rheidae**					
Puna Rhea	*Pterocnemia tarapacensis*	E		3	Peru, Bolivia, Argentina, Chile	68
KIWIS	**Order APTERYGIFORMES** **Family Apterygidae**					
Little Spotted Kiwi	*Apteryx owenii*	K*		6	New Zealand	176
TINAMOUS	**Order TINAMIFORMES** **Family Tinamidae**					
Solitary Tinamou	*Tinamus solitarius*	K*	I	3	Argentina, Brazil, Paraguay	92
Black Tinamou	*Tinamus osgoodi*	K*		3	Colombia, Peru	92
Magdalena Tinamou	*Crypturellus saltuarius*	I		3	Colombia	69
Yellow-legged Tinamou	*Crypturellus noctivagus*	K*		3	Brazil	92
Taczanowski's Tinamou	*Nothoprocta taczanowskii*	K*		3	Peru	92
Kalinowski's Tinamou	*Nothoprocta kalinowskii*	K*		3	Peru	92
Lesser Nothura	*Nothura minor*	K*		3	Brazil	92
Dwarf Tinamou	*Taoniscus nanus*	K*		3	Argentina, Brazil	92
PENGUINS	**Order SPHENISCIFORMES** **Family Spheniscidae**					
Yellow-eyed Penguin	*Megadyptes antipodes*	K*		6	New Zealand	191
Jackass Penguin	*Spheniscus demersus*	S	II	4	Namibia, South Africa	106
Peruvian Penguin	*Spheniscus humboldti*	K*	I	3	Chile, Peru	92
GREBES	**Order PODICIPEDIFORMES** **Family Podicipedidae**					
Madagascar Little Grebe	*Tachybaptus pelzelni*	K		4a	Madagascar	126
Alaotra Grebe	*Tachybaptus rufolavatus*	E		4a	Madagascar	126
Junín Grebe	*Podiceps taczanowskii*	E		3	Peru	69
Hooded Grebe	*Podiceps gallardoi*	R		3	Argentina	69
ALBATROSSES	**Order PROCELLARIIFORMES** **Family Diomedeidae**					
Amsterdam Albatross	*Diomedea amsterdamensis*	E		4b	Amsterdam I.	145
Short-tailed Albatross	*Diomedea albatrus*	E	I	1	Japan	33
PETRELS, SHEARWATERS	**Family Procellariidae**					
Mascarene Black Petrel	*Pterodroma aterrima*	E		4b	Mauritius	131
Gon-gon	*Pterodroma feae*	R		4b	Cape Verde Is., Madeira (Portugal)	143
Freira	*Pterodroma madeira*	E		4b	Madeira (Portugal)	143
Black-capped Petrel	*Pterodroma hasitata*	V		3	Cuba, Domincan Republic, Haiti	69
Cahow	*Pterodroma cahow*	E		2	Bermuda	54
Beck's Petrel	*Pterodroma becki*	I		6	Papua New Guinea, Solomon Is.	176
Murphy's Petrel	*Pterodroma ultima*	K*		7	Pitcairn I. (UK), Tuamotu (France)	209
Magenta Petrel	*Pterodroma magentae*	E		6	Chatham Is. (New Zealand)	176
Dark-rumped Petrel	*Pterodroma phaeopygia*	E		3	Galápagos (Ecuador), Hawaiian Is. (USA)	69
Cook's Petrel	*Pterodroma cooki*	K*		6	New Zealand	191

VERNACULAR NAME	SCIENTIFIC NAME	STATUS	CITES	ZOOGEOGRAPHIC REGION RANGE	PAGE
Chatham Island Petrel	*Pterodroma axillaris*	E		6	Chatham Is. (New Zealand)	181
Defilippe's Petrel	*Pterodroma defilippiana*	K*		3	Chile	92
Pycroft's Petrel	*Pterodroma pycrofti*	K*		6	New Zealand	191
Fiji Petrel	*Pterodroma macgillivrayi*	I		7	Fiji	202
Black Petrel	*Procellaria parkinsoni*	E		6	New Zealand	181
Westland Black Petrel	*Procellaria westlandica*	V		6	New Zealand	181
Pink-footed Shearwater	*Puffinus creatopus*	K*		3	Juan Fernandez Is. (Chile)	92
Heinroth's Shearwater	*Puffinus heinrothi*	I		6	Papua New Guinea	181
Newell's Shearwater	*Puffinus newelli*	K*		7	Hawaiian Is. (USA)	209
Black-vented Shearwater	*Puffinus opisthornelas*	K*		2	Mexico	66
Townsend's Shearwater	*Puffinus auricularis*	K*		2	Mexico	66
STORM-PETRELS	**Family Hydrobatidae**				
Least Storm-petrel	*Halocyptena microsoma*	K*		2	Mexico	66
Markham's Storm-petrel	*Oceanodroma markhami*	K*		3	Eastern Pacific Ocean	92
Sooty Storm-petrel	*Oceanodroma tristrami*	K*		7	Hawaiian Is. (USA), Japan	209
Ringed Storm-petrel	*Oceanodroma hornbyi*	K*		3	Chile, Ecuador, Peru	92
Black Storm-petrel	*Oceanodroma melania*	K*		2	California, Mexico	66
DIVING-PETRELS	**Family Pelecanoididae**				
Peruvian Diving-petrel	*Pelecanoides garnoti*	K*		3	Chile, Peru	92
PELICANS	**Order PELECANIFORMES** **Family Pelecanidae**				
Dalmatian Pelican	*Pelecanus crispus*	V	I	1	Western Palaearctic	34
Spot-billed Pelican	*Pelecanus philippensis*	K*		5	Burma, China, India, Indonesia, Kampuchea, Laos, Malaysia, Thailand, Vietnam	164
BOOBIES	**Family Sulidae**				
Abbott's Booby	*Sula abbotti*	E	I	5	Christmas I. (Australia)	148
CORMORANTS	**Family Phalacrocoracidae**				
New Zealand King Cormorant	*Phalacrocorax carunculatus*	K*		6	New Zealand	191
Pygmy Cormorant	*Phalacrocorax pygmeus*	K*		1	Western Palaearctic	49
Galápagos Flightless Cormorant	*Nannopterum harrisi*	R		3	Galápagos (Ecuador)	70
FRIGATEBIRDS	**Family Fregatidae**				
Ascension Frigatebird	*Fregata aquila*	R	I	4b	Ascension I. (UK)	144
Christmas Frigatebird	*Fregata andrewsi*	V		5	Christmas I. (Australia)	148
HERONS, EGRETS	**Order CICONIIFORMES** **Family Ardeidae**				
Japanese Night-heron	*Gorsachius goisagi*	K*		1,5	China, Indonesia, Japan Philippines, Taiwan	49
White-eared Night-heron	*Gorsachius magnificus*	K*		5	China	164
Slaty Egret	*Egretta vinaceigula*	I		4	Botswana, Namibia, Zambia	106
Chinese Egret	*Egretta eulophotes*	V		1,5	China, Indonesia, Malaysia, North Korea, Philippines	34
Madagascar Heron	*Ardea humbloti*	K		4a	Madagascar, Comoros	126
White-bellied Heron	*Ardea imperialis*	K*		5	Bhutan, Burma, India, Nepal	148

VERNACULAR NAME	SCIENTIFIC NAME	STATUS	CITES	ZOOGEOGRAPHIC REGION RANGE	PAGE
SHOEBILL	**Family Balaenicipitidae**				
Shoebill	*Balaeniceps rex*	S	II	4	Central and East Africa	106
STORKS	**Family Ciconiidae**				
Milky Stork	*Mycteria cinerea*	V	I	5	Indonesia, Kampuchea, Malaysia, Vietnam	148
Storm's Stork	*Ciconia stormi*	I		5	Indonesia, Malaysia, Thailand	148
White Stork	*Ciconia ciconia*	K*		1,4,5		35
Oriental White Stork	*Ciconia boyciana*	E	I	1,5	China, Japan, South Korea, USSR	35
Greater Adjutant	*Leptoptilos dubius*	K*		5	Bangladesh, Burma, India, Kampuchea, Laos, Thailand, Vietnam	164
IBISES, SPOONBILLS	**Family Threskiornithidae**				
White-shouldered Ibis	*Pseudibis davisoni*	I		5	Burma, Indonesia, Kampuchea, Laos, Thailand, Vietnam	149
Giant Ibis	*Pseudibis gigantea*	R		5	Kampuchea, Laos, Thailand, Vietnam	149
Northern Bald Ibis	*Geronticus eremita*	E	I	1	North-west Africa, Turkey, Ethiopia, North Yemen	35
Southern Bald Ibis	*Geronticus calvus*	R	II	4	Lesotho, South Africa, Swaziland	107
Crested Ibis	*Nipponia nippon*	E	I	1	China, Japan	36
Dwarf Olive Ibis	*Bostrychia bocagei*	I		4b	São Tomé	141
Black-faced Spoonbill	*Platalea minor*	K*		1,5	China, Japan, North Korea, Philippines, Taiwan, Vietnam	49
FLAMINGOS	**Family Phoenicopteridae**				
Andean Flamingo	*Phoenicoparrus andinus*	K*	II	3	Argentina, Bolivia, Chile, Peru	
Puna Flamingo	*Phoenicoparrus jamesi*	K*	II	3	Argentina, Bolivia, Chile, Peru	92
SCREAMERS	**Order ANSERIFORMES** **Family Anhimidae**				
Northern Screamer	*Chauna chavaria*	K*		3	Colombia, Venezuela	92
WATERFOWL	**Family Anatidae**				
West Indian Whistling Duck	*Dendrocygna arborea*	V	II	3	Caribbean Islands	70
Lesser White-fronted Goose	*Anser erythropus*	K*		1	Western Palaearctic	36
Hawaiian Goose or Nene	*Branta sandvicensis*	V	I	7	Hawaiian Is. (USA)	206
Freckled Duck	*Stictonetta naevosa*	K*		6	Australia	191
Crested Shelduck	*Tadorna cristata*	K*		1	South Korea, USSR	36
White-winged Wood Duck	*Cairina scutulata*	V	I	5	Bangladesh, Burma, India, Indonesia, Thailand	149
Mandarin Duck	*Aix galericulata*	K*		1,5	China, Japan, North Korea, South Korea, USSR	49
Baikal Teal	*Anas formosa*	K*		1,5	China, Japan, North Korea, South Korea, USSR	49

VERNACULAR NAME	SCIENTIFIC NAME	STATUS	CITES	ZOOGEOGRAPHIC REGION	RANGE	PAGE
Madagascar Teal	*Anas bernieri*	V		4a	Madagascar	127
New Zealand Brown Teal	*Anas aucklandica*	V	II	6	New Zealand	181
Marbled Teal	*Marmaronetta angustirostris*	K*	I/II	1,5	Western Palaearctic	49
Madagascar Pochard	*Aythya innotata*	E		4a	Madagascar	127
Brazilian Merganser	*Mergus octosetaceus*	I		3	Argentina, Brazil, Paraguay	70
Scaly-sided Merganser	*Mergus squamatus*	I	II	1,5	China, USSR	37
White-headed Duck	*Oxyura leucocephala*	K*		1	Western Palaearctic	49

Order FALCONIFORMES

VERNACULAR NAME	SCIENTIFIC NAME	STATUS	CITES	ZOOGEOGRAPHIC REGION	RANGE	PAGE
NEW WORLD VULTURES	**Family Cathartidae**					
California Condor	*Gymnogyps californianus*	E	I	2	USA	55
OLD WORLD VULTURES, HAWKS, EAGLES	**Family Accipitridae**					
Cuban Kite	*Chondrohierax wilsonii*	R	I	3	Cuba	71
Black Honey Buzzard	*Henicopernis infuscata*	K*	II	6	Papua New Guinea	192
Red Kite	*Milvus milvus*	K*	II	1	Western Palaearctic	49
Sandford's Fish-eagle	*Haliaeetus sanfordi*	K*	II	6	Solomon Is.	192
Madagascar Fish-eagle	*Haliaeetus vociferoides*	E	II	4a	Madagascar	127
Pallas's Fish-eagle	*Haliaeetus leucoryphus*	K*	II	1,5	Burma, China, India, Iran, Pakistan, USSR	49
White-tailed Fish-eagle	*Haliaeetus albicilla*	V	I	1,2,5	Palaearctic	37
Steller's Fish-eagle	*Haliaeetus pelagicus*	K*	II	1	Japan, Korea, USSR	49
Cape Vulture	*Gyps coprotheres*	R	II	4	Southern Africa	107
Black or Cinerous Vulture	*Aegypius monachus*	K*	II	1,5	Palaearctic	49
Nicobar Serpent Eagle	*Spilornis klossi*	K*	II	5	Nicobar Is. (India)	164
Kinabalu Serpent Eagle	*Spilornis kinabaluensis*	K*	II	5	Malaysia	164
Dark Serpent Eagle	*Spilornis elgini*	K*	II	5	Andaman Is. (India)	164
Madagascar Serpent Eagle	*Eutriorchis astur*	E	II	4a	Madagascar	127
Red Goshawk	*Erythrotriorchis radiatus*	K*	II	6	Australia	192
Small Sparrowhawk	*Accipiter nanus*	K*	II	5	Indonesia	164
New Britain Sparrowhawk	*Accipiter brachyurus*	K*	II	6	Papua New Guinea	192
Imitator Sparrowhawk	*Accipiter imitator*	K*	II	6	Papua New Guinea, Solomon Is.	192
Semi-collared Sparrowhawk	*Accipiter collaris*	K*	II	3	Colombia, Ecuador, Peru, Venezuela	92
Gundlach's Hawk	*Accipiter gundlachii*	K*	II	3	Cuba	92
Grey-bellied Hawk	*Accipiter poliogaster*	K*	II	3	South America	93
Plumbeous Hawk	*Leucopternis plumbea*	K*	II	3	Colombia, Ecuador, Panama, Peru	93
White-necked Hawk	*Leucopternis lacernulata*	K*	II	3	Brazil	93
Grey-backed Hawk	*Leucopternis occidentalis*	I	II	3	Ecuador	71
Mantled Hawk	*Leucopternis polionota*	I	II	3	Argentina, Brazil, Paraguay	71
Solitary Eagle	*Harpyhaliaetus solitarius*	K*	II	3	Colombia, Costa Rica, Ecuador, Guatemala, Honduras, Mexico	93
Crowned Eagle	*Harpyhaliaetus coronatus*	K*	II	3	Argentina, Bolivia, Brazil, Paraguay, Uruguay	93
Ridgway's Hawk	*Buteo ridgwayi*	K*	II	3	Dominican Republic, Haiti, Galápagos (Ecuador)	93
Galápagos Hawk	*Buteo galapagoensis*	R	II	3	Galápagos (Ecuador)	71
Hawaiian Hawk	*Buteo solitarius*	R	II	7	Hawaiian Is. (USA)	206
Red-tailed Hawk	*Buteo ventralis*	K*	II	3	Argentina, Chile	93
Crested Eagle	*Morphnus guianensis*	R	II	3	South and Central America	72
Harpy Eagle	*Harpia harpyja*	R	I	3	South and Central America	72

Vernacular Name	Scientific Name	Status	CITES	Zoogeographic Region	Range	Page
New Guinea Harpy Eagle	Harpyopsis novaeguineae	K*	II	6	Indonesia, Papua New Guinea	192
Philippine Eagle	Pithecophage jefferyi	E	I	5	Philippines	149
Spanish Imperial Eagle	Aquila adalberti	E	I	1	Portugal, Spain	38
Imperial Eagle	Aquila heliaca	K*	I	1	Western Palaearctic	49
Javan Hawk-eagle	Spizaetus bartelsi	K*	II	5	Indonesia	164
Philippine Hawk-eagle	Spizaetus philippensis	K*	II	5	Philippines	164
FALCONS	**Family Falconidae**					
Plumbeous Forest-falcon	Micrastur plumbeus	K*	II	3	Brazil, Colombia, Ecuador	93
Traylor's Forest-falcon	Micrastur buckleyi	K*	II	3	Ecuador, Peru	93
Mauritius Kestrel	Falco punctatus	E	I	4b	Mauritius	131
Grey Falcon	Falco hypoleucos	K*	II	6	Australia	192
Orange-breasted Falcon	Falco deiroleucus	K*	II	3	South and Central America	93
Peregrine Falcon	Falco peregrinus	V	I	1,2,3, 4a,4b, 5,6,7	Worldwide	38, 56
MEGAPODES	**Order GALLIFORMES** **Family Megapodiidae**					
Nicobar Scrubfowl	Megapodius nicobariensis	K*		5	Nicobar Is. (India)	164
Sula Scrubfowl	Megapodius bernsteinii	K*		5	Indonesia	164
Micronesian Scrubfowl	Megapodius laperouse	R		7	Belau, Northern Mariana Is. (USA)	202
Niuafo'ou Scrubfowl	Megapodius pritchardii	K*		7	Tonga	209
Moluccan Scrubfowl	Megapodius wallacei	K*		5	Indonesia	164
Malleefowl	Leipoa ocellata	K*		6	Australia	182
Waigeo Brush-turkey	Aepypodius bruijnii	K*		6	Indonesia	182
Maleo	Macrocephalon maleo	V	I	5	Indonesia	150
GUANS, CURASSOWS	**Family Cracidae**					
Rufous-headed Chachalaca	Ortalis erythroptera	K*		3	Ecuador, Peru	93
Bearded Guan	Penelope barbata	K*		3	Ecuador, Peru	93
Red-faced Guan	Penelope dabbenei	K*		3	Argentina, Bolivia	93
White-winged Guan	Penelope albipennis	E	I	3	Peru	72
Cauca Guan	Penelope perspicax	E		3	Colombia	72
White-browed Guan	Penelope jacucaca	K*		3	Brazil	93
Chestnut-bellied Guan	Penelope ochrogaster	K*		3	Brazil	93
Black-fronted Piping Guan	Pipile jacutinga	E	I	3	Argentina, Brazil, Paraguay	72
Highland Guan	Penelopina nigra	K*	III	3	Guatemala, Honduras, Mexico, Nicaragua,	93
Horned Guan	Oreophasis derbianus	E	I	3	Guatemala, Mexico	72
Alagoas Curassow	Mitu mitu	E	I	3	Brazil	73
Northern Helmeted Curassow	Pauxi pauxi	K*		3	Colombia, Venezuela	93
Southern Helmeted Curassow	Pauxi unicornis	K*		3	Bolivia, Peru	93
Blue-billed Curassow	Crax alberti	V		3	Colombia	73
Wattled Curassow	Crax globulosa	K*		3	Bolivia, Brazil, Colombia, Ecuador, Peru	93
Red-billed Curassow	Crax blumenbachii	E	I	3	Brazil	73
TURKEYS	**Family Meleagridae**					
Ocellated Turkey	Agriocharis ocellata	K*	III	3	Mexico, Guatemala, Belize	93
GROUSE	**Family Tetraonidae**					
Caucasian Black Grouse	Tetrao mlokosiewiczi	K*	II	1	Iran, Turkey, USSR	49

Vernacular Name	Scientific Name	Status	CITES	Zoogeographic Region Range	Page
PHEASANTS, QUAIL, PARTRIDGES	**Family Phasianidae**				
Bearded Wood Partridge	Dendrortyx barbatus	K*		Mexico	66
Chestnut Wood Quail	Odontophorus hyperythrus	K*		Colombia	94
Gorgeted Wood Quail	Odontophorus strophium	E		Colombia	72
Altai Snowcock	Tetraogallus altaicus	K*		Mongolia, USSR	50
Djibouti Francolin	Francolinus ochropectus	E	II	Djibouti	107
Mount Cameroon Francolin	Francolinus camerunensis	R		Cameroon	108
Swierstra's Francolin	Francolinus swierstrai	I	II	Angola	108
Nahan's Francolin	Francolinus nahani	R		Uganda, Zaire	108
Swamp Partridge	Francolinus gularis	K*		Bangladesh, India, Nepal	164
Black Wood Partridge	Melanoperdix nigra	K*	III	Malaysia	
Manipur Bush Quail	Perdicula manipurensis	K*		Bangladesh, India	164
White-cheeked Partridge	Arborophila atrogularis	K*		India, Burma	164
Sichuan Partridge	Arborophila rufipectus	K*		China	50
Rickett's Partridge	Arborophila gingica	K*		China	164
Orange-necked Partridge	Arborophila davidi	K*		Vietnam	164
Chestnut-headed Partridge	Arborophila cambodiana	K*		Kampuchea, Thailand	165
White-eared Partridge	Arborophila ardens	K*		China	165
Chestnut-necklaced Partridge	Arborophila charltonii	K*	III	Malaysia	165
Western Tragopan	Tragopan melanocephalus	E	I	India, Pakistan	154
Blyth's Tragopan	Tragopan blythi	R	I	Bhutan, Burma, China, India	154
Cabot's Tragopan	Tragopan caboti	E	I	China	152
Sclater's Monal	Lophophorus sclateri	R	I	Burma, China, India	152
Chinese Monal	Lophophorus lhuysii	E	I	China	38
Imperial Pheasant	Lophura imperialis	V	I	Laos, Vietnam	153
Edwards's Pheasant	Lophura edwardsi	V	I	Vietnam	153
Vietnam Pheasant	Lophura hatinhensis	K*		Vietnam	165
Swinhoe's Pheasant	Lophura swinhoii	V	I	Taiwan	151
Crested Fireback	Lophura ignita	K*		Burma, Indonesia, Malaysia, Thailand	165
Siamese Fireback	Lophura diardi	K*		Kampuchea, Laos, Thailand, Vietnam	165
Bulwer's Pheasant	Lophura bulweri	V		Indonesia, Malaysia	152
White Eared Pheasant	Crossoptilon crossoptilon	V	I	Burma, China, India	152
Brown Eared Pheasant	Crossoptilon mantchuricum	E	I	China	38
Blue Eared Pheasant	Crossoptilon auritum	K*	I	China	50
Cheer Pheasant	Catreus wallichi	E	I	India, Nepal, Pakistan	150
Elliot's Pheasant	Syrmaticus ellioti	E	I	China	151
Hume's Pheasant	Syrmaticus humiae	R	I	Burma, China, India	151
Mikado Pheasant	Syrmaticus mikado	V	I	Taiwan	151
Reeve's Pheasant	Syrmaticus reevesi	K*	I	China	50
Lady Amherst's Pheasant	Chrysolophus amherstiae	K*	I	China	50
Germain's Peacock-pheasant	Polyplectron germaini	K*	II	Vietnam	165
Malaysian Peacock-pheasant	Polyplectron malacense	K*	II	Burma, Malaysia, Thailand	165
Bornean Peacock-pheasant	Polyplectron schleiermacheri	K*		Indonesia	165
Palawan Peacock-pheasant	Polyplectron emphanum	V	I	Philippines	154
Crested Argus	Rheinardia ocellata	R	I	Laos, Malaysia, Vietnam	152
Green Peafowl	Pavo muticus	V	II	Kampuchea, Laos, Thailand, Vietnam	154
Congo Peacock	Afropavo congensis	S		Zaire	108
GUINEAFOWL	**Family Numididae**				
White-breasted Guineafowl	Agelastes meleagrides	E	III†	West Africa (†Ghana)	108

218

VERNACULAR NAME	SCIENTIFIC NAME	STATUS	CITES	ZOOGEOGRAPHIC REGION RANGE	PAGE
MESITES	**Order GRUIFORMES** **Family Mesitornithidae**				
White-breasted Mesite	*Mesitornis variegata*	R		4a	Madagascar	128
Brown Mesite	*Mesitornis unicolor*	K		4a	Madagascar	128
Subdesert Mesite	*Monias benschi*	R		4a	Madagascar	128
BUTTONQUAILS	**Family Turnicidae**				
Sumba Buttonquail	*Turnix everetti*	K*		5	Indonesia	165
Worcester's Buttonquail	*Turnix worcesteri*	K*		5	Philippines	165
Black-breasted Buttonquail	*Turnix melanogaster*	K*	II	6	Australia	192
PLAINS-WANDERER	**Family Pedionomidae**				
Plains-wanderer	*Pedionomus torquatus*	K*	II	6	Australia	192
CRANES	**Family Gruidae**				
Black-necked Crane	*Grus nigricollis*	V	I	1,5	China, India, Bhutan, Burma, Vietnam	45

Hooded Crane	*Grus monacha*	V	I	1	China, Japan, North
					  Korea, South Korea,
					  USSR
						40

Red-crowned Crane	*Grus japonesis*	V	I	1	China, Japan, North
					  Korea, South Korea,
					  USSR
						39

Whooping Crane	*Grus americana*	E	I	2	Canada, USA	57

White-naped Crane	*Grus vipio*	V	I	1	China, Japan, North
					  Korea, South Korea,
					  USSR
						45

Siberian Crane	*Grus leucogeranus*	E	I	1,5	Afghanistan, China, India, Iran, USSR	40
Wattled Crane	*Bugeranus carunculatus*	S	II	4	Ethiopia, Central and Southern Africa	109
RAILS	**Family Rallidae**				
Okinawa Rail	*Rallus okinawae*	K*		5	Japan	162
Plain-flanked Rail	*Rallus wetmorei*	K*		3	Venezuela	94
Austral Rail	*Rallus antarcticus*	K*		3	Argentina, Chile	94
Bogotá Rail	*Rallus semiplumbeus*	V		3	Colombia	73
Guam Rail	*Rallus owstoni*	V		7	Guam (USA)	202
Inaccessible Rail	*Atlantisia rogersi*	R		4b	Inaccessible I. (UK)	144
Lord Howe Island Woodhen	*Tricholimnas sylvestris*	E	I	6	Lord Howe I. (Australia)	182
Snoring Rail	*Aramidopsis plateni*	K*		5	Indonesia	165
Zapata Rail	*Cyanolimnas cerverai*	R		3	Cuba	74
Woodford's Rail	*Nesoclopeus woodfordi*	K*		6	Papua New Guinea, Solomon Is.	192
Barred-wing Rail	*Nesoclopeus poeciloptera*	E		7	Fiji	202
Bald-faced Rail	*Gymnocrex rosenbergii*	K*		5	Indonesia	165
Invisible Rail	*Habroptila wallacii*	K*		5	Indonesia	165
Corncrake	*Crex crex*	K*		1,4	Africa, Western Palaearctic	46
Dot-winged Crake	*Porzana spiloptera*	K*		3	Argentina, Uruguay	94
Henderson Rail	*Nesophylax ater*	K*		7	Henderson I. (UK)	209
Horqueta or Rufous-faced Crake	*Laterallus xenopterus*	K*		3	Brazil, Paraguay	94
Rusty-flanked Crake	*Laterallus levraudi*	K*		3	Venezuela	94
Siberian Crake	*Coturnicops exquisita*	K*		1,5	China, Japan, South Korea, USSR	50
White-winged Flufftail	*Sarothrura ayresi*	I		4	Ethiopia, Southern Africa	109
Slender-billed Flufftail	*Sarothrura watersi*	I		4a	Madagascar	128

VERNACULAR NAME	SCIENTIFIC NAME	STATUS	CITES	ZOOGEOGRAPHIC REGION RANGE	PAGE
Sakalava Rail	Amaurornis olivieri	K		4a	Madagascar	128
Gough Moorhen	Gallinula comeri	R		4b	Gough I. (UK)	145
San Cristóbal Mountain Rail	Gallinula sylvestris	I		6	Solomon Is.	182
Takahe	Notornis mantelli	E		6	New Zealand	182
Horned Coot	Fulica cornuta	R		3	Argentina, Bolivia, Chile	74
FINFOOTS	**Family Heliornithidae**					
Masked Finfoot	Heliopais personata	K*		5	Bangladesh, Burma, India, Indonesia, Malaysia, Thailand	165
KAGU	**Family Rhynochetidae**					
Kagu	Rhynochetos jubatus	E	I	6	New Caledonia (France)	183
BUSTARDS	**Family Otididae**					
Little Bustard	Tetrax tetrax	K*	II	1	Western Palaearctic	50
Great Bustard	Otis tarda	K*	II	1	Palaearctic	46
Great Indian Bustard	Ardeotis nigriceps	E	I	5	India	155
Houbara Bustard	Chlamydotis undulata	K*	I	1	Western Palaearctic	46
Bengal Florican	Houbaropsis bengalensis	K*	I	5	India, Kampuchea, Nepal	156
Lesser Florican	Sypheotides indica	K*	II	5	India	155
OYSTERCATCHERS	**Order CHARADRIIFORMES** **Family Haematopodidae**					
Chatham Island Oystercatcher	Haematopus chathamensis	E		6	Chatham Is. (New Zealand)	183
STILTS	**Family Recurvirostridae**					
Black Stilt	Himantopus novaezealandiae	E		6	New Zealand	183
PLOVERS	**Family Charadriidae**					
Sociable Plover	Chettusia gregaria	K*		1	Asia, North-east Africa	50
Javan Wattled Lapwing	Vanellus macropterus	I		5	Indonesia	156
Piping Plover	Charadrius melodus	K*		2	Canada, USA	66
Madagascar Plover	Charadrius thoracicus	R		4a	Madagascar	129
St. Helena Plover	Charadrius sanctaehelenae	R		4b	St. Helena (UK)	144
Hooded Plover	Charadrius rubricollis	K*		6	Australia	192
New Zealand Shore Plover	Thinornis novaeseelandiae	E		6	New Zealand	184
SNIPES, WOODCOCKS, SANDPIPERS	**Family Scolopacidae**					
Eskimo Curlew	Numenius borealis	E	I	2	Canada, USA	57
Bristle-thighed Curlew	Numenius tahitiensis	K*		2,7	Alaska, Pacific Ocean	66
Slender-billed Curlew	Numenius tenuirostris	K*	I	1	Western Palaearctic	47
Spotted Greenshank	Tringa guttifer	I	I	1,5	Bangladesh, Burma, China, Hong Kong, Japan, USSR	47
Tuamotu Sandpiper	Prosobonia cancellatus	V		7	Tuamotu Archipelago (France)	202
Sulawesi Woodcock	Scolopax celebensis	K*		5	Indonesia	165
Obi Woodcock	Scolopax rochussenii	K*		5	Indonesia	165
New Zealand Snipe	Coenocorypha aucklandica	R		6	New Zealand	184
Wood Snipe	Gallinago nemoricola	K*		5	Bhutan, India, Nepal, Pakistan	165
Asian Dowitcher	Limnodromus semipalmatus	R		1,5,6	Asia	47
Cox's Sandpiper	Calidris paramelanotos	K*		1?,5? 6	Australia	192
Spoon-billed Sandpiper	Eurynorhynchus pygmeus	K*		1,5	USSR, South-East Asia	50

VERNACULAR NAME	SCIENTIFIC NAME	STATUS	CITES	ZOOGEOGRAPHIC REGION	RANGE	PAGE
COURSERS	**Family Glareolidae**					
Jerdon's Courser	*Cursorius bitorquatus*	K*		5	India	156
GULLS, TERNS	**Family Laridae**					
Pacific Gull	*Larus pacificus*	K*		6	Australia	192
Olrog's Gull	*Larus atlanticus*	K*		3	Argentina	94
Lava Gull	*Larus fuliginosus*	K*		3	Galápagos (Ecuador)	94
White-eyed Gull	*Larus leucophthalmus*	K*		1,4	Red Sea	50
Audouin's Gull	*Larus audouinii*	R		1	Mediterranean, Morocco	47
Relict Gull	*Larus relictus*	R	I	1,5	China, Mongolia, USSR, Vietnam	48
Saunders's Gull	*Larus saundersi*	K*		1,5	China, Hong Kong, Japan, Mongolia, South Korea, Taiwan	50
Kerguelen Tern	*Sterna virgata*	K*		4b	Prince Edward I. (South Africa), Crozet and Kerguelen Is. (France)	145
Black-fronted Tern	*Sterna albostriata*	K*		6	New Zealand	192
Damara Tern	*Sterna balaenarum*	R		4	South Africa, Namibia	109
Chinese Crested Tern	*Sterna bernsteini*	I		1,5	China, Indonesia, Malaysia, Thailand	48
AUKS, MURRES	**Family Alcidae**					
Japanese Murrelet	*Synthliboramphus wumizusume*	K*		1	Japan, North Korea, South Korea, USSR	50
PIGEONS, DOVES	**Order COLUMBIFORMES** **Family Columbidae**					
Eastern Stock Dove	*Columba eversmanni*	K*		5	Afghanistan, India, Iran	50
Somali Pigeon	*Columba oliviae*	R		4	Somalia	109
Madeira Laurel Pigeon	*Columba trocaz*	R		4b	Madeira (Portugal)	143
Dark-tailed Laurel Pigeon	*Columba bollii*	R		4b	Canary Is. (Spain)	143
White-tailed Laurel Pigeon	*Columba junoniae*	R	I	4b	Canary Is. (Spain)	143
Maroon Wood Pigeon	*Columba thomensis*	V	I	4b	São Tomé	142
Nilgiri Wood Pigeon	*Columba elphinstonii*	K*		5	India	165
Sri Lanka Wood Pigeon	*Columba torringtoni*	K*		5	Sri Lanka	165
Pale-capped Wood Pigeon	*Columba punicea*	K*		5	Bhutan, Burma, China, India, Thailand	166
Grey Wood Pigeon	*Columba argentina*	K*		5	Indonesia, Malaysia	166
Yellow-legged Wood Pigeon	*Columba pallidiceps*	K*		6	Papua New Guinea, Solomon Is.	192
Ring-tailed Wood Pigeon	*Columba caribaea*	K*		3	Jamaica	94
Pink Pigeon	*Nesoenas mayeri*	E	III	4b	Mauritius	132
Socorro Dove	*Zenaida graysoni*	K*		2	Mexico	66
Blue-eyed Ground Dove	*Columbina cyanopis*	K*		3	Brazil	94
Purple-winged Ground Dove	*Claravis godefrida*	V		3	Argentina, Brazil, Paraguay	74
Grenada Dove	*Leptotila wellsi*	I		3	Grenada	74
Ochre-bellied Dove	*Leptotila ochraceiventris*	K*		3	Ecuador, Peru	94
Tolima Dove	*Leptotila conoveri*	I		3	Colombia	74
Grey-headed Quail Dove	*Geotrygon caniceps*	K*		3	Cuba, Dominican Republic	
Blue-headed Quail Dove	*Starnoenas cyanocephala*	K*		3	Cuba	94
Mindoro Bleeding-heart	*Gallicolumba platenae*	K*		5	Philippines	166
Negros Bleeding-heart	*Gallicolumba keayi*	K*		5	Philippines	166
Sulu Bleeding-heart	*Gallicolumba menagei*	K*		5	Philippines	166

VERNACULAR NAME	SCIENTIFIC NAME	STATUS	CITES	ZOOGEOGRAPHIC REGION RANGE	PAGE
Society Islands Ground Dove	Gallicolumba erythroptera	I		Society Is., Tuamotu (France)	204
Santa Cruz Ground Dove	Gallicolumba sanctaecrucis	K*		6	Solomon Is., Vanuatu	192
Thick-billed Ground Dove	Gallicolumba salamonis	K*		6	Solomon Is.,	192
Marquesas Ground Dove	Gallicolumba rubescens	I		7	Marquesas (France)	203
Wetar Ground Dove	Gallicolumba hoedtii	K*		5	Indonesia	166
Scheepmaker's Crowned Pigeon	Goura scheepmakeri	K*	II	6	Indonesia, Papua New Guinea	193
Victoria Crowned Pigeon	Goura victoria	K*	II	6	Indonesia, Papua New Guinea	193
Tooth-billed Pigeon	Didunculus strigirostris	V		7	Western Samoa	203
Sumba Green Pigeon	Treron teysmanni	K*		5	Indonesia	166
Flores Green Pigeon	Treron floris	K*		5	Indonesia	166
Timor Green Pigeon	Treron psittacea	K*		5	Indonesia	166
Large Green Pigeon	Treron capellei	K*		5	Burma, Indonesia, Malaysia, Thailand	166
Red-naped Fruit Dove	Ptilinopus dohertyi	K*		5	Indonesia	166
Flame-breasted Fruit Dove	Ptilinopus marchei	K*		5	Philippines	166
Mariana Fruit Dove	Ptilinopus roseicapilla	V		7	Guam, Northern Mariana Is. (USA)	204
Rapa Fruit Dove	Ptilinopus huttoni	R		7	Austral Is. (France)	204
Negros Fruit Dove	Ptilinopus arcanus	K*		5	Philippines	161
Cloven-feathered Dove	Drepanoptila holosericea	V		6	New Caledonia (France)	184
Mindoro Imperial Pigeon	Ducula mindorensis	K*	I	5	Philippines	166
Spotted Imperial Pigeon	Ducula carola	K*		5	Philippines	166
Society Islands Imperial Pigeon	Ducula aurorae	V		7	Society Is., Tuamotu (France)	203
Marquesas Imperial Pigeon	Ducula galeata	E		7	Marquesas Is. (France)	203
Island Imperial Pigeon	Ducula pistrinaria	K*		6	Papua New Guinea, Solomon Is.	193
Christmas Imperial Pigeon	Ducula whartoni	V		5	Christmas I. (Australia)	161
Giant Imperial Pigeon	Ducula goliath	V		6	New Caledonia (France)	184

LORIES, PARROTS, MACAWS — Order PSITTACIFORMES, Family Psittacidae

VERNACULAR NAME	SCIENTIFIC NAME	STATUS	CITES	ZOOGEOGRAPHIC REGION RANGE	PAGE
Biak Red Lory	Eos cyanogenia	K*	II	6	Indonesia	193
Red-and-blue Lory	Eos histrio	K*	II	5	Indonesia	166
Purple-naped Lory	Lorius domicella	K*	II	5	Indonesia	166
Tahiti Lorikeet	Vini peruviana	R	II	7	Society Is., Tuamotu (France), Cook I.	204
Ultramarine Lorikeet	Vini ultramarina	R	II	7	Marquesas Is. (France)	204
Blue-fronted Lorikeet	Charmosyna toxopei	K*	II	5	Indonesia	166
Streaked Lorikeet	Charmosyna multistriata	K*	II	6	Indonesia	193
Yellow-crested Cockatoo	Cacatua sulphurea	K*	II	5	Indonesia	166
Salmon-crested Cockatoo	Cacatua moluccensis	K*	II	5	Indonesia	166
White Cockatoo	Cacatua alba	K*	II	5	Indonesia	166
Red-vented Cockatoo	Cacatua haematuropygia	K*	II	5	Philippines	166
Tanimbar Corella	Cacatua goffini	K*	II	5	Indonesia	166
Green-crowned Racket-tailed Parrot	Prioniturus luconensis	K*	II	5	Philippines	166
Blue-headed Racket-tailed Parrot	Prioniturus discurus	K*	II	5	Philippines	166
Red-crowned Racket-tailed Parrot	Prioniturus montanus	K*	II	5	Philippines	167
Vulturine Parrot	Psittrichas fulgidus	K*	II	6	Indonesia, Papua New Guinea	185
Princess Parrot or Pilpul	Polytelis alexandrae	K*	II	6	Australia	185
Hooded Parrot	Psephotus dissimilis	K*	I	6	Australia	193
Golden-shouldered Parrot	Psephotus chrysopterygius	R	I	6	Australia	184
Paradise Parrot	Psephotus pulcherrimus	E	I	6	Australia	185
Antipodes Island Parrot	Cyanoramphus unicolor	K*	II	6	New Zealand	193

VERNACULAR NAME	SCIENTIFIC NAME	STATUS	CITES	ZOOGEOGRAPHIC REGION RANGE	PAGE
Orange-fronted Parakeet	Cyanoramphus malherbi	E	II	New Zealand	185
Orange-bellied Parrot	Neophema chrysogaster	R	I	Australia	185
Scarlet-chested Parakeet	Neophema splendida	R	II	Australia	185
Ground Parrot	Pezoporus wallicus	E	I	Australia	187
Night Parrot	Geopsittacus occidentalis	I	I	Australia	186
Black-cheeked Lovebird	Agapornis nigrigenis	R	II	Zambia	109
Wallace's Hanging Parrot	Loriculus flosculus	K*	II	Indonesia	167
Sangihe Hanging Parrot	Loriculus catamene	K*	II	Indonesia	167
Rothschild's Parakeet	Psittacula intermedia	K*	II	India	167
Nicobar Parakeet	Psittacula caniceps	K*	II	Nicobar Is. (India)	167
Mauritius Parakeet	Psittacula eques	E	I	Mauritius	132
Hyacinth Macaw	Anodorhynchus hyacinthinus	K*	I	Bolivia, Brazil, Paraguay	74
Indigo Macaw	Anodorhynchus leari	E	I	Brazil	75
Little Blue Macaw	Cyanopsitta spixii	E	I	Brazil	75
Blue-throated Macaw	Ara glaucogularis (= A. caninde)	I	I	Bolivia	75
Red-fronted Macaw	Ara rubrogenys	K*	I	Bolivia	94
Blue-winged Macaw	Ara maracana	K*	II	Argentina, Brazil, Paraguay	94
Golden Conure	Aratinga guarouba	V	I	Brazil	76
Cuban Conure	Aratinga euops	K*	II	Cuba	94
Golden-capped Conure	Aratinga auricapilla	K*	II	Brazil	94
Golden-plumed Conure	Leptosittaca branickii	K*	II	Colombia, Ecuador, Peru	76
Yellow-eared Conure	Ognorhynchus icterotis	V	II	Colombia, Ecuador	76
Thick-billed Parrot	Rhynchopsitta pachyrhyncha	V	I	Mexico	58
Maroon-fronted Parrot	Rhynchopsitta terrisi	E	I	Mexico	58
Blue-chested Parakeet	Pyrrhura cruentata	R	I	Brazil	76
Pearly Conure	Pyrrhura perlata	K*	II	Brazil	94
White-necked Conure	Pyrrhura albipectus	K*	II	Ecuador	94
Brown-breasted Conure	Pyrrhura calliptera	K*	II	Colombia	94
Slender-billed Conure	Enicognathus leptorhynchus	K*	II	Chile	94
Rufous-fronted Parakeet	Bolborhynchus ferrugineifrons	I	II	Colombia	76
Grey-cheeked Parakeet	Brotogeris pyrrhopterus	K*	II	Ecuador, Peru	95
Brown-backed Parrotlet	Touit melanonota	R	II	Brazil	76
Golden-tailed Parrotlet	Touit surda	I	II	Brazil	77
Spot-winged Parrotlet	Touit stictoptera	K*	II	Colombia, Ecuador	95
Pileated Parrot	Pionopsitta pileata	K*	I	Argentina, Brazil, Paraguay	95
Rusty-faced Parrot	Hapalopsittaca amazonina	K*	II	Colombia, Ecuador, Venezuela	77
Puerto Rican Amazon	Amazona vittata	E	I	Puerto Rico	77
Red-spectacled Amazon	Amazona pretrei	V	I	Argentina, Brazil, Paraguay, Uruguay	77
Red-crowned or Green-cheeked Amazon	Amazona viridigenalis	K*	II	Mexico	66
Red-tailed Amazon	Amazona brasiliensis	E	I	Brazil	78
Red-browed Amazon	Amazona rhodocorytha	K*	I	Brazil	78
Yellow-faced Amazon	Amazona xanthops	K*	II	Brazil	95
Vinaceous Amazon	Amazona vinacea	K*	I	Argentina, Brazil, Paraguay	95
St. Lucia Amazon	Amazona versicolor	E	I	St. Lucia	78
Red-necked Amazon	Amazona arausiaca	E	I	Dominica	78
St. Vincent Amazon	Amazona guildingii	E	I	St. Vincent	79
Imperial Amazon	Amazona imperialis	E	I	Dominica	78
Purple-bellied Parrot	Triclaria malachitacea	K*	II	Brazil	95
Kakapo	Strigops habroptilus	E	I	New Zealand	186

VERNACULAR NAME	SCIENTIFIC NAME	STATUS	CITES	ZOOGEOGRAPHIC REGION	RANGE	PAGE
TURACOS	**Order Cuculiformes** **Family Musophagidae**					
Bannerman's Turaco	*Tauraco bannermani*	E		4	Cameroon	110
Prince Ruspoli's Turaco	*Tauraco ruspolii*	R		4	Ethiopia	110
CUCKOOS	**Family Cuculidae**					
Green-cheeked Bronze Cuckoo	*Chrysococcyx rufomerus*	K*		5	Indonesia	167
Cocos Cuckoo	*Coccyzus ferrugineus*	K*		3	Costa Rica	95
Red-faced Malkoha	*Phaenicophaeus pyrrhocephalus*	K*		5	India, Sri Lanka	167
Banded Ground Cuckoo	*Neomorphus radiolosus*	K*		3	Colombia, Ecuador	95
Sunda Ground Cuckoo	*Carpococcyx radiceus*	K*		5	Indonesia, Malaysia	167
Green-billed Coucal	*Centropus chlororhynchus*	K*		5	Sri Lanka	167
Steere's Coucal	*Centropus steerii*	K*		5	Philippines	167
Javan Coucal	*Centropus nigrorufus*	K*		5	Indonesia	167
BARN OWLS	**Order STRIGIFORMES** **Family Tytonidae**					
Madagascar Red Owl	*Tyto soumagnei*	I	I	4a	Madagascar	129
Taliabu Owl	*Tyto nigrobrunnea*	K*	II	5	Indonesia	167
Minahassa Owl	*Tyto inexspectata*	K*	II	5	Indonesia	167
Lesser Masked Owl	*Tyto sororcula*	K*	II	5	Indonesia	167
Golden Owl	*Tyto aurantia*	K*	II	6	Papua New Guinea	193
Itombwe Owl	*Phodilus prigoginei*	I	II	4	Burundi, Zaire	110
OWLS	**Family Strigidae**					
White-fronted Scops Owl	*Otus sagittatus*	K*	II	5	Burma, Indonesia, Malaysia, Thailand	167
Sokoke Scops Owl	*Otus ireneae*	E	II	4	Kenya	110
Sumatran Scops Owl	*Otus stresemanni*	K*	II	5	Indonesia	167
Javan Scops Owl	*Otus angelinae*	K*	II	5	Indonesia	167
Flores Scops Owl	*Otus alfredi*	K*	II	5	Indonesia	167
Mindoro Scops Owl	*Otus mindorensis*	K*	II	5	Philippines	167
Grand Comoro Scops Owl	*Otus pauliani*	R	II	4b	Comoro Is.	141
Biak Scops Owl	*Otus beccari*	K*	II	5	Biak Is, Iriangya	193
Seychelles Scops Owl	*Otus insularis*	R	II	4b	Seychelles	136
São Tomé Scops Owl	*Otus hartlaubi*	R	II	4b	São Tomé	142
Usambara Eagle Owl	*Bubo vosseleri*	R	II	4	Tanzania	111
Philippine Eagle Owl	*Bubo philippensis*	K*	II	5	Philippines	167
Blakiston's Fish Owl	*Ketupa blakistoni*	K*	II	I	China, Japan, USSR	
Rufous Fishing Owl	*Scotopelia ussheri*	R	II	4	West Africa	111
Albertine Owlet	*Glaucidium albertinum*	R	II	4	Rwanda, Zaire	110
Forest Owlet	*Athene blewitti*	I	II	5	India	161
David's Owl	*Strix davidi*	K*	II	5	China	167
Fearful Owl	*Nesasio solomonensis*	K*	II	6	Solomon Is.	193
FROGMOUTHS	**Order CAPRIMULGIFORMES** **Family Podargidae**					
Dulit Frogmouth	*Batrachostomus harterti*	K*		5	Indonesia, Malaysia	167
POTOOS	**Family Nyctibiidae**					
Long-tailed Potoo	*Nyctibius aethereus*	K*		3	Brazil, Colombia, Ecuador, Guyana, Paraguay, Peru, Venezuela	95
White-winged Potoo	*Nyctibius leucopterus*	K*		3	Brazil	95
Rufous Potoo	*Nyctibius bracteatus*	K*		3	Colombia, Ecuador, Guyana, Peru	95

224

Vernacular Name	Scientific Name	Status	CITES	Zoogeographic Region Range	Page
NIGHTJARS	**Family Caprimulgidae**				
Satanic Nightjar	*Eurostopodus diabolicus*	K*		5	Indonesia	167
Puerto Rican Nightjar	*Caprimulgus noctitherus*	R		3	Puerto Rico	79
White-winged Nightjar	*Caprimulgus candicans*	K*		3	Brazil, Paraguay	95
Roraiman Nightjar	*Caprimulgus whitelyi*	K*		3	Venezuela	95
Pygmy Nightjar	*Caprimulgus hirundinaceus*	K*		3	Brazil	95
Red-necked Nightjar	*Caprimulgus ruficollis*	K*		1	Spain, Portugal, West Africa	50
Vaurie's Nightjar	*Caprimulgus centralasicus*	K*		1	China	48
Salvadori's Nightjar	*Caprimulgus pulchellus*	K*		5	Indonesia	168
Long-trained Nightjar	*Macropsalis creagra*	K*		3	Argentina, Brazil	95
Sickle-winged Nightjar	*Eleothreptus anomalus*	K*		3	Argentina, Brazil, Paraguay, Uruguay	95
	Order APODIFORMES				
SWIFTS	**Family Apodidae**				
White-chested Swift	*Cypseloides lemosi*	K*		3	Colombia	95
Giant Swiftlet	*Hydrochous gigas*	K*		5	Indonesia, Malaysia	168
Seychelles Swiftlet	*Collocalia elaphra*	R		4b	Seychelles	134
Tahiti Swiftlet	*Aerodramus leucophaeus*	K*		7	Society Is. (France)	209
Atiu Swiftlet	*Aerodramus sawtelli*	K*		7	Cook I.	210
Schouteden's Swift	*Schoutedenapus schoutedeni*	I		4	Zaire	111
Fernando Po Swift	*Apus sladeniae*	K		4	Angola, Cameroon, Fernando Po (Equatorial Guinea), Nigeria	111
Dark-rumped Swift	*Apus acuticauda*	K*		5	India	168
HUMMINGBIRDS	**Family Trochilidae**				
Hook-billed Hermit	*Glaucis dohrnii*	E	I	3	Brazil	79
Sooty Barbthroat	*Threnetes niger*	K*	II	3	French Guiana	95
Black-billed Hermit	*Phaethornis nigrirostris*	R	II	3	Brazil	80
Minute Hermit	*Phaethornis idaliae*	K*	II	3	Brazil	95
White-tailed Sabrewing	*Campylopterus ensipennis*	K*	II	3	Tobago (Trinidad), Venezuela	95
Napo Sabrewing	*Campylopterus villaviscensio*	K*	II	3	Ecuador	95
Fiery-tailed Awlbill	*Avocettula recurvirostris*	K*	II	3	Brazil, French Guiana, Guyana, Venezuela	95
Coppery Thorntail	*Popelairia letitiae*	K*	II	3	Bolivia	95
Sapphire-bellied Hummingbird	*Lepidopyga lilliae*	K*	II	3	Colombia	96
Honduran Emerald	*Amazilia luciae*	K*	II	3	Honduras	96
Tachira Emerald	*Amazilia distans*	K*	II	3	Venezuela	96
Mangrove Hummingbird	*Amazilia boucardi*	K*	II	3	Costa Rica	96
Chestnut-bellied Hummingbird	*Amazilia castaneiventris*	K*	II	3	Colombia	96
White-tailed Hummingbird	*Eupherusa poliocerca*	K*	II	3	Mexico	96
Oaxaca or Blue-capped Hummingbird	*Eupherusa cyanophrys*	K*	II	3	Mexico	96
Blossomcrown	*Anthocephala floriceps*	K*	II	3	Colombia	96
Ecuadorean Piedtail	*Phlogophilus hemileucurus*	K*	II	3	Ecuador	96
Peruvian Piedtail	*Phlogophilus harterti*	K*	II	3	Peru	95
Pink-throated Brilliant	*Helidoxa gularis*	K*	II	3	Ecuador, Peru	96
Scissor-tailed Hummingbird	*Hylonympha macrocerca*	K*	II	3	Venezuela	96
Purple-backed Sunbeam	*Aglaeactis aliciae*	K*	II	3	Peru	96
Black Inca	*Coeligena prunellei*	I	II	3	Colombia	80
Juan Fernandez Firecrown	*Sephanoides fernandensis*	K*	II	3	Juan Fernandez Is. (Chile)	80
Purple-throated Sunangel	*Heliangelus viola*	K*	II	3	Ecuador, Peru	96
Royal Sunangel	*Heliangelus regalis*	K*	II	3	Peru	96

225

Vernacular Name	Scientific Name	Status	CITES	Zoogeographic Region	Range	Page
Black-breasted Puffleg	*Eriocnemis nigrivestris*	K*	II	3	Ecuador	96
Turquoise-throated Puffleg	*Eriocnemis godini*	K*	II	3	Ecuador	96
Colourful Puffleg	*Eriocnemis mirabilis*	K*	II	3	Colombia	96
Black-thighed Puffleg	*Eriocnemis derbyi*	K*	II	3	Colombia, Ecuador	96
Hoary Puffleg	*Haplophaedia lugens*	K*	II	3	Colombia, Ecuador	96
Neblina Metaltail	*Metallura odomae*	K*	II	3	Peru	96
Violet-throated Metaltail	*Metallura baroni*	K*	II	3	Ecuador	96
Grey-bellied Comet	*Taphrolesbia griseventris*	K*	II	3	Peru	96
Hyacinth Visorbearer	*Augastes scutatus*	K*	II	3	Brazil	96
Hooded Visorbearer	*Augastes lumachellus*	K*	II	3	Brazil	96
Marvellous Spatuletail	*Loddigesia mirabilis*	K*	II	3	Peru	96
Bee Hummingbird	*Calypte helenae*	K*	II	3	Cuba	97
Chilean Woodstar	*Eulidia yarrellii*	R	II	3	Chile	80
Little Woodstar	*Acestrura bombus*	K*	II	3	Ecuador, Peru	97
Esmeraldas Woodstar	*Acestura berlepschi*	K*	II	3	Ecuador	97
Glow-throated Hummingbird	*Selasphorus ardens*	K*	II	3	Panama	97

TROGONS

Order   TROGONIFORMES
Family   Trogonidae

Vernacular Name	Scientific Name	Status	CITES	Zoogeographic Region	Range	Page
Resplendent Quetzal	*Pharomachrus mocinno*	V	I	3	Central America	85
Eared Trogon	*Euptilotis neoxenus*	K*		2	Mexico, USA	66
Baird's Trogon	*Trogon bairdii*	K*		3	Costa Rica, Panama	97

KINGFISHERS

Order   CORACIIFORMES
Family   Alcedinidae

Vernacular Name	Scientific Name	Status	CITES	Zoogeographic Region	Range	Page
Blyth's Kingfisher	*Alcedo hercules*	K*		5	Bhutan, Burma, China, India, Nepal, Vietnam	168
Jungle Kingfisher	*Ceyx melanurus*	K*		5	Philippines	168
Winchell's Kingfisher	*Halcyon winchelli*	K*		5	Philippines	168
Lazuli Kingfisher	*Halcyon lazuli*	K*		5	Indonesia	168
New Britain Kingfisher	*Halcyon albonotata*	K*		6	Papua New Guinea	193
Cinnamon-banded Kingfisher	*Halcyon australasia*	K*		5	Indonesia	168
Mangaia Kingfisher	*Halcyon ruficollaris*	K*		7	Cook Is.	210
Tuamotu Kingfisher	*Halcyon gambieri*	K*		7	Tuamotu Archipelago (France)	210
Marquesas Kingfisher	*Halcyon godeffroyi*	K*		7	Marquesas Is. (France)	210
Moustached Kingfisher	*Halcyon bougainvillei*	K*		6	Papua New Guinea, Solomon Is.	193
Blue-capped Wood Kingfisher	*Halcyon hombroni*	K*		5	Philippines	167
Biak Paradise Kingfisher	*Tanysiptera riedelii*	K*		6	Indonesia	193

MOTMOTS

Family   Momotidae

Vernacular Name	Scientific Name	Status	CITES	Zoogeographic Region	Range	Page
Keel-billed Motmot	*Electron carinatum*	K*		3	Central America	97

GROUND-ROLLERS

Family   Brachypteraciidae

Vernacular Name	Scientific Name	Status	CITES	Zoogeographic Region	Range	Page
Short-legged Ground-roller	*Brachypteracias leptosomus*	R		4a	Madagascar	129
Scaly Ground-roller	*Brachypteracias squamiger*	R		4a	Madagascar	129
Rufous-headed Ground-roller	*Atelornis crossleyi*	R		4a	Madagascar	129
Long-tailed Ground-roller	*Uratelornis chimaera*	R		4a	Madagascar	129

HORNBILLS

Family   Bucerotidae

Vernacular Name	Scientific Name	Status	CITES	Zoogeographic Region	Range	Page
Brown Hornbill	*Ptilolaemus tickelli*	K*		5	Burma, India, Laos, Thailand, Vietnam	168
Rufous-necked Hornbill	*Aceros nipalensis*	K*		5	Bhutan, Burma, India, Kampuchea, Laos, Nepal, Thailand, Vietnam	168

VERNACULAR NAME	SCIENTIFIC NAME	STATUS	CITES	ZOOGEOGRAPHIC REGION RANGE	PAGE
Plain-pouched Hornbill	Aceros subruficollis	K*		Burma, Indonesia, Malaysia, Thailand	168
Narcondam Hornbill	Aceros narcondami	K*	II	5 Andaman Is. (India)	168
Sumba Hornbill	Rhyticeros everetti	K*		5 Indonesia	168
Sulu Hornbill	Anthracoceros montani	K*		5 Philippines	168
Helmeted Hornbill	Rhinoplax vigil	I	I	5 Burma, Indonesia, Malaysia, Thailand	162
JACAMARS	**Family Galbulidae**				
Three-toed Jacamar	Jacamaralcyon tridactyla	K*		3 Brazil	97
BARBETS	**Family Capitonidae**				
White-mantled Barbet	Capito hypoleucus	K*		3 Colombia	97
Toucan Barbet	Semnornis ramphastinus	V		3 Colombia, Ecuador	85
Black-banded Barbet	Megalaima javensis	K*		5 Indonesia	168
White-chested Tinkerbird	Pogoniulus makawai	I		4 Zambia	111
HONEYGUIDES	**Family Indicatoridae**				
Yellow-footed Honeyguide	Melignomon eisentrauti	K		4 Cameroon, Ghana, Liberia	111
TOUCANS	**Family Ramphastidae**				
Yellow-browed Toucanet	Aulacorhynchus huallagae	K*		3 Peru	97
WOODPECKERS	**Family Picidae**				
Speckle-chested Piculet	Picumnus steindachneri	K*		3 Peru	97
Red-cockaded Woodpecker	Picoides borealis	V		2 USA	59
Helmeted Woodpecker	Dryocopus galeatus	E		3 Argentina, Brazil, Paraguay	86
Black-bodied Woodpecker	Dryocopus schulzi	K*		3 Argentina, Paraguay	97
Robust Woodpecker	Campephilus robustus	K*		3 Argentina, Brazil, Paraguay	97
Ivory-billed Woodpecker	Campephilus principalis	E		2,3 Cuba, USA	58, 86
Imperial Woodpecker	Campephilus imperialis	E	I	2 Mexico	58
Red-collared Woodpecker	Picus rabieri	K*		5 Laos, Vietnam	168
Okinawa Woodpecker	Sapheopipo noguchii	E		5 Japan	162
BROADBILLS	**Order PASSERIFORMES** **Family Eurylaimidae**				
African Green Broadbill	Pseudocalyptomena graueri	R		4 Uganda, Zaire	112
Wattled Broadbill	Eurylaimus steeri	K*		5 Philippines	168
WOODCREEPERS	**Family Dendrocolaptidae**				
Snethlage's Woodcreeper	Xiphocolaptes franciscanus	K*		3 Brazil	97
OVENBIRDS, SPINETAILS	**Family Furnariidae**				
White-bellied Cinclodes	Cinclodes palliatus	K*		3 Peru	97
Stout-billed Cinclodes	Cinclodes aricomae	K*		3 Peru	97
Masafuera Rayadito	Aphrastura masafuerae	K*		3 Chile	97
White-browed Tit Spinetail	Leptasthenura xenothorax	K*		3 Peru	97
Plain Spinetail	Synallaxis infuscata	K*		3 Brazil	97
Apurimac Spinetail	Synallaxis courseni	K*		3 Peru	97
Chestnut-throated Spinetail	Synallaxis cherriei	K*		3 Brazil, Ecuador, Peru	97
Russet-bellied Spinetail	Synallaxis zimmeri	K*		3 Peru	98
Austral Canastero	Asthenes anthoides	K*		3 Argentina, Chile	98
Line-fronted Canastero	Asthenes urubambensis	K*		3 Peru	98
Orinoco Softtail	Thripophaga cherriei	K*		3 Venezuela	98

VERNACULAR NAME	SCIENTIFIC NAME	STATUS	CITES	ZOOGEOGRAPHIC REGION RANGE	PAGE
Striated Softtail	Thripophaga macroura	K*	3	Brazil	98
Chestnut-backed Thornbird	Phacellodomus dorsalis	K*	3	Peru	98
Canebrake Groundcreeper	Phacellodomus dendrocolaptoides	K*	3	Argentina, Brazil, Paraguay	98
White-throated Barbtail	Margarornis tatei	K*	3	Venezuela	98
White-browed Foliage-gleaner	Philydor amaurotis	K*	3	Argentina, Brazil	98
Alagoas Foliage-gleaner	Philydor novaesi	K*	3	Brazil	98
Russet-mantled Foliage-gleaner	Philydor dimidiatus	K*	3	Brazil, Paraguay	98
Rufous-necked Foliage-gleaner	Automolus ruficollis	K*	3	Ecuador, Peru	98
Chestnut-capped Foliage-gleaner	Automolus rectirostris	K*	3	Brazil	98
Henna-hooded Foliage-gleaner	Automolus erythrocephalus	K*	3	Ecuador, Peru	98
Great Xenops	Megaxenops parnaguae	K*	3	Brazil	98
ANTBIRDS	**Family Formicariidae**				
White-bearded Antshrike	Biatas nigropectus	K*	3	Argentina, Brazil	98
Cocha Antshrike	Thamnophilus praecox	K*	3	Ecuador, Peru	98
Recurve-billed Bushbird	Clytoctantes alixii	K*	3	Colombia, Venezuela	98
Plumbeous Antshrike	Thamnomanes plumbeus	K*	3	Brazil	98
Klages's Antwren	Myromtherula klagesi	K*	3	Brazil	98
Black-hooded Antwren	Myromtherula erythronotos	E	3	Brazil	86
Salvadori's Antwren	Myromtherula minor	K*	3	Brazil	98
Ashy Antwren	Myromtherula grisea	K*	3	Bolivia	98
Black-capped Antwren	Herpsilochmus pileatus	K*	3	Brazil	98
Ash-throated Antwren	Herpsilochmus parkeri	K*	3	Peru	99
Narrow-billed Antwren	Formicivora iheringi	V	3	Brazil	86
Rufous-tailed Antbird	Drymophila genei	K*	3	Brazil	99
Yellow-rumped Antwren	Terenura sharpei	K*	3	Bolivia, Peru	99
Orange-bellied Antwren	Terenura sicki	K*	3	Brazil	99
Rio de Janeiro Antbird	Cercomacro brasiliana	K*	3	Brazil	99
Rio Branco Antbird	Cercomacro carbonaria	K*	3	Brazil	99
Fringe-backed Fire-eye	Pyriglena atra	E	3	Brazil	87
Slender Antbird	Rhopornis ardesiaca	V	3	Brazil	87
Scalloped Antbird	Myrmeciza ruficauda	K*	3	Brazil	99
Grey-headed Antbird	Myrmeciza griseiceps	K*	3	Ecuador, Peru	99
Spot-breasted Antbird	Myrmeciza stictothorax	K*	3	Brazil	99
Bare-eyed Antbird	Rhegmatorhina gymnops	K*	3	Brazil	99
Rufous-fronted Antthrush	Formicarius rufifrons	K*	3	Peru	99
Giant Antpitta	Grallaria gigantea	K*	3	Colombia, Ecuador	99
Great Antpitta	Grallaria excelsa	K*	3	Venezuela	99
Moustached Antpitta	Grallaria alleni	I	3	Colombia	87
Tachira Antpitta	Grallaria chthonia	K*	3	Venezuela	99
Bicolored Antpitta	Grallaria rufocinerea	K*	3	Colombia	87
Brown-banded Antpitta	Grallaria milleri	I	3	Colombia	87
Scallop-breasted Antpitta	Grallaricula loricata	K*	3	Venezuela	99
Hooded Antpitta	Grallaricula cucullata	K*	3	Colombia, Venezuela	99
GNATEATERS	**Family Conopophagidae**				
Hooded Gnateater	Conopophaga roberti	K*	3	Brazil	99
TAPACULOS	**Family Rhinocryptidae**				
Stresemann's Bristlefront	Merulaxis stresemanni	I	3	Brazil	87
Brasília Tapaculo	Scytalopus novacapitalis	I	3	Brazil	87
COTINGAS	**Family Cotingidae**				
Shrike-like Cotinga	Laniisoma elegans	K*	3	Bolivia, Brazil, Colombia, Ecuador, Peru, Venezuela	99

VERNACULAR NAME	SCIENTIFIC NAME	STATUS	CITES	ZOOGEOGRAPHIC REGION RANGE	PAGE
Grey-winged Cotinga	Tijuca condita	K*		3	Brazil	99
Black-headed Berryeater	Carpornis melanocephalus	K*		3	Brazil	99
White-cheeked Cotinga	Ampelion stresemanni	K*		3	Peru	99
Buff-throated Purpletuft	Iodopleura pipra	K*		3	Brazil	99
Kinglet Cotinga	Calyptura cristata	I		3	Brazil	88
Cinnamon-vented Piha	Lipaugus lanioides	K*		3	Brazil	99
Turquoise Cotinga	Cotinga ridgwayi	K*		3	Costa Rica, Panama	99
Banded Cotinga	Cotinga maculata	V	I	3	Brazil	88
White-winged Cotinga	Xipholena atropurpurea	V	I	3	Brazil	88
Yellow-billed Cotinga	Carpodectes antoniae	K*		3	Costa Rica, Panama	100
White Cotinga	Carpodectes hopkei	K*		3	Colombia, Ecuador, Panama	100
Bare-necked Umbrellabird	Cephaloptuers glabricollis	K*		3	Costa Rica, Panama	88
Long-wattled Umbrellabird	Cephalopterus penduliger	V		3	Colombia, Ecuador	88
MANAKINS	**Family Pipridae**				
Black-capped Manakin	Piprites pileatus	K*		3	Argentina, Brazil	100
Golden-crowned Manakin	Pipra vilasboasi	K*		3	Brazil	100
TYRANT FLYCATCHERS	**Family Tyrannidae**				
White-tailed Shrike Tyrant	Agriornis albicauda	K*		3	Argentina, Bolivia, Chile	100
Cock-tailed Tyrant	Alectrurus tricolor	K*		3	Argentina, Bolivia, Brazil, Paraguay	100
Strange-tailed Tyrant	Yetapa risoria	K*		3	Argentina, Brazil, Paraguay, Uruguay	100
Grey-breasted Flycatcher	Empidonax griseipectus	K*		3	Ecuador, Peru	100
Belted Flycatcher	Xenotriccus callizonus	K*		3	Guatemala, Mexico	100
Tawny-chested Flycatcher	Aphanotriccus capitalis	K*		3	Costa Rica, Nicaragua	100
Russet-winged Spadebill	Platyrinchus leucoryphus	K*		3	Venezuela	100
Short-tailed Tody Flycatcher	Todirostrum viridanum	K*		3	Venezuela	100
Fork-tailed Pygmy Tyrant	Ceratotriccus furcatus	K*		3	Brazil	100
Kaempfer's Tody Tyrant	Idioptilon kaempferi	K*		3	Brazil	100
Southern Bristle Tyrant	Pogonotriccus eximius	K*		3	Argentina, Brazil, Paraguay	100
Venezuelan Bristle Tyrant	Pogonotriccus venezuelanus	K*		3	Venezuela	100
Minas Gerais Tyrannulet	Phylloscartes roquettei	K*		3	Brazil	100
São Paulo Tyrannulet	Phylloscartes paulistus	K*		3	Brazil, Paraguay	100
Long-tailed Tyrannulet	Phylloscartes ceciliae	K*		3	Brazil	100
Bearded Tachuri	Polystictus pectoralis	K*		3	Argentina, Bolivia, Brazil, Colombia, Guyana, Paraguay, Suriname, Venezuela	100
Grey-backed Tachuri	Polystictus superciliaris	K*		3	Brazil	100
Sharp-tailed Tyrant	Culicivora caudacuta	K*		3	Argentina, Bolivia, Brazil, Paraguay	100
Ash-breasted Tit Tyrant	Anairetes alpinus	K*		3	Bolivia, Peru	100
PLANTCUTTERS	**Family Phytotomidae**				
Peruvian Plantcutter	Phytotoma raimondii	K*		3	Peru	100
PITTAS	**Family Pittidae**				
Schneider's Pitta	Pitta schneideri	K*		5	Indonesia	168
Whiskered Pitta	Pitta kochi	K*	I	5	Philippines	168
Giant Pitta	Pitta caerulea	K*		5	Kampuchea, Laos, Vietnam	168
Bar-bellied Pitta	Pitta ellioti	K*		5	Burma, Thailand	169
Gurney's Pitta	Pitta gurneyi	E		5	Indonesia	162

229

VERNACULAR NAME	SCIENTIFIC NAME	STATUS	CITES	ZOOGEOGRAPHIC REGION RANGE	PAGE
Blue-headed Pitta	*Pitta baudi*	K*		5	China, Japan, Korea	169
Fairy Pitta	*Pitta nympha*	K*		5	Borneo, Taiwan, Indo-China	169
Superb Pitta	*Pitta superba*	K*		6	Manus I. (Papua New Guinea)	193
Solomon Islands Pitta	*Pitta anerythra*	K*		6	Papua New Guinea, Solomon Is.	193
NEW ZEALAND WRENS	**Family Acanthisittidae**				
New Zealand Bush Wren	*Xenicus longpipes*	E*		6	New Zealand	187
SUNBIRD-ASITY	**Family Philepittidae**				
Yellow-bellied Sunbird-asity	*Neodrepanis hypoxantha*	I		4a	Madagascar	129
SCRUB-BIRDS	**Family Atrichornithidae**				
Rufous Scrub-bird	*Atrichornis rufescens*	R		6	Australia	187
Noisy Scrub-bird	*Atrichornis clamosus*	E	I	6	Australia	187
LARKS	**Family Alaudidae**				
Ash's Lark	*Mirafra ashi*	K		4	Somalia	112
Degodi Lark	*Mirafra degodiensis*	K		4	Ethopia	112
Somali Long-clawed Lark	*Heteromirafra archeri*	I		4	Somalia	112
Sidamo Long-clawed Lark	*Heteromirafra sidamoensis*	I		4	Ethiopia	112
South African Long-clawed lark	*Heteromirafra ruddi*	I		4	Lesotho, South Africa, Swaziland	112
Botha's Lark	*Spizocorys fringillaris*	I		4	South Africa	112
Raso Lark	*Alauda razae*	E		4b	Raso (Cape Verde Is.)	143
SWALLOWS	**Family Hirundinidae**				
White-eyed River Martin	*Pseudochelidon sirintarae*	I	II	5	Thailand	163
Golden Swallow	*Kalochelidon euchrysea*	K*		3	Jamaica, Haiti, Dominican Repubic	88
Bahama Swallow	*Callichelidon cyaneoviridis*	K*		3	Bahama Is.	101
White-tailed Swallow	*Hirundo megaensis*	R		4	Ethiopia	112
Red Sea Cliff Swallow	*Hirundo perdita*	K*		4	Sudan	125
PIPITS	**Family Motacillidae**				
Sokoke Pipit	*Anthus sokokensis*	V		4	Kenya, Tanzania	113
Yellow-breasted Pipit	*Anthus chloris*	K*		4	Lesotho, South Africa	125
Chaco Pipit	*Anthus chacoensis*	K*		3	Argentina, Paraguay	101
Ochre-breasted Pipit	*Anthus nattereri*	K*		3	Argentina, Brazil, Paraguay	101
CUCKOO-SHRIKES	**Family Campephagidae**				
Caledonian Greybird	*Coracina analis*	K*		6	New Caledonia	193
Mauritius Cuckoo-shrike	*Coracina typica*	V		4b		
Réunion Cuckoo-shrike	*Coracina newtoni*	V		4b	Mauritius	133
Blackish Cuckoo-shrike	*Coracina coerulescens*	K*		5	Réunion (France)	133
White-winged Cuckoo-shrike	*Coracina ostenta*	K*		5	Philippines	169
				Philippines	169
Western Wattled Cuckoo-shrike	*Campephaga lobata*	V		4	West Africa	113
BULBULS	**Family Pycnonotidae**				
Wattled Bulbul	*Pycnonotus nieuwenhuisi*	K*		5	Indonesia	169
Spot-winged Bulbul	*Pycnonotus leucolepis*	K*		4	Liberia	125
Prigogine's Greenbul	*Chlorocichla prigoginei*	V		4	Zaire	113

VERNACULAR NAME	SCIENTIFIC NAME	STATUS	CITES	ZOOGEOGRAPHIC REGION RANGE	PAGE
Appert's Greenbul	*Phyllastrephus apperti*	R	4a	Madagascar	129
Dusky Greenbul	*Phyllastrephus tenebrosus*	R	4a	Madagascar	129
Grey-crowned Greenbul	*Phyllastrephus cinereiceps*	R	4a	Madagascar	129
Yellow-throated Olive Greenbul	*Criniger olivaceus*	V	4	West Africa	113
Mottled-breasted Bulbul	*Hypsipetes siquijorensis*	K*	5	Philippines	169
Mauritius Black Bulbul	*Hypsipetes olivaceus*	V	4b	Mauritius	133
SHRIKES	**Family Laniidae**				
Gabela Helmet-shrike	*Prionops gabela*	I	4	Angola	113
Mount Kupe Bush-shrike	*Malaconotus kupeensis*	I	4	Cameroon	113
Green-breasted Bush-shrike	*Malaconotus gladiator*	R	4	Cameroon, Niger	114
Uluguru Bush-shrike	*Malaconotus alius*	R	4	Tanzania	114
Monteiro's Bush-shrike	*Malaconotus monteiri*	I	4	Angola, Cameroon	113
São Tomé Fiscal Shrike	*Lanius newtoni*	I	4b	São Tomé	142
VANGAS	**Family Vangidae**				
Van Dam's Vanga	*Xenopirostris damii*	R	4a	Madagascar	129
Pollen's Vanga	*Xenopirostris polleni*	R	4a	Madagascar	130
DIPPERS	**Family Cinclidae**				
Rufous-throated Dipper	*Cinclus schulzi*	I	3	Argentina	89
WRENS	**Family Troglodytidae**				
Slender-billed Wren	*Hylorchilus sumichrasti*	K*	3	Mexico	101
Apolinar's Wren	*Cistothorus apolinari*	V	3	Colombia	89
Zapata Wren	*Ferminia cerverai*	R	3	Cuba	89
Niceforo's Wren	*Thryothorus nicefori*	K*	3	Colombia	101
Clarion Wren	*Troglodytes tanneri*	K*	2	Mexico	66
THRASHERS, MOCKINGBIRDS	**Family Mimidae**				
Socorro Mockingbird	*Mimodes graysoni*	K*	2	Mexico	66
White-breasted Thrasher	*Ramphocinclus brachyurus*	E	3	Martinique, St. Lucia	89
THRUSHES	**Family Muscicapidae Subfamily Turdinae**				
Rusty-bellied Shortwing	*Brachypteryx hyperythra*	K*	5	China, India	169
Swynnerton's Forest Robin	*Swynnertonia swynnertoni*	R	4	Mozambique, Tanzania, Zimbabwe	114
Gabela Akalat	*Sheppardia gabela*	I	4	Angola	114
East Coast Akalat	*Sheppardia gunningi*	R	4	Kenya, Mozambique, Tanzania	114
Rufous-headed Robin	*Erithacus ruficeps*	K*	1,5	China, Malaysia	51
Black-throated Robin	*Erithacus obscurus*	K*	1,5	China, Thailand	51
White-headed Robin-chat	*Cossypha heinrichi*	I	4	Angola, Zaire	114
Dappled Mountain Robin	*Modulatrix orostruthus*	R	4	Mozambique, Tanzania	114
Usambara Ground Robin	*Dryocichloides montanus*	R	4	Tanzania	114
Iringa Ground Robin	*Dryocichloides lowei*	R	4	Tanzania	115
Thyolo Alethe	*Alethe choloensis*	E	4	Malawi, Mozambique	115
Seychelles Magpie-robin	*Copsychus sechellarum*	E	4b	Seychelles	134
Black Shama	*Copsychus cebuensis*	K*	5	Philippines	169
Luzon Redstart	*Rhyacornis bicolor*	K*	5	Philippines	169
Blue-fronted Robin	*Cinclidium frontale*	K*	5	China, India, Laos, Nepal, Thailand, Vietnam	169
Green Cochoa	*Cochoa viridis*	K*	5	China, Laos, Thailand, Vietnam	169

231

VERNACULAR NAME	SCIENTIFIC NAME	STATUS	CITES	ZOOGEOGRAPHIC REGION RANGE	PAGE
Sumatran Cochoa	*Cochoa beccari*	K*	5	Indonesia	169
Javan Cochoa	*Cochoa azurea*	K*	5	Indonesia	169
Rufous-brown Solitaire	*Myadestes leucogenys*	K*	3	Brazil, Ecuador, Guyana, Peru, Venezuela	101
Kamao	*Myadestes myadestinus*	K*	7	Hawaiian Is. (USA)	210
Olomao	*Myadestes lanaiensis*	K*	7	Hawaiian Is. (USA)	210
Puaiohi	*Myadestes palmeri*	E	7	Hawaiian Is. (USA)	206
White-browed Bushchat	*Saxicola macrorhyncha*	K*	5	India, Pakistan	
Hodgson's Bushchat	*Saxicola insignis*	K*	1,5	China, India, Mongolia, Nepal	163 51
Fuerteventura Stonechat	*Saxicola dacotiae*	R	4b	Canary Is. (Spain)	144
Benson's Rockthrush	*Monticola bensoni*	R	4a	Madagascar	130
Sri Lanka Whistling-thrush	*Myiophoneus blighi*	K*	5	Sri Lanka	169
Geomalia	*Geomalia heinrichi*	K*	5	Indonesia	169
Slaty-backed Thrush	*Zoothera schistacea*	K*	5	Indonesia	169
Red-backed Thrush	*Zoothera erythronota*	K*	5	Indonesia	169
Orange-banded Thrush	*Zoothera peronii*	K*	5	Indonesia	169
Everett's Thrush	*Zoothera everetti*	K*	5	Indonesia, Malaysia	169
Spot-winged Thrush	*Zoothera spiloptera*	K*	5	Sri Lanka	169
Fawn-breasted Thrush	*Zoothera machiki*	K*	5	Indonesia	170
Amami Thrush	*Zoothera amami*	K*	1	Japan	51
San Cristóbal Thrush	*Zoothera margaretae*	K*	6	Solomon Is.	193
Forest Ground-thrush	*Turdus oberlaenderi*	R	4a	Madagascar	115
Kibale Ground-thrush	*Turdus kibalensis*	I	4	Uganda	115
Spotted Ground-thrush	*Turdus fischeri*	R	4	East Africa, South Africa, Zaire	115
Taita Thrush	*Turdus helleri*	E	4	Kenya	115
Yemen Thrush	*Turdus menachensis*	K*	1	North Yemen, Saudi Arabia	51
Grey-sided Thrush	*Turdus feae*	K*	5	Burma, China, India, Thailand	170
BABBLERS	**Subfamily Timaliinae**				
Marsh Babbler	*Pellorneum palustre*	K*	5	Bangladesh, India	170
Black-browed Babbler	*Trichastoma perspicillatum*	K*	5	Indonesia	170
Bagobo Babbler	*Leonardina woodi*	K*	5	Philippines	170
Short-tailed Scimitar-babbler	*Jabouilleia danjoui*	K*	5	Vietnam	170
Bornean Wren-babbler	*Ptilocichla leucogrammica*	K*	5	Indonesia, Malaysia	170
Striated Wren-babbler	*Ptilocichla mindanensis*	K*	5	Philippines	170
Rabor's Wren-babbler	*Napothera rabori*	K*	5	Philippines	170
Marbled Wren-babbler	*Napothera marmorata*	K*	5	Malaysia	170
Rusty-throated Wren-babbler	*Spelaeornis badeigularis*	K*	5	India	163
Deignan's Babbler	*Stachyris rodolphei*	K*	5	Thailand	170
Striped Babbler	*Stachyris striata*	K*	5	Philippines	170
White-breasted Babbler	*Stachyris grammiceps*	K*	5	Indonesia	170
Sooty Babbler	*Stachyris herberti*	K*	5	Laos	170
Miniature Tit-babbler	*Micromacronus leytensis*	K*	5	Philippines	170
Jerdon's Moupinia	*Moupinia altirostris*	K*	5	Burma, India, Pakistan	170
Hinde's Pied Babbler	*Turdoides hindei*	V	4	Kenya	116
Ashy-headed Laughingthrush	*Garrulax cinereifrons*	K*	5	Sri Lanka	170
Black-hooded Laughingthrush	*Garrulax milleti*	K*	5	Vietnam	170
Grey Laughingthrush	*Garrulax maesi*	K*	5	China, Laos	170
White-cheeked Laughingthrush	*Garrulax vassali*	K*	5	Laos, Vietnam	170
Yellow-throated Laughingthrush	*Garrulax galbanus*	K*	5	Bangladesh, China, India	170
White-speckled Laughingthrush	*Garrulax bieti*	K*	5	China	170

Vernacular Name	Scientific Name	Status	CITES	Zoogeographic Region Range	Page
Nilgiri Laughingthrush	*Garrulax cachinnans*	K*		5	India	170
Collared Laughingthrush	*Garrulax versini*	K*		5	Vietnam	170
Red-winged Laughingthrush	*Garrulax formosus*	K*		5	China, Vietnam	171
Omei Shan Liocichla	*Liocichla omeiensis*	K*		1	China	51
Doubtful Leiothrix	*Leiothrix astleyi*	K*		6	China	163
Gold-fronted Fulvetta	*Alcippe variegaticeps*	K*		1,5	China	171
White-throated Mountain Babbler	*Lioptilus gilberti*	R		4	Cameroon, Nigeria	116
Grey-crowned Crocias	*Crocias langbianis*	K*		5	Vietnam	171
Madagascar Yellowbrow	*Crossleyia xanthophrys*	I		4a	Madagascar	130
PARROTBILLS	**Subfamily Panurinae**				
Greater Rufous-headed Parrotbill	*Paradoxornis ruficeps*	K*		5	Bhutan, Burma, China, India, Laos, Vietnam	171
Black-breasted Parrotbill	*Paradoxornis flavirostris*	K*		5	India, Burma, China	171
Eye-browed Parrotbill	*Paradoxornis heudi*	I		1	China, USSR	48
PICATHARTES	**Subfamily Picathartinae**				
White-necked Picathartes	*Picathartes gymnocephalus*	V	I	4	West Africa	116
Grey-necked Picathartes	*Picathartes oreas*	R	I	4	Cameroon, Equatorial Guinea, Gabon, Nigeria	116
GNATCATCHERS	**Subfamily Polioptilinae**				
Cuban Gnatcatcher	*Polioptila lembeyei*	K*		3	Cuba	101
OLD WORLD WARBLERS	**Subfamily Sylviinae**				
Grauer's Swamp Warbler	*Bradypterus graueri*	V		4	Burundi, Rwanda, Uganda, Zaire	121
Dja River Warbler	*Bradypterus grandis*	K		4	Cameroon, Gabon	121
Large-billed Bush Warbler	*Bradypterus major*	K*		5	China, India, Nepal, Pakistan	171
Sri Lanka Bush Warbler	*Bradypterus palliseri*	K*		5	Sri Lanka	171
Aquatic Warbler	*Acrocephalus paludicola*	K*		1,4	Western Palaearctic, Southern Africa	51
Speckled Warbler	*Acrocephalus sorghopilus*	K*		1,5	China	51
Nauru Warbler	*Acrocephalus rehsei*	K*		7	Nauru	210
Nihoa Warbler	*Acrocephalus familiaris*	R		7	Hawaiian Is. (USA)	207
Rodrigues Warbler	*Acrocephalus rodericanus*	E	III	4b	Mauritius	133
Seychelles Warbler	*Acrocephalus sechellensis*	R		4b	Seychelles	135
Aldabra Warbler	*Nesillas aldabranus*	E		4b	Aldabra (Seychelles)	136
Papyrus Yellow Warbler	*Chloropeta gracilirostris*	R		4	Burundi, Kenya, Rwanda, Uganda, Zaire, Zambia	121
Kolombangara Warbler	*Phylloscopus amoenus*	K*		6	Solomon Is.	193
Socotra Cisticola	*Cisticola haesitata*	K*		1	Socotra (South Yemen)	51
Tana River Cisticola	*Cisticola restricta*	K*		4	Kenya	122
River Prinia	*Prinia fluviatilis*	K		4	Cameroon, Chad, Nigeria	122
Long-tailed Prinia	*Prinia burnesi*	K*		5	India, Pakistan	171
White-winged Apalis	*Apalis chariessa*	K*		4	Kenya, Malawi, Mozambique, Tanzania	125
Karamoja Apalis	*Apalis karamojae*	K		4	Tanzania, Uganda	122
Kungwe Apalis	*Apalis argentea*	R		4	Burundi, Rwanda, Tanzania, Zaire	122
Kabobo Apalis	*Apalis kaboboensis*	R		4	Zaire	122
Long-billed Apalis	*Apalis moreaui*	R		4	Mozambique, Tanzania	122
Mrs Moreau's Warbler	*Bathmocercus winifredae*	R		4	Tanzania	122
Turner's Eremomela	*Eremomela turneri*	R		4	Kenya, Uganda, Zaire	122
Pulitzer's Longbill	*Macrosphenus pulitzeri*	I		4	Angola	122
São Tomé Short-tail	*Amaurocichla bocagii*			4b	São Tomé	142
Bristled Grass Warbler	*Chaetornis striatus*	K*		5	India, Nepal	171
Marshland Warbler	*Megalurus pryeri*	I			China, Japan	51
Fly River Grassbird	*Megalurus albolimbatus*	K*		6	Papua New Guinea	194
Whitney's Thicket Warbler	*Cichlornis whitneyi*	K*		6	Solomon Is., Vanuatu	194
Long-legged Warbler	*Trichocichla rufa*	E		7	Fiji	204

233

VERNACULAR NAME	SCIENTIFIC NAME	STATUS	CITES	ZOOGEOGRAPHIC REGION RANGE	PAGE
AUSTRALIAN WARBLERS	**Subfamily Malurinae**				
Purple-crowned Fairy-wren	*Malurus coronatus*	K*		6	Australia	194
Thick-billed Grass-wren	*Amytornis textilis*	K*		6	Australia	194
Eyrean Grass-wren	*Amytornis goyderi*	I		6	Australia	188
Grey Grass-wren	*Amytornis barbatus*	K*		6	Australia	194
Carpentarian Grass-wren	*Amytornis dorotheae*	K*		6	Australia	194
Eastern Bristlebird	*Dasyornis braachypterus*	K*		6	Australia	188
Western Bristlebird	*Dasyornis longirostris*	R	I	6	Australia	188
Chestnut-breasted Whiteface	*Aphelocephala pectoralis*	K*		6	Australia	194
OLD WORLD FLYCATCHERS	**Subfamily Muscicapinae**				
Nimba Flycatcher	*Melaenornis annamarulae*	I		4	Ivory Coast, Liberia	122
Streaky-breasted Jungle-flycatcher	*Rhinomyias addita*	K*		5	Indonesia	171
Brown-chested Jungle-flycatcher	*Rhinomyias brunneata*	K*		5	China, India, Indonesia	171
Henna-tailed Jungle-flycatcher	*Rhinomyias colonus*	K*		5	Indonesia	171
White-throated Jungle-flycatcher	*Rhinomyias albigularis*	K*		5	Philippines	171
White-browed Jungle-flycatcher	*Rhinomyias insignis*	K*		5	Philippines	171
Lompobattang Flycatcher	*Ficedula bonthaina*	K*		5	Indonesia	171
Sumba Flycatcher	*Ficedula harterti*	K*		5	Indonesia	171
Cryptic Flycatcher	*Ficedula crypta*	K*		5	Philippines	171
Damar Blue Flycatcher	*Ficedula henrichi*	K*		5	Indonesia	171
Black-banded Flycatcher	*Ficedula timorensis*	K*		5	Indonesia	171
Matinan Flycatcher	*Cyornis sandfordi*	K*		5	Indonesia	171
Rueck's Blue Flycatcher	*Cyornis ruecki*	K*	II	5	Indonesia	171
Blue-breasted Flycatcher	*Cyornis herioti*	K*		5	Philippines	171
Chapin's Flycatcher	*Muscicapa lendu*	R		4	Kenya, Zaire, Uganda	122
Grand Comoro Flycatcher	*Humblotia flavirostris*	R		4b	Comoro Is.	141
Red-tailed Newtonia	*Newtonia fanovanae*	I		4a	Madagascar	130
Chatham Island Black Robin	*Petroica traversi*	E		6	Chatham Is. (New Zealand)	188
WATTLE-EYES	**Subfamily Platysteirinae**				
Banded Wattle-eye	*Platysteira laticincta*	E		4	Cameroon	122
MONARCHS	**Subfamily Monarchinae**				
Seychelles Black Paradise-flycatcher	*Terpsiphone corvina*	R		4b	Seychelles	136
Caerulean Flycatcher	*Eutrichomyias rowleyi*	K*		5	Indonesia	172
Short-crested Monarch	*Hypothymis helenae*	K*		5	Philippines	172
Celestial Monarch	*Hypothymis coelestis*	K*		5	Philippines	172
Rarotonga Flycatcher	*Pomarea dimidiata*	V		7	Cook I.	205
Tahiti Monarch	*Pomarea nigra*	E		7	Society Is. (France)	205
Marquesas Monarch	*Pomarea mendozae*	K*		7	Marquesas Is. (France)	210
Versicolor Flycatcher	*Mayrornis versicolor*	K*		7	Fiji	210
Rennell Shrikebill	*Clytorhynchus hamlini*	K*		7	Solomon Is.	194
Truk Monarch	*Metabolus rugensis*	R		7	Federated States of Micronesia (USA)	205
White-tipped Monarch	*Monarcha everetti*	K*		5	Indonesia	172
Black-chinned Monarch	*Monarcha boanensis*	K*		5	Indonesia	172
Flores Monarch	*Monarcha sacerdotum*	K*		5	Indonesia	172
White-tailed Monarch	*Monarcha leucurus*	K*		5	Indonesia	172
Biak Monarch	*Monarcha brehmii*	K*		6	Indonesia	194
Guam Flycatcher	*Myiagra freycineti*	K*		7	Guam (USA)	210
Biak Black Flycatcher	*Myiagra atra*	K*		6	Indonesia	194

VERNACULAR NAME	SCIENTIFIC NAME	STATUS	CITES	ZOOGEOGRAPHIC REGION RANGE	PAGE
FANTAILS	**Subfamily Rhipidurinae**				
Tawny-backed Fantail	*Rhipidura superflua*	K*	5	Indonesia	172
St. Matthias Fantail	*Rhipidura matthiae*	K*	6	Papua New Guinea	194
WHISTLERS	**Subfamily Pachycephalinae**				
Vogelkop Whistler	*Pachycephala meyeri*	K*	6	Indonesia	194
Sangihe Shrike-thrush	*Colluricincla sanghirensis*	K*	5	Indonesia	172
TITS	**Family Paridae**				
White-winged Tit	*Parus nuchalis*	K*	5	India	172
Yellow Tit	*Parus holsti*	K*	5	Taiwan	172
NUTHATCHES	**Family Sittidae**				
White-browed Nuthatch	*Sitta victoriae*	K*	5	Burma	172
Corsican Nuthatch	*Sitta whiteheadi*	K*	1	Corsica (France)	51
Algerian Nuthatch	*Sitta ledanti*	R	1	Algeria	48
Black-masked Nuthatch	*Sitta yunnanensis*	K*	5	China	172
Yellow-billed Nuthatch	*Sitta solangiae*	K*	5	Vietnam	172
Giant Nuthatch	*Sitta magna*	K*	5	Burma, China, Thailand	172
Beautiful Nuthatch	*Sitta formosa*	K*	5	Bhutan, Burma, China, India, Laos, Vietnam	172
PHILIPPINE TREECREEPERS	**Family Rhabdornithidae**				
Long-billed Rhabdornis	*Rhabdornis grandis*	K*	5	Philippines	172
FLOWERPECKERS	**Family Dicaeidae**				
Brown-backed Flowerpecker	*Dicaeum everetti*	K*	5		172
Legge's Flowerpecker	*Dicaeum vincens*	K*	5	Indonesia, Malaysia	172
Forty-spotted Pardalote	*Pardalotus quadragintus*	K*	6	Sri Lanka	172
				Australia	189
SUNBIRDS	**Family Nectariniidae**				
Banded Green Sunbird	*Anthreptes rubritorques*	R	4	Tanzania	123
Amani Sunbird	*Anthreptes pallidigaster*	R	4	Kenya, Tanzania	123
Giant Sunbird	*Dreptes thomensis*	K*	4b	São Tomé	145
Apricot-breasted Sunbird	*Nectarinia buettikoferi*	K*	5	Indonesia	173
Rockefeller's Sunbird	*Nectarinia rockefelleri*	R	4	Zaire	123
Marunga Sunbird	*Nectarinia prigoginei*	E	4	Zaire	122
Rufous-winged Sunbird	*Nectarinia rufipennis*	R	4	Tanzania	123
Elegant Sunbird	*Aethopyga duyvenbodei*	K*	5	Indonesia	173
WHITE-EYES	**Family Zosteropidae**				
Javan White-eye	*Zosterops flava*	K*	5	Indonesia, Malaysia	173
Biak White-eye	*Zosterops mysorensis*	K*	6	Indonesia	194
Sudest White-eye	*Zosterops meeki*	K*	6	Papua New Guinea	194
Ambon Yellow White-eye	*Zosterops kuehni*	K*	5	Indonesia	173
Gezo White-eye	*Zosterops luteirostris*	K*	6	Solomon Is.	194
Nendo White-eye	*Zosterops sanctaecrucis*	K*	6	Solomon Is.	194
Small Lifou White-eye	*Zosterops minuta*	K*	7	Loyalty Is. (France)	210
White-breasted White-eye	*Zosterops albogularis*	E	I	6	Norfolk I. (Australia)	189
Large Lifou White-eye	*Zosterops inornata*	K*	7	Loyalty Is. (France)	210
Seychelles White-eye	*Zosterops modestus*	E	4b	Seychelles	135
Mount Karthala White-eye	*Zosterops mouroniensis*	R	4b	Comoro Is.	141
Mauritius Olive White-eye	*Zosterops chloronothus*	V	4b	Mauritius	133
Fernando Po Speirops	*Speirops brunneus*	R	4b	Bioko (Equatorial Guinea)	142
Príncipe Speirops	*Speirops leucophaeus*	K*	4b	Principe (São Tomé)	145

235

Vernacular Name	Scientific Name	Status	CITES	Zoogeographic Region Range	Page
Black-masked Finch	*Coryphaspiza melanotis*	K*		Argentina, Bolivia, Brazil, Paraguay	102
Yellow Cardinal	*Gubernatrix cristata*	K*	II	Argentina, Brazil, Uruguay	102
CARDINAL GROSBEAKS	**Subfamily Cardinalinae**				
Black-cowled Saltator	*Saltator nigriceps*	K*		Ecuador, Peru	102
Masked Saltator	*Saltator cinctus*	K*		Ecuador	102
TANAGERS	**Subfamily Thraupinae**				
Cone-billed Tanager	*Conothraupis mesoleuca*	K*		Brazil	102
Yellow-green Bush Tanager	*Chlorospingus flavovirens*	K*		Colombia, Ecuador	102
Cherry-throated Tanager	*Nemosia rourei*	E		Brazil	90
Black-cheeked Ant Tanager	*Habia atrimaxillaris*	K*		Costa Rica	102
Sooty Ant Tanager	*Habia gutturalis*	K*		Colombia	102
Black-and-gold Tanager	*Buthraupis melanochlamys*	K*		Colombia	102
Gold-ringed Tanager	*Buthraupis aureocincta*	K*		Colombia	102
Golden-backed Mountain Tanager	*Buthraupis aureodorsalis*	K*		Peru	102
Green-throated Euphonia	*Euphonia chalybea*	K*		Argentina, Brazil, Paraguay	102
Multicoloured Tanager	*Chlorochrysa nitidissima*	K*		Colombia	102
Azure-rumped Tanager	*Tangara cabanisi*	I		Guatemala, Mexico	90
Seven-coloured Tanager	*Tangara fastuosa*	V		Brazil	90
Black-backed Tanager	*Tangara peruviana*	K*		Brazil	102
Green-capped Tanager	*Tangara meyerdeschauenseei*	K*		Peru	102
White-bellied Dacnis	*Dacnis albiventris*	K*		Brazil, Colombia, Ecuador, Peru, Venezuela	102
Turquoise Dacnis	*Dacnis hartlaubi*	K*		Colombia	102
Black-legged Dacnis	*Dacnis nigripes*	K*		Brazil	102
Scarlet-breasted Dacnis	*Dacnis berlepschi*	K*		Colombia, Ecuador	102
Venezuelan Flowerpiercer	*Diglossa venezuelensis*	K*		Venezuela	103
WOOD WARBLERS	**Family Parulidae**				
Bachman's Warbler	*Vermivora bachmanii*	E	2,3	Cuba, USA	65
Golden-cheeked Warbler	*Dendroica chrysoparia*	K*	2,3	USA, Central America	66
Kirtland's Warbler	*Dendroica kirtlandii*	E	2,3	Bahama Is., USA	60
Whistling Warbler	*Catharopeza bishopi*	K*		St. Vincent	103
Altamira Yellowthroat	*Geothlypis flavovelata*	K*	2	Mexico	66
Black-polled Yellowthroat	*Geothlypis speciosa*	K*		Mexico	103
Semper's Warbler	*Leucopeza semperi*	E		St. Lucia	91
Yellow-faced Redstart	*Myioborus pariae*	K*		Venezuela	103
Grey-throated Warbler	*Basileuterus cinereicollis*	K*		Colombia, Venezuela	103
Pirre Warbler	*Basileuterus ignotus*	K*		Panama	103
Grey-headed Warbler	*Basileuterus griseiceps*	K*		Venezuela	103
White-striped Warbler	*Basileuterus leucophrys*	K*		Brazil	103
White-winged Ground Warbler	*Xenoligea montana*	K*		Dominican Republic, Haiti	103
Pearly-breasted Conebill	*Conirostrum margaritae*	K*		Brazil, Peru	103
HAWAIIAN HONEYCREEPERS	**Family Drepanididae**				
Kauai Creeper	*Oreomystis bairdi*	K*	7	Hawaiian Is. (USA)	210
Hawaii Creeper	*Oreomystis mana*	K*	7	Hawaiian Is. (USA)	210
Oahu Creeper	*Paroreomyza maculata*	K*	7	Hawaiian Is. (USA)	210
Maui Creeper	*Paroreomyza montana*	K*	7	Hawaiian Is. (USA)	210
Akepa	*Loxops coccinea*	K*	7	Hawaiian Is. (USA)	210

VERNACULAR NAME	SCIENTIFIC NAME	STATUS	CITES	ZOOGEOGRAPHIC REGION RANGE	PAGE
Akialoa	*Hemignathus obscurus*	E		7	Hawaiian Is. (USA)	207
Nukupuu	*Hemignathus lucidus*	E		7	Hawaiian Is. (USA)	207
Akiapolaau	*Hemignathus munroi*	E		7	Hawaiian Is. (USA)	208
Maui Parrotbill	*Pseudonestor xanthophrys*	V		7	Hawaiian Is. (USA)	208
Nihoa Finch	*Telespyza ultima*	K*		7	Hawaiian Is. (USA)	210
Laysan Finch	*Telespyza cantans*	K*		7	Hawaiian Is. (USA)	210
Ou	*Psittirostra psittacea*	E		7	Hawaiian Is. (USA)	208
Palila	*Psittirostra bailleui*	E		7	Hawaiian Is. (USA)	208
Poo Uli	*Melamprosops phaeosoma*	R		7	Hawaiian Is. (USA)	208
Crested Honeycreeper	*Palmeria dolei*	V		7	Hawaiian Is. (USA)	208
VIREOS	**Family Vireonidae**				
Black-capped Vireo	*Vireo atricapillus*	K*		2	Mexico, USA	66
San Andres Vireo	*Vireo caribaeus*	K*		3	San Andres Is. (Colombia)	103
AMERICAN BLACKBIRDS	**Family Icteridae**				
Chestnut-mantled Oropendola	*Psarocolius cassini*	K*		3	Colombia	103
Selva Cacique	*Cacicus koepckeae*	K*		3	Peru	103
Martinique Oriole	*Icterus bonana*	K*		3	Martinique (France)	103
Montserrat Oriole	*Icterus oberi*	K*		3	Monserrat (UK)	103
Saffron-cowled Blackbird	*Agelaius flavus*	K*	III	3	Uruguay	103
Yellow-shouldered Blackbird	*Agelaius xanthomus*	V		3	Puerto Rico	91
Lesser Red-breasted Meadowlark	*Sturnella defilippi*	K*		3	Argentina, Brazil, Uruguay	103
Red-bellied Grackle	*Hypopyrrhus pyrohypogaster*	K*		3	Colombia	103
Forbes's Blackbird	*Curaeus forbesi*	K*		3	Brazil	103
FINCHES	**Family Fringillidae**				
Blue Chaffinch	*Fringilla teydea*	R		4b	Canary Is. (Spain)	144
Ankober Serin	*Serinus ankoberensis*	R		4	Ethiopia	123
Yellow-throated Serin	*Serinus flavigula*	I		4	Ethiopia	123
Grosbeak Bunting	*Neospiza concolor*	I		4b	São Tomé	142
Yellow-faced Siskin	*Carduelis yarrellii*	K*	II	3	Brazil, Venezuela	103
Red Siskin	*Carduelis cucullata*	E	I	3	Venezuela	91
Saffron Siskin	*Carduelis siemiradzkii*	K*		3	Ecuador	103
Warsangli Linnet	*Acanthis johannis*	R		4	Somalia	123
WAXBILLS	**Family Estrildidae**				
Anambra Waxbill	*Estrilda poliopareia*	K		4	Nigeria	123
Black-lored Waxbill	*Estrilda nigriloris*	K		4	Zaire	123
Green Munia	*Estrilda formosa*	K*		5	India	173
Green-faced Parrotfinch	*Erythrura viridifacies*	K*		5	Philippines	173
Red-eared Parrotfinch	*Erythrura coloria*	K*		5	Philippines	173
Pink-eared Parrotfinch	*Erythrura kleinschmidti*	R		7	Fiji	205
Gouldian Finch	*Erythrura gouldiae*	K*		6	Australia	195
Timor Sparrow	*Padda fuscata*	K*		5	Indonesia	173
WEAVERS	**Family Ploceidae**				
Bannerman's Weaver	*Ploceus bannermani*	V		4	Cameroon, Nigeria	124
Bates's Weaver	*Ploceus batesi*	R		4	Cameroon	124
Black-chinned Weaver	*Ploceus nigrimentum*	R		4	Angola, Congo	124
Loango Slender-billed Weaver	*Ploceus subpersonatus*	R		4	Angola, Congo, Zaire	124
Lake Lufira Weaver	*Ploceus ruweti*	R		4	Zaire	124
Clarke's Weaver	*Ploceus golandi*	E		4	Kenya	124
Golden-naped Weaver	*Ploceus aureonucha*	R		4	Zaire	124
Finn's Baya Weaver	*Ploceus megarhynchus*	K*		5	India	173
Yellow-legged Weaver	*Ploceus flavipes*	R		4	Zaire	124

VERNACULAR NAME	SCIENTIFIC NAME	STATUS	CITES	RANGE	PAGE
Tanzanian Mountain Weaver	*Ploceus nicolli*	R		4	Tanzania	124
Entebbe Weaver	*Ploceus victoriae*	K*		4	Uganda	125
Ibadan Malimbe	*Malimbus ibadanensis*	E		4	Nigeria	124
Gola Malimbe	*Malimbus ballmani*	I		4	Liberia, Sierra Leone	124
Mauritius Fody	*Foudia rubra*	E		4a	Mauritius	134
Seychelles Fody	*Foudia sechellarum*	R		4b	Seychelles	136
Rodrigues Fody	*Foudia flavicans*	E		4b	Rodrigues (Mauritius)	134
STARLINGS	**Family Sturnidae**				
Rusty-winged Starling	*Aplonis zelandica*	K*		6	Solomon Is., Vanuatu	195
Santo Mountain Starling	*Aplonis santovestris*	R		6	Vanuatu	205
Rarotonga Starling	*Aplonis cinerascens*	K*		7	Cook I.	210
Abbott's Starling	*Cinnyricinclus femoralis*	K*		4	Kenya, Tanzania	125
Sri Lanka White-headed Myna	*Sturnus senex*	K*		5	Sri Lanka	173
Bali Starling	*Leucopsar rothschildi*	E	I	5	Indonesia	163
ORIOLES	**Family Oriolidae**				
Isabela Oriole	*Oriolus isabellae*	K*		5	Philippines	173
Silver Oriole	*Oriolus mellianus*	K*		5	China, Thailand	173
Príncipe Drongo	*Dicrurus modestus*	K*		4b	Príncipe (São Tomé)	145
Grand Comoro Drongo	*Dicrurus fuscipennis*	R		4b	Comoro Is.	141
Mayotte Drongo	*Dicrurus waldeni*	R		4b	Mayotte (France)	141
NEW ZEALAND WATTLEBIRDS	**Family Callaeidae**			New Zealand	190
Kokako	*Callaeas cinerea*	E		6	New Zealand	190
Saddleback	*Creadion carunculatus*	K*		6		
BELL MAGPIES	**Family Cracticidae**			Papua New Guinea	195
Sudest Butcherbird	*Cracticus louisiadensis*	K*		6		
BOWERBIRDS	**Family Ptilonorhynchidae**			Papua New Guinea	191
Adelbert Bowerbird	*Sericulus bakeri*	K*		6		
BIRDS OF PARADISE	**Family Paradisaeidae**				
Macgregor's Bird of Paradise	*Macregoria pulchra*	K*	II	6	Indonesia, Papua New Guinea	195
Wallace's Standardwing	*Semioptera wallacei*	K*		6	Moluccas	191
Long-tailed Paradigalla	*Paradigalla carunculata*	K*	II	6	Indonesia	195
Black Sicklebill	*Epimachus fastuosus*	K*	II	6	Indonesia, Papua New Guinea	195
Brown Sicklebill	*Epimachus meyeri*	K*	II	6	Indonesia, Papua New Guinea	195
Ribbon-tailed Astrapia	*Astrapia mayeri*	K*	II	6	Indonesia, Papua New Guinea	195
Huon Bird of Paradise	*Astrapia rothschildi*	K*	II	6	Papua New Guinea	195
Wahnes's Parotia	*Parotia wahnesi*	K*	II	6	Papua New Guinea	195
Goldie's Bird of Paradise	*Paradisaea decora*	K*	II	6	New Caledonia	195
Emperor of Germany Bird of Paradise	*Paradisaea guilielmi*	K*	II	6	New Caledonia	195
Blue Bird of Paradise	*Paradisaea rudolphi*	K*	II	6	Papua New Guinea	195

VERNACULAR NAME	SCIENTIFIC NAME	STATUS	CITES	ZOOGEOGRAPHIC REGION RANGE	PAGE
CROWS	**Family Corvidae**				
Beautiful Jay	*Cyanolyca pulchra*	K*	3	Colombia, Ecuador	103
Dwarf Jay	*Cyanolyca nana*	K*	3	Mexico	103
White-throated Jay	*Cyanolyca mirabilis*	K*	3	Mexico	103
Azure Jay	*Cyanocorax caeruleus*	K*	3	Argentina, Brazil	103
Sichuan Jay	*Perisoreus internigrans*	K*	1	China	51
Sri Lanka Magpie	*Urocissa ornata*	K*	5	Sri Lanka	173
Hooded Treepie	*Crypsirina cucullata*	K*	5	Burma	173
Ratchet-tailed Treepie	*Temnurus temnurus*	K*	5	China, Vietnam	173
Ethiopian Bush Crow	*Zavattariornis stresemanni*	R	4	Ethiopia	124
Banggai Crow	*Corvus unicolor*	K*	5	Indonesia	173
Flores Crow	*Corvus florensis*	K*	5	Indonesia	173
Marianas Crow	*Corvus kubaryi*	E	7	Guam, Northern Mariana Is. (USA)	205
Hawaiian Crow	*Corvus tropicus*	E	7	Hawaiian Is. (USA)	209

Appendix II

A Systematic List of Birds Presumed to have Become Extinct since 1600

Compiled by Alison Stattersfield, ICBP, December 1987

This table is based on a review of selected references (for main sources see bibliography). It is not a rigorous analysis of the original source material. Except for the very well documented Réunion Dodo, only species represented by specimens are included. In many cases the date of extinction is an approximation corresponding to the date of the last sighting, capture, record etc. A series of new species, descriptions of which have yet to be published, is not included in the list. These birds are all from Mauritius and include a petrel, night-heron, stork, shelduck, falcon, babbler and a bulbul.

The definition of "extinct" is obviously highly emotive and equivocal. The commonly used criterion that a species is extinct if it has not been seen in the wild during the past 50 years is not followed here. Many birds, not on this list, would fall into this category; they often inhabit remote areas unfrequented by ornithologists, and thus the paucity of information may be a function of the inacessability of their terrain rather than of their true rarity. These little-recorded species which may be threatened are afforded a Red Data Book status, and appear elsewhere in this book.

An asterisk indicates birds that are generally regarded as extinct but for which there may still be some chance of survival.

Species	Estimated date of extinction	From
Dromaiidae Emus		
Kangaroo Island Black Emu *Dromaius diemenianus*	1803	Kangaroo Island (Australia)
Aepyornithidae Elephantbirds		
Great Elephantbird *Aepyornis maximus*	1650	Madagascar
Podicipedidae Grebes		
Atitlán Grebe *Podilymbus gigas*	1980	Guatemala
Colombian Grebe *Piodiceps andinus*	1977	Colombia
Anomalopterygidae Moas		
Brawny Great Moa *Dinornis torosus*	1670	New Zealand
Burly Lesser Moa *Eurapteryx gravis*	1640	New Zealand
South Island Tokoweka *Megalapteryx didinus*	ca. 1785	New Zealand
Hydrobatidae Storm-petrels		
Guadalupe Storm-petrel *Oceanodroma macrodactyla*	1912	Guadalupe (Mexico)
Phalacrocoracidae Cormorants		
Spectacled Cormorant *Phalacrocorax perspicillatus*	1852	Beringa Island (USSR)
Threskiornithidae Ibises		
Réunion Flightless Ibis *Borbonibis latipes*	1773	Réunion (France)
Ardeidae Herons		
New Zealand Little Bittern *Ixobrychus novaezelandiae*	1900	New Zealand
Mauritius Night-heron *Nycticorax mauritianus*	by 1700	Mauritius
Rodrigues Night-heron *Nycticorax megacephalus*	1761	Rodrigues (Mauritius)
Anatidae Waterfowl		
Chatham Island Swan *Cygnus sumnerensis*	1590–1690	Chatham Island (New Zealand)
Mauritian Shelduck *Alopochen mauritianus*	1698	Mauritius
Mauritian Duck *Anas theodori*	1696	Mauritius, Réunion (France)
Labrador Duck *Camptorhynchus labradorius*	1875	Canada, USA
* Pink-headed Duck *Rhodonessa caryophyllacea*	1935	India, Burma
Auckland Island Merganser *Mergus australis*	1905	New Zealand
Falconidae Falcons		
Guadalupe Caracara *Polyborus lutosus*	1900	Guadalupe (Mexico)
Phasianidae Pheasants, quails		
New Zealand Quail *Coturnix novaezelandiae*	1875	New Zealand
* Himalayan Mountain Quail *Ophrysia superciliosa*	1868	Himalayas (India)
Rallidae Rails		
Wake Island Rail *Rallus wakensis*	1945	Wake Island (USA)
Chatham Island Banded Rail *Rallus dieffenbachii*	1840	Chatham Island (New Zealand)
Chatham Island Rail *Rallus modestus*	1900	Chatham Island (New Zealand)
Ascension Flightless Crake *Atlantisia elpenor*	1656	Ascension Island (UK)
* New Caledonia Wood Rail *Tricholimnas lafresnayanus*	1904	New Caledonia (France)
Laysan Rail *Porzanula palmeri*	1944	Laysan (Hawaiian Islands)
Hawaiian Rail *Porzana sandwichensis*	1884	Hawaii
Kosrae Crake *Aphanolimnas monasa*	1827	Kosrae (Caroline Islands)
Tristan Moorhen *Gallinula nesiotis*	1875–1900	Tristan da Cunha (UK)
Samoan Woodhen *Gallinula pacifica*	1908	Samoan Islands
Lord Howe Purple Gallinule *Porphyrio albus*	1834	Lord Howe Island (Australia)
Red Rail *Aphanapteryx bonasia*	1693	Mauritius

Species	Estimated date of extinction	From
Rodrigues Rail *Aphanapteryx leguati*	1761	Rodrigues (Mauritius)
Mascarene Coot *Fulica newtoni*	1693	Mauritius, Réunion (France)
Haematopodidae Oystercatcher		
* Canarian Black Oystercatcher *Haematopus meadewaldoi*	1913	Canary Islands (Spain)
Scolopacidae Sandpipers		
Tahiti Sandpiper *Prosobonia leucoptera*	1773	Tahiti (Society Islands)
Alcidae Auks		
Great Auk *Alca impennis*	1844	Funk Island (Canada), Iceland, Faeroes, St. Kilda, Orkney Islands
Raphidae Dodos, solitaires		
Dodo *Raphus cucullatus*	1665	Mauritius
Réunion Dodo *'Ornithaptera' solitara*	1710–1715	Réunion (France)
Rodrigues Solitaire *Pezophaps solitarius*	1765	Rodrigues (Mauritius)
Columbidae Pigeons		
Bonin Wood Pigeon *Columba versicolor*	1889	Bonin Islands (Japan)
Ryukyu Wood Piegon *Columba jouyi*	1936	Ryukyu Islands (Japan)
Passenger Pigeon *Ectopistes migratorius*	1914	USA
Solomon Island Crowned Pigeon *Microgoura meeki*	1904	Solomon Islands
* Red-moustached Fruit-dove *Ptilinopus mercierii*	1922	Marquesas (France)
Hollandais Pigeon *Alectroenas nitidissima*	1835	Mauritius
Rodrigues Pigeon *'Alectroenas' rodericana*	1726	Rodrigues (Mauritius)
Psittacidae Lories, parrots, macaws		
* New Caledonia Lorikeet *Charmosyna diadema*	1860	New Caledonia (France)
Norfolk Island Kaka *Nestor productus*	1851	Phillip Island (Australia)
Black-fronted Parakeet *Cyanoramphus zealandicus*	1844	Tahiti (Society Islands)
Raiatea Parakeet *Cyanoramphus ulietanus*	1773	Raiatea (Society Islands)
Mauritius Parrot *Lophopsittacus mauritianus*	1680	Mauritius
Mauritius Grey Parrot *'Lophopsittacus' bensoni*	1765	Mauritius
Rodrigues Parrot *'Necropsittacus' rodericanus*	1761	Rodrigues (Mauritius)
Mascarene Parrot *Mascarinus mascarinus*	1834	Réunion (France)
Seychelles Alexandrine Parrot *Psittacula wardi*	1870	Seychelles
Rodrigues Ring-necked Parakeet *Psittacula exsul*	1876	Rodrigues (Mauritius)
* Glaucous Macaw *Anodorhynchus glaucus*	1955	Brazil, Uruguay
Cuban Red Macaw *Ara tricolor*	1885	Cuba
Carolina Parakeet *Conurposis carolinensis*	1914	USA
Cuculidae Cuckoos		
* Snail-eating Coua *Coua delalandei*	1930	Madagascar
Strigidae Owls		
Rodrigues Little Owl *'Athene' murivora*	1726	Rodrigues (Mauritius)
Laughing Owl *Sceloglaux albifacies*	1910	New Zealand
Aegothelidae Owlet-frogmouths		
New Caledonian Owlet-frogmouth *Aegotheles savesi*	1880	New Caledonia
Caprimulgidae Nightjars		
*Jamaican Least Pauraque *Siphonorhis americanus*	1859	Jamaica
Alcedinidae Kingfishers		
Ryukyu Kingfisher *Halcyon miyakoensis*	1841	Ryuku Islands (Japan)
Acanthisittidae New Zealand wrens		
New Zealand Bush Wren *Xenicus longipes*	1972	New Zealand
Stephen Island Wren *Xenicus lyalli*	1874	Stephen Island (New Zealand)

Species	Estimated date of extinction	From
(Muscicapidae) Turdinae Thrushes		
Kittlitz's Thrush *Zoothera terrestris*	1828	Bonin Islands (Japan)
Grand Cayman Thrush *Turdus ravidus*	1938	Grand Cayman Island (UK)
(Muscicapidae) Sylviinae Old world warblers		
Laysan Millerbird *Acrocephallus familiaris*	1912–1923	Laysan (Hawaiian Islands)
(Muscicapidae) Pachycephalinae		
Whistlers		
Pipio or New Zealand Thrush *Dicaeum quadracolor*	1906	New Zealand
Dicaeidae Flowerpeckers		
Four-coloured Flowerpecker *Turnagra capensis*	1963	Cebu Island (Philippines)
Zosteropidae White-eyes		
Lord Howe White-eye *Zosterops strenua*	1928	Lord Howe Island (Australia)
Meliphagidae Honeyeaters		
Oahu Oo *Moho apicalis*	1837	Oahu (Hawaiian Islands)
*Hawaii Oo *Moho noblis*	1934	Hawaii
Kioea *Chaetoptila angustilpluma*	1860	Hawaii
Drepanidae Hawaiian honeycreepers		
*Kakawihie *Paroreomyza flammea*	1963	Hawaii
Greater Amakihi *Hemignathus Sagittirostris*	1900	Hawaiian Islands
Greater Koa-finch *Rhodacanthis palmeri*	1896	Hawaii
Lesser Koa-finch *Rhodacanthis flaviceps*	1891	Hawaii
Kona Grosbeak *Chloridops kona*	1894	Hawaii
Ula-ai-hawane *Ciridops anna*	1892	Hawaii
Hawaii Mamo *Drepanis pacifica*	1899	Hawaii
Black Mamo *Drepanis funerea*	1907	Molokai (Hawaiian Islands)
(Emberizidae) Cardinalinae		
Cardinal-grosbeaks		
Townsend's Finch *Spiza townsendi*	1833	USA
Icteridae Blackbirds, troupials		
Slender-billed Grackle *Quiscalus palustris*	1910	Mexico
Fringillidae Finches		
Bonin Grosbeak *Chaunoproctus ferreorostris*	1890	Bonin Islands (Japan)
Sturnidae Starlings		
*Pohnpei Mountain Starling *Aplonis pelzelni*	1956	Pohnpei (Caroline Islands)
Kosrae Mountain Starling *Aplonis corvina*	1828	Kosrea (Caroline Islands)
Mysterious Starling *Aplonis mavornata*	1774	Raiatea (Society Islands)
Norfolk Island Starling *Aplonis fusca*	1925	Norfolk Island (Australia)
Rodrigues Starling *Necrospar rodericanus*	1726	Rodrigues (Mauritius)
Réunion Starling *Fregilupus varius*	1850–1860	Réunion (France)
Callaeidae New Zealand		
wattlebirds		
Huia *Heteralocha acutirostris*	1907	New Zealand

Bibliography

Authorative field guides, or at least check-lists of birds are now available for most countries. The following is a selective list of more detailed works which have been consulted and which the reader may find useful.

Ali, S. and Ripley, S. D. (1968–74). *A Handbook of the Birds of India and Pakistan*. 10 vols. London: Oxford University Press.

Austin, L. A. Jr (1961). *Birds of the World*. London: Paul Hamlyn.

Anon (1974). *A World Atlas of Birds*. London: Mitchell Beazley.

Beehler, B. M., Pratt, T. K. and Zimmerman, D. A. (1986). *Birds of New Guinea*. Princeton: Princeton University Press.

Blakers, M., Davies, S. J. J. F. and Reilly, P. N. (1984). *The Atlas of Australian Birds*. Victoria: Royal Australasian Ornithologists' Union.

Collar, N. J. and Stuart, S. N. (1985). *Threatened Birds of Africa and Related Islands*. The ICBP/IUCN Red Data Book, Part 1, 3rd Edition. Cambridge: ICBP.

Collar, N. J. and Andrew, P. (1988). *Birds to Watch: The ICBP World Checklist of Threatened Birds*. Cambridge: ICBP.

Cramp, S. (ed.) (1977–87). *The Birds of the Western Palaearctic*. 5 vols. London: Oxford University Press.

Croxall, J. P., Evans, P. G. H. and Schreiber, R. W. (eds) (1984). *Status and Conservation of the World's Seabirds*. Norwich: ICBP.

Diamond, A. W. (ed.) (1987). *Studies of Mascarene Island Birds*. Cambridge: Cambridge University Press.

Fisher, J. and Peterson, R. T. (1964). *The World of Birds*. London: MacDonald.

Fuller, E. R. (1987). *Extinct Birds*. London: Viking.

Glenister, A. G. (1971). *Birds of the Malay Peninsula, Singapore and Penang*. London: Oxford University Press.

Greenway, J. C. (1967). *Extinct and Vanishing Birds of the World*, 2nd Edition. London: Dover Publications.

Hilty, S. L. and Brown, W. L. (1986). *A Guide to the Birds of Colombia*. Princeton: Princeton University Press.

King, W. B. (1978). *Red Data Book*, 2. Aves, 2nd Edition. Morges, Switzerland: IUCN.

Macdonald, J. D. (1973). *Birds of Australia*. Sydney: A. H. & A. W. Reed.

Morony, J. J., Bock, W. J. and Farrand, J. (1975). *Reference List of the Birds of the World*. New York: American Museum of Natural History.

Mountfort, G. (1974). *So Small a World*. London: Hutchinson.

Mountfort, G. (1978). *Back from the Brink*. London: Hutchinson.

Pratt, H. D., Bruner, P. L. and Berrett, D. G. (1987). *The Birds of Hawaii and the Tropical Pacific*. New Jersey: Princeton University Press.

Schauensee, R. M. de (1982). *A Guide to the Birds of South America*. Philadelphia: Academy of Natural Sciences (reprinted by Pan American section, ICBP).

Schauensee, R. M. de (1984). *The Birds of China*. Oxford: Oxford University Press.

Stuart, S. N. and Johnson, T. (eds) (1986). *World Checklist of Threatened Species*. Peterborough: Natural Conservancy Council.

White, C. M. N. and Bruce, M. D. (1986). *The Birds of Wallacea*. London: British Ornithologists Union.

Index of Vernacular Names

INDEX

Index of Scientific Names